Career
Counseling

Elizabeth B. Yost
M. Anne Corbishley

Career Counseling

❧ ❧ ❧ ❧

A *Psychological* *Approach*

 Jossey-Bass Publishers · San Francisco

A Psychological Approach
  by Elizabeth B. Yost and M. Anne Corbishley

Copyright © 1987 by: Jossey-Bass Inc., Publishers
                       350 Sansome Street
                       San Francisco, California 94104
                       &
                       Jossey-Bass Limited
                       Headington Hill Hall
                       Oxford OX3 0BW

Library of Congress Cataloging-in-Publication Data

Yost, Elizabeth B.
    Career Counseling.

    (The Jossey-Bass social and behavioral science series)
    Bibliography: p. 253
    Includes index.
    1. Vocational guidance   I. Corbishley, M. Anne.
II. Title.   III. Series.
HF5381.Y58   1987   158.6   86-46335
ISBN 1-55542-035-4
ISBN 1-55542-420-1 (paperback)

Manufactured in the United States of America

The paper used in this book meets the
State of California requirements for recycled paper
(50 percent recycled waste, including 10 percent
postconsumer waste), which are the strictest
guidelines for recycled paper currently in
use in the United States.

FIRST EDITION
 HB Printing   10 9 8 7 6 5 4 3
 First paperback printing: January 1992

Code 8711
Code 9215   (paperback)

The Jossey-Bass
Social and Behavioral Science Series
and
The Jossey-Bass
Higher Education Series

Consulting Editor
Counseling Psychology

Gary R. Hanson
University of Texas, Austin

This book is dedicated to our parents,
Virginia and Jack Bravinder
Mary and William Corbishley,
with love and gratitude

Contents

❧ ❧ ❧ ❧

Preface

For most people, work is a vital part of psychological functioning. Job-related concerns can, and usually do, have an impact on physical and mental health and on intimate and social relationships; in turn, problems outside the workplace affect a person's productivity and satisfaction on the job. As a result, therapists and other helping professionals often find that many of their clients' problems include and may even be caused by difficulty in deciding on a career or finding a job. Similarly, career specialists often have clients whose career decision-making ability is hampered by psychological problems.

In this book, we take a unique approach to clients' career problems by integrating traditional career counseling techniques with psychological methods of assessment and intervention. We present this approach in the form of a step-by-step process that allows counselors to lead clients from the initial interview to job placement, confident that the final career choice will have been made within the full context of the client's life, including ambitions for the future, personal style, psychological blocks, and the needs of significant others. Although the method we propose is soundly based on theoretical principles, we devote no more than 10 percent of the text to career theory and research.

We imposed this limitation on ourselves in an effort to meet the goal of practicality—an important consideration for busy professionals.

Throughout the book we present a rationale for our suggestions, together with ways for the counselor to evaluate the career counseling process and recognize when consultation with experts in particular areas might be needed. We also make every effort to help counselors individualize the various stages, rather than simply lead clients through a preset program. Within the logical order suggested by the process we describe, there is ample room for flexibility, and we encourage counselors to use their own techniques, to adapt the exercises, or to be creative in developing new ones.

Who Should Read This Book?

The book should be valuable for several groups of people. Clinical psychologists, social workers, and others with no training specific to career counseling will appreciate the unity and the self-sufficiency of the model and the detailed explanations of the process it presents. The volume will provide a thorough grounding in the principles and techniques necessary for offering career counseling services.

Counselors, counseling psychologists, and other mental health workers who already have training in career counseling will appreciate the unique integration of vocational and psychological material and should find the exercises and worksheets a useful resource. Despite the structured approach of this model, there is room for the application of techniques from different psychological schools, so that counselors are not asked to renounce adherence to any psychological approach.

For career specialists such as employment service counselors, vocational counselors, and college placement counselors, the material on psychological issues should provide a rich source of insight into difficulties clients can have while making a career choice. These counselors might also find the Work-Related Preferences a new and valuable way to conceptualize the assessment and implementation of career counseling. Some of the exercises might also prove to be useful supplementary material.

Finally, this volume should be of value in counselor education programs for course work and practica in career counseling. The model we present is comprehensive and detailed; we have drawn from many sources a mass of information and material and integrated it in a readily accessible form. The book should provide a solid basis for counselors in training who have not had time enough in the field to develop their own approaches to career counseling.

Overview of the Contents

In Chapter One, we provide a necessarily brief overview of career theories to establish a context for the model of career decision making we offer in this book. The model is then outlined, as are some of the psychological issues and constraints typically encountered in career counseling—for example, anxieties, cognitive blocks, maladaptive behaviors, and social and environmental problems. Chapters Two and Three address the work-related evaluation and psychological assessment necessary for career counseling, including methods for setting goals and separating personal from career problems. In Chapter Four, we discuss ways to help clients develop a list of possible career alternatives, then narrow the list to the most desirable options. Chapter Five presents methods of amassing and evaluating information about the client's selected alternatives and describes how to help clients make a final choice. Chapter Six is devoted to solving the many problems that can arise during the stages discussed in the previous two chapters: lack of interests, unrealistic self-assessment, and dissatisfaction with one's alternatives. In Chapter Seven, we discuss how to help clients decide what type of plan they need to make in order to meet their career goal and how to formulate and evaluate the plan. Chapters Eight and Nine consider job search skills—that is, how clients should prepare for and handle all aspects of obtaining further training or a job itself, such as writing the cover letter and résumé and being interviewed.

For ease of use, each chapter conforms to the same outline. First, we explain the tasks that need to be accomplished and the rationale for those tasks. We follow this with an extensive set of sample methods and procedures that can be used to accomplish the tasks. Most often, these are methods that we and others have used and found successful, but we make no claim that they are the only or even the best methods, and we encourage practitioners to use their creativity in developing new techniques to help clients complete the necessary tasks. Finally, where appropriate, we offer suggestions for homework assignments to help clients complete the stage and move on. Throughout, we have used case examples, charts, lists, and exercises to illustrate and complement the text.

The final section of each chapter reflects our belief that career counseling is more challenging than at first may appear and that it tends to involve the client's personality characteristics, significant others, and any psychological difficulties the client may be experiencing. In this section, we identify problems, pitfalls, and psychological blocks that can occur for both client and counselor. Here again, we offer sample tested ways to handle such difficulties as perfectionism, fear of failure, performance anxiety, resistance, and family dynamics, while encouraging practitioners to use their own techniques.

Acknowledgments

We would like to acknowledge our indebtedness and appreciation to the following people who contributed, knowingly or not, to this venture: to Susan Gilmore, who convincingly demonstrated the value of career counseling by her competence and commitment; to Doug Sprague, who brought an original style, admirable ideas, and a delightful sense of humor to the initial planning of this book; to the clients and university and high school students who helped us to develop and test the ideas and materials presented here; and to the students in career counseling classes who provided feedback on the practicality of the techniques and the viability of the approach.

Tucson, Arizona　　　　　　　　　　Elizabeth B. Yost
March 1987　　　　　　　　　　　　 M. Anne Corbishley

The Authors

❧ ❧ ❧ ❧

Elizabeth B. Yost is visiting professor in the Counseling Psychology Program at the University of California, Santa Barbara. She received her Ph.D. degree (1973) in counseling psychology from the University of Oregon. She is a Diplomate in Counseling Psychology of the American Board of Professional Psychology (ABPP) and is coauthor of *Effective Personal and Career Decision Making* (1976, with K. Bartsch and K. Girrell) and of *Group Cognitive Therapy: A Treatment Approach for Depressed Older Adults* (1986, with L. E. Beutler, M.A. Corbishley, and J. R. Allender).

She was formerly associate professor in the Department of Psychology at the University of Arizona and research associate in the Department of Psychiatry at the Arizona College of Medicine. She also worked at the Department of Counseling and Guidance at the University of Arizona, where for eleven years she taught courses in career counseling, psychological assessment, cognitive behavior therapy, and behavior modification. Before that, she worked as a staff psychologist at the Career Development and Placement Center at Pennsylvania State University.

M. Anne Corbishley teaches in the Counselling Psychology Program in the Faculty of Education at Simon Fraser University in

British Columbia, Canada. She received her Ph.D. degree (1987) in counseling and guidance from the University of Arizona. She is coauthor, with Elizabeth B. Yost and others, of several books and articles on depression, cognitive therapy, and career counseling.

For seventeen years she taught and counseled in elementary, middle, and high schools in England and Canada. She also served for two years as career counseling consultant to undergraduate students in the Department of Secondary Education at the University of Arizona.

Career
Counseling

❧ 1 ❧

The Process of
Career Counseling

Michael Aronsen is senior editor and part owner of a highly respected and thriving specialty publishing house. His work presents him with variety, challenge, and excellent pay, and prospects for the business could not be better. On this fine fall day, however, he is distracted from his work, something that seems to be happening a lot lately. Across from his open office window, a modern building of unusual design is being built, and Michael watches with barely acknowledged envy as the architect strolls around his creation, admiring, inspecting, instructing.

When Michael was a child, he spent much of his spare time sketching and working with modeling clay, deriving great satisfaction from seeing his daydreams take visible form. Michael's parents regarded his artistic interest and ability as a hobby, and it never occurred to them, or to Michael, that he would do anything other than follow his father into the family's publishing business. Although Michael appreciates the many advantages to his present position, more and more often he finds himself aware that something is missing. Now that he has overcome the challenge to perform well in his career, he realizes that the printed word has never held much interest for him. His wife senses his restlessness and is concerned by his increasing petty grumbles about his work, and even more by his occasional wild ideas about "giving it all up and doing something interesting."

Michael's situation is not unusual. He finds himself in an occupation that is not as satisfactory as he would like. Because

1

his job does have many advantages, his dissatisfaction is rather vague, formed out of hazy feelings of frustration, loss, lack of fulfillment. As he approaches the middle years of life, when people often begin to assess past achievements and reevaluate goals, his feelings become stronger and begin to add a gray tinge to much of his life outside work.

And yet Michael is one of the lucky ones, having found a career that is not unpleasant and that provides some valuable rewards. For many people, work is an irritation—a constant source of pain, boredom, and frustration. Doris, for example, is a cashier in a supermarket. She works quickly and accurately and the pay is good enough for now, but she dislikes working with numbers and money, and she hates standing on her feet all day. She is good with her hands and would prefer to use them, as she does in her leisure time, to make clothing. Thomas, too, is unhappy in his work as packing supervisor for a mail order business. He enjoys the organizational aspects of his job but has never learned to like supervising others. He prefers to work alone and accomplish goals he sets for himself, without the responsibility for making sure that others perform well.

Dissatisfaction with one's job might appear to some to be a relatively minor problem when compared with, for example, severe marital difficulties, but a closer examination of the place of work in most people's lives reveals that career choice has the potential for affecting all aspects of a person's existence. In Western society, work is a major source of status, identity, and gratification. Its pervasiveness can be demonstrated in conversations overheard both at ceremonial occasions and in everyday life: at engagement parties ("What does your fiancé do, dear?"), at christenings ("Now you've got someone to carry on after you, George"), at funerals ("For forty years he dedicated his life to the schoolchildren whose lives he directed"), on the playground ("My Dad's a pilot"), on campus ("I think I'll go into business for myself").

This preoccupation with work is understandable when we consider the time involved and the needs work can meet. In a lifetime the average person spends more time at work than at any other single activity except sleep. Furthermore, the work people do largely determines their standard of living, including where they live, their recreational activities, the schools their children attend, the car they drive—even their clothing and food choices. Psychologically, work has the potential to fulfill the needs to be competent and productive, to function as a member of a team in a joint enterprise, to contribute to the welfare of the group, and to have some control over the means of one's existence. In fact, people who are unemployed or retired tend to complain more about the loss of self-respect and meaning in their lives than about the loss of income. For the majority of people in many societies today, work is the most important avenue to making their dreams come true.

Clearly, work is an important part of the lives of most people and, not surprisingly, gives rise to a variety of problems. In this book we are particularly concerned with problems relating to career choice. How is it, for example, that so many people end up in jobs that neither please nor suit them? For some people, career choice is dictated by economic necessity, and they must take whatever job is available at the time; yet the state of the economy does not explain why the many who have a greater number of options often choose one that is less than satisfactory. For others, the problem is making any choice at all. These people often avoid or postpone making a career decision by spending their time in alternative ways—for example, by extended travel or perpetual studenthood—or by taking on a series of short-lived positions that are often below their ability level and outside their range of interests.

For decades, researchers have investigated issues related to career choice and job satisfaction, seeking answers to such questions as: How do people get their ideas about what sort of work they want to do? What is it that makes work satisfactory or unsatisfactory? What is the best way to help people decide on a career? Is there a "right" job for each person, or can people adapt to anything?

Answers to these questions are important not just to researchers but ultimately to each individual client faced with a career decision upon which hang self-esteem, enjoyment, and life-style. Because helping a client through the complexities of career choice is at best difficult, we feel strongly about the need for a coherent model of career counseling. We also believe that it is foolish to either reinvent the wheel or ignore the wheels that already exist. Therefore, we acknowledge with gratitude the efforts that have been made by countless theorists and researchers to clarify questions about career choice. Although this is primarily a practical manual, not a theoretical review, we consider it important to present here below a brief overview of the major career theories of this century, with apologies for the occasions when brevity inevitably results in oversimplification.

Theories of Career Development and Choice

The major career theories described in this section have stimulated considerable efforts, and several are still in the process of elaboration and refinement. The collective result of these theories is a sometimes bewildering array of assessment instruments and counseling models, many of which have proven useful in clinical work.

Trait Factor. The trait factor model had its start in Parsons's 1909 book *Choosing a Vocation,* in which he outlined his theory of matching personal traits to job characteristics. A number of subsequent researchers, led principally by Paterson and colleagues (1941) and Williamson (1939, 1965), continued and developed the model, with a primary focus in two areas: the use of psychological tests to measure traits, and the classification of occupations. It is to the trait factor school that we owe the *Dictionary of Occupational Titles* (1972), a compendium of more than 40,000 jobs, each one described and classified.

The trait factor theory is based on the assumption that people possess stable and relatively unchanging characteristics (traits), including interests, special talents, and intelligence. Because jobs can be differentiated in terms of their need for different skills and levels of ability, high job satisfaction and performance should be expected if people are matched with jobs that "fit" them. Accordingly, trait factor theorists have devoted immense efforts to the measurement of individual traits, encouraging the widespread use of tests such as the General Aptitude Test Battery (GATB) and the Differential Aptitude Test (DAT). Among implications of the theory are that there exists one ideal job for each person, that people's interests and abilities do not change over time, and that these are the two factors most responsible for career choice and satisfaction.

The trait factor model of career counseling assumes that clients have one of four possible problems: (1) lack of career choice, (2) uncertainty about career choice, (3) unwise career choice, or (4) discrepancy between interests and aptitudes. The first two may be a result of insufficient information about self and work or of personal barriers such as fear of failure and insecurity about one's ability. These factors may also be responsible for the third problem, unwise career choice, meaning that the person and the job are mismatched in some way. For example, the person does not have the intelligence or personality traits to perform the job satisfactorily, or the job is not challenging or interesting enough for the person. An example of the fourth problem, discrepancy between interests and aptitudes, would be a person with few verbal skills wanting to become a lawyer. For all four types of problems, the counseling approach is to help the person with self-analysis, to provide adequate information about occupations, and to combine these two sets of data to find the fit between client and job. These basic counseling tasks may need to be supplemented with decision-making skills, reality testing, and so on.

Although the heyday of trait factor counseling was over by the 1950s, its influence is still apparent today. Few counselors now would accept the rather mechanistic proposal that tests can play the greatest role in choosing a career, but equally few would deny that some people are better suited to certain jobs than to others. In recent decades, more sophisticated research methodology and more elaborate ways of viewing human behavior have led to greater complexity in career theory, spurring attempts to incorporate not just interests and abilities but also factors such as family background, developmental stages, personality traits less specifically concerned with work, and sociological conditions into career analyses. The concern with these complexities reflects a general view that the trait factor theory as originally developed was too narrow. In today's less stable world, the emphasis is on flexibility and adaptability rather than on a "one hole, one peg" approach.

Ginzberg. In a radical departure from trait factor theory, Ginzberg, Ginsburg, Axelrad, and Herma (1951) introduced a developmental theory derived from Buehler's (1933) life stage schema. Despite Ginzberg's reformulation of the theory in 1972, his work and that of his colleagues is generally regarded as an incomplete approach to the developmental concept.

According to Ginzberg and his colleagues, vocational choice is the result of a developmental process that occurs in three periods, each with separate substages. Up to the age of about eleven, children are in the *fantasy* period, where their career interests are unrealistic. The second period, called *tentative,* is divided into four stages (interest, capacity, values, and transition) and lasts from about age eleven to age seventeen. During the tentative period, young people define and clarify their interests, their work-related skills and abilities, and the values they attach to work, and they become aware of the necessity to make a vocational decision.

As a result of the self-awareness and maturation that occur in this period, individuals narrow down their vocational choices to some extent, rejecting those choices that are obvious misfits. In the third, *realistic,* period, the three stages are exploration, crystallization, and specification. During this period, individuals first narrow their choices but remain ambivalent, they next select a career field, and finally they opt for a specific job or type of training leading to a particular career choice. This period typically concludes between late adolescence and early adulthood, although some people keep their options open much longer.

Ginzberg and his colleagues made no attempt to explain how career development occurs within each stage or what might promote a move from stage to stage. Nor did they investigate the consequences of failure to complete the stages. In addition, the original research was conducted on small and limited samples, mostly affluent white males (Brown, 1984). Studies of boys of lower socioeconomic status and women appeared to provide support for the existence of periods and stages, but other factors, such as social role expectations and lack of economic opportunities, played a stronger role (Ginzberg, 1984). Ginzberg increasingly conceded that vocational development is not as rigid, irreversible, or independent of the economy as early formulations of the theory might have suggested.

Super. A major contribution to developmental career theory has been made by Donald Super (1957, 1969). With his colleagues in the longitudinal Career Pattern Study, begun in 1957 and still in the process of analysis, he has evolved a complex model of career development that has stimulated a great deal of research and produced concepts and instruments of value to career counselors.

A fundamental aspect of Super's model is self-concept. As people grow up, they develop a view of their own roles, personality traits, and abilities. They then compare this self-view with what they know about various occupations and try to translate their self-concept into an occupational concept. In other words, they ask, "What role can a person like me play in this occupation?" Thus, Super's theory is also a matching one, in that he believes people organize their vocational choices to find the occupation that will best allow them to express their self-concept—that is, to find satisfactory outlets for their values, interests, abilities, and personality characteristics.

The developmental aspect of Super's model consists of five stages. In a person's lifetime ("maxicycle") these are *growth* (0–14 years), *exploration* (14–25), *establishment* (25–45), *maintenance* (45–65), and *decline* or *disengagement* (over 65). However, the same stages can also be experienced in "minicycles" within each of the "maxicycle" stages. For example, a man entering the life stage of *exploration*, embarking on a new career, might first go through a *growth* stage in which he learns to relate to others in the work situation and then proceed to *explore* how he can best operate in this new situation, *establish* a permanent place for himself, *maintain* the place securely for some time, and eventually *disengage,* or reduce his participation in the job.

Throughout all these stages, people play various roles—roles that can change over their life span and that will assume different salience at various points. Similarly, interests and values do not always remain static. In Super's model, then, life is seen as a process of change, marked by multiple decision points. Career selection is not a single relatively stable choice but the cumulative result of past decisions, subject to redecision if the chosen career does not provide satisfaction.

One concept treated extensively by Super is *career maturity,* or the extent to which a person has completed stage-appropriate career developmental tasks in comparison with his or her peers. Factors involved might be the realism, consistency, and certainty of a person's career choice, or the career-planning and information-seeking behavior demonstrated by the individual. Several instruments, including the Career Development Inventory (Super and others, 1979) and the Career Maturity Inventory (Crites, 1978), have been developed to measure career maturity and to guide subsequent interventions. For example, a teenager who shows a high level of career maturity is deemed ready to make a career choice, while a peer with less awareness of and interest in careers will probably need to be taken through several preparatory steps before making an actual choice. In adults, Super recognizes that there is a more tenuous link between developmental stages and career choice. He indicates that adult readiness for career decision making should be referred to as *career adaptability.*

Throughout his extensive work on this model, Super has attempted to incorporate ever more factors, including those often ignored by other theorists, such as socioeconomic status, gender, social change, and the process of choice. His theory has become correspondingly more complex, offering at this point more in the way of conceptual challenge than practical use.

Roe. Trained as a clinical psychologist, Anne Roe developed a theory of career development based on her research investigations of the personality traits of eminent artists and scientists. Roe's (1956) theory asserts that occupational choice is the result of personality, which in turn is largely the product of early parent-child relationships. Roe based her ideas on Maslow's (1954) proposition that everyone has five basic needs that are arranged in a hierarchy of importance: physiological, safety, belongingness and love, self-esteem, and self-actualization. Not until the needs on the lower end of the hierarchy are satisfied will a person seek to satisfy the higher-order needs. According to Roe, an individual's need structure, which is greatly influenced by early childhood frustrations and satisfactions, can best be satisfied by his or her occupation.

Roe further hypothesized that there are two basic orientations: toward other people or not toward other people. She proposed that individuals who enjoy working with others were raised by warm and accepting parents and are drawn toward people because of their strong need for affection and belongingness. On the other hand, people raised by parents who neglected or rejected them have security needs that are met by selecting non-person-oriented occupations. Roe also contended that although the selection of an occupational category is primarily a function of the individual's needs, the level of attainment within the category is more likely to depend on the individual's abilities and socioeconomic background.

In accordance with her theory, Roe developed a classification system for occupations that includes eight groups: service, business contact, organization, technology, outdoor, science, general culture, and arts and entertainment. Each group has eight levels based on the degree of responsibility, skill, and ability required.

In 1972, Roe modified her view, taking the position that early parent-child relations combine with other environmental experiences and with genetic influences to produce needs. She suggested that occupational choice depends on how the individual learns to satisfy these needs through two types of activities, those involving and those excluding interactions with people.

Roe's theory has generated considerable research, which nevertheless has provided little support for her ideas (Osipow, 1973), partly because her belief that different child-rearing practices produce different vocational choices is difficult to validate. Parental behavior is usually inconsistent, both between parents and within the same parent, and there are many other influences on a child besides the parent. Most research testing Roe's hypotheses has used either adult subjects who recall their childhood family climate or child subjects who report their current family climate in simplistic terms. The ability of the adults to recall accurately and the usefulness of the terms used by the children are both questionable.

Roe's major contributions to career counseling have been her occupational classification system and the fact that she drew attention to the importance of early childhood influences in career development.

Tiedeman and O'Hara. Tiedeman and his colleagues (Tiedeman, 1961; Tiedeman and O'Hara, 1963) drew on the work of Super and Ginzberg in formulating their view of career development as the process of building a personal vocational identity; in this process, the individual strives to strike a balance between integration, or becoming part of a career field, and differentiation—retaining individuality and not losing uniqueness.

Tiedeman and his colleagues identified the series of decisions a person makes in the course of his or her career development. They divided the process of vocational decision making into two periods, each with several stages. The first period, *anticipation* or *preoccupation,* includes four stages: exploration, crystallization, choice, and clarification. During the exploration stage, the person considers and becomes familiar with the career options available, mentally trying out work roles and weighing the desirability of each in relation to his or her values, abilities, and interests. The individual next enters the crystallization period, assessing options and narrowing the total number, accepting some as feasible, rejecting others as unobtainable or inappropriate. During the choice stage, the person decides which vocational alternative he or she wants to follow, and during the clarification phase, the person focuses on the behaviors necessary to reach the chosen goal, working out how he or she will implement the choice. Any uncertainties about the choice are resolved in this stage.

The second period, called *implementation* or *adjustment,* consists of three stages: induction, reformation, and integration. In the induction stage, the person enters the work situation and tries to become part of the new career group, hoping to gain approval and recognition. At this point the person is extremely receptive to the demands of the work situation and is more concerned with meeting the needs of the organization than in meeting his or her own needs. In the reformation stage, the individual begins to influence the group as well as being influenced by it. The person becomes more assertive, expressing views and needs, and the career group comes to accept him or her. During the integration phase, the person becomes a working member of the career group, having achieved a balance between the demands of the group and his or her own needs.

Tiedeman's decision-making paradigm was used as the basis for a computer-assisted career counseling program, the Information System for Vocational Decisions (ISVD), which was introduced in 1969. The system allowed the client to relate self-descriptive information to extensive data on military service and occupational and educational opportunities. Although not widely adopted because it was not cost effective in terms of computer time, the ISVD has served as a prototype for computer-aided counseling.

Although there are few empirical data to support Tiedeman's theory, his views have been important in directing attention to the significance of self-awareness in career decision making.

Holland. John Holland (1985) has devoted his career to what he calls a "theory of vocational personalities and work environments," which he has revised five times since 1959.

Holland began with the principle that people with certain personality traits are attracted to and suited for jobs with certain specific definable characteristics. Therefore, if we know what a person is like, we can predict what sort of occupation is most likely to produce satisfaction and achievement for that person. Conversely, if we can delineate a particular job clearly enough, we can assess what sort of person we should look for to fill that slot.

From this simple trait factor premise, Holland developed a typology of personalities and work environments that can be used to categorize particular persons or jobs. The six main categories he created are realistic (R), investigative (I), artistic (A), social (S), enterprising (E), and conventional (C). This typology is summarized in Exhibit 1. The categorizing or coding can be done by using one of Holland's own instruments, such as the Vocational Preference Inventory or the Self Directed Search.

Exhibit 1. Holland's Personality Types and Work Environments.

- *Realistic.* The work requires mechanical, manual, technical, or agricultural skills and practical, concrete problem solving. Realistic people tend to be practical, materialistic, and uninvolved with others. They value strength and tangible results and lack interpersonal skills.
- *Investigative.* The work requires scientific and mathematical abilities and intellectual problem solving. Investigative people tend to be analytical, introspective, complex. They value the scientific approach to life and lack social and leadership skills.
- *Artistic.* The work requires the use of creative skills in an unsystematized environment. Artistic people are usually imaginative, expressive, sensitive, nonconforming. They value freedom, ambiguity, and esthetics and lack skills in the orderly manipulation of data.
- *Social.* The work requires social, educational, and therapeutic skills. Social people tend to be cooperative, ethical, responsible, understanding, and friendly. They value interpersonal relationships and lack mechanical and scientific skills.
- *Enterprising.* The work involves persuasive, manipulative, and leadership skills. Enterprising people tend to be ambitious, extraverted, domineering, and self-confident. They value success in the political and economic fields and lack scientific abilities.
- *Conventional.* The work involves the systematic organization and manipulation of data. Conventional people tend to be methodical, conforming, conscientious, unimaginative, and practical. They value organization and achievement in business and lack artistic skills.

Because it would be altogether too simplistic to believe that people can be categorized in no more than six ways, Holland assumes that most people have a dominant type and one or two other types of some, but lesser, importance. It would, for example, be extremely rare to find a person who is a pure realistic type—that is, asocial, practical, conforming, valuing concrete objects, preferring to work with machines rather than with people. It would be more common to find a person with characteristics and interests of two groups: for example, realistic and investigative (RI), where the R type is influenced by the rational, curious, symbolic, analytical aspects of the I type; it would be even more likely to find people with a third major code, such as realistic investigative artistic (RIA), with idealistic, impulsive, and emotional characteristics.

As a further complication of the coding system, Holland argues that some types are more compatible with each other and some are less compatible. To reflect this compatibility ("consistency" in Holland's terminology), he has arranged the types in a particular order around a hexagon (Figure 1). The closer together the types are on the hexagon, the greater the consistency. In career terms, this means that, for example, a person with a largely realistic personality would probably resemble more closely the workers and prefer the work in the nearby investigative and conventional categories rather than in the more dis-

**Figure 1. Holland's Model of Relationships
Among Personality Types and Work Environments.**

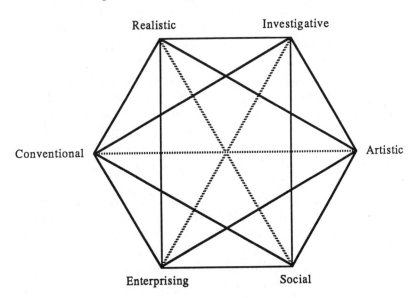

Source: From John L. Holland, *Making Vocational Choices: A Theory of Vocational Personalities & Work Environments.* 2/E, 1985, p. 29. Reprinted by permission of Prentice-Hall, Inc., Englewood Cliffs, New Jersey.

tant social, artistic, or enterprising categories. Holland claims that people with inconsistent personality codes (for example, RS, AC, and IE combinations) have lower job achievement and satisfaction and less stable vocational choices and personalities.

In the latest formulation of his theory, Holland has attempted to answer many of his critics' complaints about the biases and shortcomings of earlier versions, although in essence the theory retains its original premises, only somewhat expanded. He has attempted to account for not only the existence but also the development of career preferences and of personality, and he has tried to incorporate into his theory the vocational effects of variables he previously neglected, including socioeconomic status, gender, ability, and upbringing. He now acknowledges that both personality traits and career interests do change over time, and he provides an explanation for such change.

In his latest version, Holland (1985) theorizes about how personality types develop and change. To a certain extent, parents, especially those who are themselves consistent types, produce similar types in their children, both by modeling and by encouraging certain behaviors and preferences. As early preferences crystallize into interests, children learn the competencies appropriate to those interests, but at the same time they miss the opportunities to learn skills that would fit with other types of interests. Gradually, a child acquires a familiar and reinforcing behavioral repertoire that leaves neither time nor motivation to explore other preferences. The child's acquired abilities and interests eventually lead to a consistent self-perception, so that the child comes to believe: "I am the type of person who is good with my hands," "I am the type of person who is very creative," and so on.

According to Holland, a person's basic personality type stabilizes between the ages of eighteen and thirty and thereafter is rather difficult to change. The more consistent a person's type is, the more likely it is that he or she will find a satisfactory job environment. Consistent types are more apt to deal with job dissatisfaction by altering the work environment than by changing their own personalities. Because the familiar is usually comfortable, few people are eager to make changes, especially if, as is likely, their support system is also comfortable with the status quo and reluctant to encourage change. The need for a new repertoire of skills, new training, and new credentialing when making drastic career changes also tends to reduce the amount of personality change people make.

Despite difficulties, however, change does occur. People whose personalities are inconsistent or undifferentiated (that is, have no clearly distinguished dominant or secondary types) tend to change themselves to fit the job rather than alter the environment to suit them. Sometimes the marketplace dictates a move to work in a different environment, and, if the person acquires the requisite skills and experiences job satisfaction, he or she will come to resemble more closely the personalities of those who work in that environment. Thus, a man trained as an accountant, code CIS, forced to work as a taxi driver, code RSE, could conceivably, if he were successful and learned to enjoy his work, develop the traits and interests common to many cab drivers.

Holland's theory has inspired extensive research efforts, and many aspects of the theory have received positive, though variable, support. From the clinician's point of view, the theory has probably had the greatest impact through the instrumentation that has developed. The Self Directed Search (Holland, 1977b), for example, is widely used as a simple and effective way to introduce people to the subject of career choice. It represents Holland's enduring beliefs that career choice need not be as complex as is often maintained and that effective self-help is to be preferred to invasive and unnecessary career counseling.

Krumboltz. Krumboltz's theory of career counseling (Krumboltz and Thoresen, 1969; Krumboltz, 1976) is grounded in social learning theory and in classical behaviorism. It also incorporates more recent ideas from cognitive behavior therapy (Beck and others, 1979; Ellis, 1962). According to behavioral theory, personality develops not out of innate psychic drives or in developmental stages but as a result of idiosyncratic interactions with the environment. These interactions are a two-way street: people learn both by responding to and by acting on the environment. Furthermore, the learning process is lawful; that is, learning occurs or fails to occur under certain specifiable conditions and in predictable ways.

For the purpose of career theory, the most important "laws" of learning are instrumental and associative. *Instrumental learning* is familiar to most people as reward and punishment. People tend to repeat and enjoy behavior that has pleasing consequences for them and to avoid and dislike behavior that produces unpleasant results. *Associative learning* occurs when people transfer the emotional import of one event to another event that up until then had little or no emotional significance. For example, a young girl's new stepfather is a farmer, so the family moves from the city to the country. She has no interest in animals but enjoys her stepfather's company and comes to associate caring for animals with a feeling of being loved. In time, caring generalizes from animals to people and forms the basis of a later career in child welfare.

People do not require firsthand experience to learn and to modify their own responses. Thus, a young woman contemplating medical school might come to fear and avoid such training after watching a friend suffer through unpleasant experiences in medical school.

Cognitive behavior therapy (Beck and others, 1979; Mahoney, 1974; Meichenbaum, 1977) holds that learning is mediated by what people say to themselves, whether consciously or not. People not only respond to and act on the environment, they also process experiences mentally, drawing conclusions that may or may not be accurate and forming attitudes and expectations that may or may not be functional. These cognitive processes can be accessed and influenced directly in order to alter both behavior and emotion.

On the basis of these ideas, Krumboltz has built a coherent and relatively comprehensive model to explain career preferences and choice. He argues that career decision making is influenced by several factors, each of which has a different impact in different lives. First, genetic endowment expands or limits options to a greater or lesser degree in each individual. Included in genetic endowment are unavoidable factors (sex, race, disabilities) and factors such as special talents that a person can choose to develop. Some of these characteristics are unalterable, while others can be changed. Being female, for example, can reduce the opportunities for risk taking and skill building to which a child is exposed, but these deficits can be made up later in life. Second, career decisions are influenced by environmental conditions and events beyond individual control. This category includes socioeconomic status, educational experiences, the state of the economy, family and cultural norms—in fact, anything that could affect the work field, from obsolescence to drought.

A third factor influencing career development and choice is individual learning. Heritage and the environment influence a person's responses, and each interaction in turn influences subsequent responses. A lifetime of these individual learning experiences provides a person with a unique repertoire of interests, of career information, and of occupational stereotypes (''world view generalizations'') that increase or decrease the attractiveness of an occupation. Learning can occur instrumentally. For example, successfully building a treehouse can lead to increased carpentry activity, and being rewarded for playing the piano might encourage interest in a musical career. (Krumboltz notes the importance of genetic factors in such cases, since the child most likely to be rewarded for piano playing is the one born with musical talent.) The environment has an impact on instrumental learning by providing both the range of activities for a child to try and the external rewards for the child's efforts. Learning can also be associative. For example, watching a movie in which a firefighter hero is painfully injured might reduce the desire to pursue dangerous occupations. Among a person's multitudinous learning experiences, he or she acquires or fails to acquire task approach skills, such as work habits, performance standards, career decision-making skills, and problem-solving abilities.

Fourth, Krumboltz places special emphasis on what he calls self-observation generalizations; that is, people compare their own performance and skills with some standard and draw conclusions about themselves and their competence. These conclusions then guide future responses to situations. Problems do not arise as long as people have reasonable standards, observe themselves accurately, and draw rational conclusions. Frequently, however, people compare themselves to standards that are unrealistic, idealized, or inappropriate for the particular situation. Sometimes they do not perceive their performance accurately, or they believe someone else's (inaccurate or biased) judgment of their performance. The result is often a set of unwarranted conclusions, whether unduly negative or positive, that form the basis of a potentially damaging image of themselves as a worker. It is not difficult to see the effect on career behavior of an inaccurate negative conclusion about self-efficacy drawn from an idealized standard. For example, a five-year-old boy makes a model boat. His father criticizes it because it is not as good as models made by the boy's eight-year-old brother. The child concludes that he is hopelessly clumsy and incapable of working with his hands.

For many people, self-observations are covert. As a result, they behave according to hidden beliefs, without being aware of the attitudes and behavior patterns that are developing. A woman who has been extravagantly and unrealistically praised for childhood performance might come to view herself as capable of succeeding at all tasks, regardless of the difficulty involved or the effort she makes. When she encounters a more demanding set of standards—in her first job, for example—she is likely to experience considerable distress. If she decides to blame her critics for not understanding her great potential, she will make no changes in her self-observation generalizations. Yet change can occur if she is able to take an objective look at the standards and at her own performance and draw some accurate conclusions. For many people, therefore, it is important to make explicit the self-beliefs that form part of their response system, in order to remove barriers to career selection.

In summary, Krumboltz has attempted to incorporate into his model all possible influences on career development and choice. In his view, the unique nature of each individual's experience precludes the concept of sequential developmental stages. This emphasis on uniqueness also means that Krumboltz's model is applicable to all persons, including women and others of minority status who often do not "fit" career models developed on a population of middle-class white males. He sees life as involving a dynamic interaction between person and environment, which means that change is constantly occurring or is at least able to occur. In other words, personality traits, interests, and even self-concept are capable of alteration at any point in life.

From Theory to Practice

Several common beliefs emerge from an overview of career theories. We will discuss four that, apart from their commonsense appeal, have practical implications that need to be incorporated into a model of counseling for career choice.

— First, it is reasonable to assume that people make career decisions not at a single isolated moment but out of the context of a whole lifetime of experiences. Therefore, even though counselors may not be able to reliably identify specific developmental stages, it can still be an important career counseling activity to explore a client's past, at least insofar as elements from that past seem to influence current career difficulties. A second point is that, although theoreticians may not yet have established all the needs that work can satisfy (and these needs may yet turn out to be quite idiosyncratic), it is clear that many people do have strong expectations of the work that occupies at least half of their waking lives. For most people, life is either enriched or impoverished by the work they do and by their work environments; it is wise, therefore, to spend time in career counseling exploring in depth the interpersonal and intrapersonal satisfactions clients derive or expect to derive from work.

A third point emphasized by many theorists is the need for skills specific to job selection, acquisition, and retention. As society becomes more complex, the need for specialized skills can be expected to increase, and career counselors can anticipate spending time assessing and, if necessary, teaching career-appropriate skills. Almost all theories acknowledge the importance of career information, which assumes a central place in career counseling in today's world of information overload and rapid change. Jobs are constantly being created, replaced, and altered, so that, even more than in earlier decades, clients need up-to-date information. Counselors must be able to help clients find the information in the first place and then keep it current, since good decisions cannot be made on the basis of poor information.

Finally, several theorists recognize what clinicians know from experience—namely, that however attractive or suitable available options might be, some clients are not in a position to make a career choice. Whether this lack of readiness is caused by immaturity, environmental constraints, personality flaws, or yet undiscovered factors, barriers to career decision making need to be explored in counseling and either removed or circumvented. This requirement implies that the career counselor cannot afford to ignore either the psychological make-up of the client or the world of interpersonal relationships in which he or she lives.

Despite these commonalities among theories, it is apparent that unresolved contradictions still exist among theories and that a comprehensive career theory remains to be developed. Deterministic theories imply relatively unchanging, even unchangeable, needs and traits and are at odds with contextual theories, which in their turn ignore developmental issues. To further confuse the situation, research has failed to support some aspects of each theory and has supported other aspects, but to different degrees with different populations. What is of perhaps greatest significance for relating theory to practice is that most theorists in this field acknowledge the existence and the force of many variables as yet insufficiently explored. Thus, factors such as sex, race, socioeconomic status, age, cultural background, and even luck play some part in career development and choice. In other words, theory cannot explain the idiosyncrasies of an individual client, and as yet there is no way to determine the extent to which any individual conforms to or deviates from the norms indicated by theory and research.

Nonetheless, clients still require help with career problems. In the absence of a fully integrated model, but convinced of the need for a structured approach to ensure coverage of all issues related to career choice, we have elected to present in this text a decision-making model similar to the one articulated by Krumboltz. This is not an arbitrary choice. A first advantage of the decision-making approach is that it focuses on the acknowledged core of career choice. Since 1909, when Parsons assumed that if a person has good information he or she will naturally make a good career choice, there has been increasing recognition of the centrality of decision making. Mendonca and Siess (1976), for example, identified this skill as the key to effective career exploration and choice. Hazler and Roberts (1984) maintain that the decision-making process "might be defined not as the heart of vocational choice, but instead as the whole process" (p. 409).

Second, the decision-making model has considerable face validity for clients, in that decision-making skills can be used in other areas of life and at other times. Because many clients can expect to make career decisions several times in their lives, effective counseling should be able to prepare them for independent future decision making.

A third advantage of using a decision-making model in career counseling is that it allows considerable flexibility. The model provides a road map marked with beginning and end points and major stages along the route, but client needs and idiosyncratic styles and counselor orientation and preferred techniques will dictate the paths by which each stage is reached and how long the journey takes.

A Systematic Model

Many systematic models of career decision making have been developed, and the differences among them tend to be relatively minor, as the various steps of the process follow a logical sequence, representing the areas to be explored, the information to be gathered, and the activities to be undertaken if the client is to reach his or her particular career counseling goal. The steps or stages we use throughout this book are a composite of decision-making models and systematic career counseling processes developed over the last fifty years and currently in common use (Hazler and Roberts, 1984; Yost, 1976). The eight stages are listed below.

Initial Assessment. The purpose of this stage is to gather personal and employment information about the client and to arrive, in collaboration with the client, at a feasible career counseling goal that the client is motivated to pursue. If possible, a time frame for reaching the goal is decided. The counselor explains what career counseling involves and what the role of the client will be in the process, and a working partnership is established.

Self-Understanding. At this stage, the client explores his or her values, interests, experience, and abilities that relate to the present goal. In addition, assessment is made of psychological issues that may affect career counseling.

Making Sense of Self-Understanding Data. The purpose of this stage is to synthesize the information gathered in the previous stage into a coherent set of statements that indicate the client's desired outcomes for a career choice. These statements will be used as a reference point and yardstick at future stages. A second purpose is to summarize personal and environmental barriers to success in pursuing the desired career.

Generating Alternatives. Using the information acquired thus far, counselor and client develop a list of possible career alternatives, without making any judgments about the value of the options.

Obtaining Occupational Information. The purpose of this stage is to learn as much about each option as is necessary to make an informed choice. The list of options is narrowed.

Making the Choice. At this stage, the client makes a choice among options. This is quite often a difficult task, as various psychological problems can arise and must be dealt with.

Making Plans. The purpose of this stage is to make plans to reach the career choice goal. If necessary, contingency plans are worked out to handle any setbacks that might arise.

Implementing Plans. During this stage, the client takes whatever action is necessary to achieve the selected career goal. This may include further training or education, learning how to present oneself on paper and in person to prospective employers, and conducting a job search.

For the most part, you and your clients will complete the stages in sequence, simply because nothing else makes as much sense. It is difficult to imagine, for example, how a client could make a reasonable choice without some self-understanding or make plans without first having made a definite choice. There will be occasions, however, when the stages shift position or overlap, and it is important to be responsive to times when it would be appropriate to complete the stages in a different order or to go back to a stage a second time. Obviously, too, clients require different amounts of time at each stage, according to their unique needs.

Each chapter begins with a brief section that explains what tasks need to be accomplished at that stage, together with the logic behind those tasks. This section is followed by an extensive set of sample methods and procedures that can be used to accomplish the tasks. Most often these are methods that we have used and found successful, but we make no claims that they are the only or the best ways to do what has to be done. Hopefully, they will act as a guide toward the development of your own methods. Because it is our belief that career counseling is more challenging than it at first may appear, we also include in each chapter a section that identifies problems and pitfalls that can occur for both client and counselor at this stage of counseling. Here again we offer sample and tested ways to handle the various difficulties but encourage you to use or develop your own methods as well. Finally, in each chapter we offer ideas for homework assignments to help clients complete the tasks.

Psychological and Social Aspects of Career Counseling

Although the model we have described takes a rational step-by-step approach to the problem of choosing a career, making a satisfactory choice is not solely an intellectual task but rather an emotional, cognitive, and psychological process that involves the whole person, including the environment in which he or she lives.

Decision making must therefore be interpreted in the broadest possible terms if individual client needs, styles, and characteristics are to be accommodated. Inevitably, any efforts to include intrapsychic and interpersonal elements in career counseling can lead to problems of emphasis, and the boundary between personal and career counseling becomes unclear. Traditionally, counselors have attempted to separate the two types of counseling, mainly by promoting the idea that a certain level of mental health is required before the client can proceed with career counseling (Crites, 1981). Among others, Brown (1985) challenges this assumption, pointing out that for many clients an unsuitable work environment alone can produce symptoms that would appear to indicate severe psychological disorder. For these people, career counseling to alter or remove them from the disturbing environment may be the most appropriate intervention.

Brown also makes the point that there is usually an interaction between a person's work and other areas of life, so that stress in one area affects other areas as well. The implication here is that even when the chief source of the problem is not the client's career, work may well be affected to the extent that career counseling is needed. For example, a woman in a low-paying job whose husband has just left her will probably have to address her need for a more lucrative job at the same time that she is dealing with her feelings about the separation. In her case, career and personal counseling will probably be concurrent, rather than sequential.

Most clinicians are well aware that career counseling frequently involves other concerns. In the course of pursuing a career choice, clients often clarify values unrelated to careers, reassess general life goals, learn new interpersonal skills, and increase their self-esteem. For these clients, career and personal counseling are virtually synonymous.

The question of what issues, personal or career, to address in counseling, and in what order, is an important one to answer in the initial assessment stage if both client and counselor wish to maintain focus and direction in their joint endeavor. Because, despite clear initial goals, personal and psychological issues often arise at various stages of career counseling, these issues are given major emphasis throughout this book. The nature of decision making allows counselors to identify certain styles or patterns of reacting that have the potential for serious impact on career counseling from the start. We present some of these common psychological constraints here so that counselors will be in a position to recognize them more easily and to proceed with assessment or intervention specifically related to these issues and thus reduce their power to disrupt or destroy the process of counseling.

The psychological constraints affecting career counseling express themselves in the form of dysfunctional emotions, behaviors, and cognitions. Although, for the sake of clarity, we will discuss each of these categories separately, in reality they are intertwined and interdependent, so that it is hard to say which, if any, started the cycle. This interdependence can be demonstrated by the case of Marianne, a client who in the first interview was unusually anxious (emotional constraint) about the prospect of making a career choice. When she returned for the second session, she had not completed her homework and responded with increasing anxiety to attempts by the counselor to actively engage her in the career choice process. This passivity (behavioral constraint) had been a long-standing habit with Marianne, who had thoroughly absorbed her mother's teaching that girls who go after things for themselves are not popular with men and will probably not get married (cognitive constraint). Marianne was, in fact, married but was terrified lest her "aggressiveness" in pursuing a career end with the loss of her spouse. The counselor needed to deal with her anxiety, passivity, and expectation of loss before proceeding with career counseling. Marianne probably came to counseling in the first place on the strength of an unusual spurt of courage or a sudden whim, and she might not have continued without a lowering of her level of psychological discomfort.

The following discussion of emotional, behavioral, and cognitive constraints is not exhaustive, since unique clients have unique concerns. The constraints we have chosen to describe are commonly seen in career counseling clients and should act as a red flag, warning you that this particular style or attitude could be detrimental to counseling.

Emotional Constraints. The emotions most likely to affect career counseling—fear, anxiety, guilt, pride, self-doubt, and discouragement—are often the result of the way the person behaves and thinks. For example, from first grade Jack's report cards said that he gave up too easily, and Jack has continued to give up on most of his adult ventures. Quitting has become a behavioral pattern with Jack, and he is, consequently, quick to feel discouraged. Harold would like to work as an electrician but is held back by pride; he believes that working with one's hands is demeaning.

Sometimes an emotion cannot be tied to a particular cognition or behavior pattern because it has become a habitual and generalized response to life. Clients say such things as "I'm terribly sensitive, I get nervous at the least little thing" or "Our whole family's guilty, but I'm the worst. Anytime anything goes wrong, I blame myself" or "I hate to try anything new because I always know I'll do it wrong, and I feel so stupid and embarrassed." If these emotions are under control and do not constrain the client, they need not be addressed in counseling, but if they are sufficiently strong or persistent to result in behavior that impedes the process of choosing a career, they cannot be ignored.

Behavioral Constraints. There are three main groups of behavior patterns that can have a deleterious effect on career choice. The first pattern involves the amount of control the client has over his or her own life. The less control the client has taken, the harder it will be for him or her to participate in what is essentially an active process. For example, Molly, raised by indulgent parents, has never lost the habit of letting life slide by, because it is simpler that way and because she loves comfort and ease. Wayne, described by his friends as "laid back," is a handsome, relatively intelligent, and popular college student whose passivity in pursuing goals conceals a fear of failure. Wendy, who tries frantically to get her life under control but lacks any knowledge of how to do so, is so disorganized that it will be next to impossible for her to gather useful career information until she has learned more self-control.

A second grouping of behavioral constraints has to do with perseverance. For career counseling to be successful (unless the client is very lucky), a certain amount of perseverance is required, because career decision making takes time and effort and can be frustrating. Some clients are more likely than others to have trouble staying the course if their lack of perseverance is not dealt with. Examples include Ken, who is impatient with delays and wants results immediately; Jackie, who takes a butterfly approach to life, flitting from one craze to another; Jack, who has a long history of giving up at the first sign of trouble; and Jo, whose lack of self-confidence allows her to perform well at familiar tasks but who falls to pieces when she starts to learn anything new and difficult.

The third group of behavior patterns revolves around experimentation. In career counseling, the client is starting out on a new venture, which entails risks and unknown factors. An inflexible style—that is, a tendency to respond in the same way to every challenge, regardless of how appropriate that response might be—is one form of constraint. Another form is a dysfunctional risk-taking style, in which the client either rushes blindly into situations without assessing risks or refuses to take any risks at all.

Cognitive Constraints. For many career counseling clients, the most serious constraints are cognitive. Much of people's fear and guilt, low self-esteem, and irrational behavior proceeds from beliefs, attitudes, and expectations that are often unconscious and unexamined yet play a considerable part in their everyday lives. The presence of a dysfunctional thought is not, in itself, automatically a problem. Cognitions become troublesome only when they give rise to strong negative emotions or dysfunctional behavior. Jennifer, for example, comes from a family where the most despised word is "failure." She has terrible memories of humiliations for mistakes and failures and is aware that she will probably never completely lose the small voice in the back of her mind that says, "You mustn't fail." Over the years, however, she has developed her own set of values and believes that failure is a necessary and acceptable part of life; she is now able to recognize the small voice when it speaks and exorcise it with her new beliefs. "Actually," says Jennifer, "it's quite a useful sort of nagging voice to have, because it probably helps me try hard and make fewer mistakes." Clearly, what might have been a highly dysfunctional belief is under Jennifer's control and will not be a constraint in counseling. Her brother, Alec, on the other hand, is still heavily influenced by his family's values and would find it difficult to make a career choice without first dealing with his fear of failure.

Cognitive constraints are so highly individual that it is almost impossible to categorize them with any precision. Nevertheless, there are three broad classifications that can be helpful in organizing dysfunctional thoughts about career goals: "I can't," "I won't," and "I shouldn't." Examples of thoughts that fall into each of these three categories are presented in Exhibit 2.

Exhibit 2. Dysfunctional Cognitions.

I Can't

I'll make a fool of myself, and I couldn't stand that.
I've never done it before, so I won't be able to.
I'll fail, or make a mistake, and that would be horrible.
No one else in my family (my age, my sex) has ever done it, so I won't
 be able to either.
I'm not strong (intelligent, talented) enough to do it.
I'm not as good as others.

I Won't

It probably won't work out, so why bother?
If it doesn't work out perfectly, I'm not interested.
It's not fair. I shouldn't have to do this.
Men (women, professionals, old people) aren't supposed to do that sort
 of thing.
You're the counselor. It's your job to get the information (make the deci-
 sion, get me a job).
People don't do it this way.
It's too hard.
It's too boring.
It'll all work out (without my effort).

Exhibit 2. Dysfunctional Cognitions, Cont'd.

I Shouldn't

It's against my upbringing.
It will displease my husband (wife, father).
I should stay home with the children.
It's not fair to ask my wife and kids to move to a small town (city, abroad).

It is important to understand that it is not because these beliefs are exaggerated or irrational that they need to be addressed but rather because they are likely to have an impact on the client's response to career counseling. In some cases, bringing cognitive constraints to light causes clients to change their beliefs, and the constraints are thereby removed. In other cases, the client takes a look at the belief and decides to retain it. The constraint then becomes one that has to be worked around.

Decision-Making Styles. Although not necessarily a matter of constraint, individual decision-making styles play a significant part in the whole process of career counseling, affecting such aspects as information gathering, creating and executing plans, choosing, and remaining satisfied with the choice (Phillips, Friedlander, Pazienza, and Kost, 1985). Perhaps the most widely recognized scheme for classifying decision-making styles has been developed by Harren (1979), who describes three styles: rational, intuitive, and dependent. The *rational* decision maker gathers information carefully, evaluates it objectively, decides on the basis of likely consequences (both positive and negative), and accepts full responsibility for making the decision. The *intuitive* decider also takes responsibility for the decision but otherwise presents a complete contrast: He or she decides impulsively and emotionally, according to current mood, and thus allows little or no time to gather and logically appraise information or to consider possible consequences. The *dependent* style characterizes the person who takes no responsibility for decisions or for active involvement in the tasks required to make a decision and who is influenced by the demands and expectations of others. Consequently, this person appears willing to please but passive, relying on external events or other people to make the decision.

Needless to say, few people are pure examples of one style; most people tend toward one style of decision making but also demonstrate some features of other styles.

Research into decision-making styles does not indicate that any one style is better or worse than the others. It is certainly possible for rational decisions to turn out bad and emotional or dependent ones to be satisfactory. The importance of assessing decision-making style lies in the interaction between the client's style and the process of career counseling. The rational decider, for example, is likely to find immediate appeal in a logical, investigative, analytical approach to career counseling such as that described in this book. This type of client will appear easy to deal with, since he or she will not only understand but also enjoy the process of making a career choice. However, enthusiasm for the task might lead the client to overlook or dismiss emotional and psychological factors important to the final decision, and the counselor's task will be to help the rational client give adequate consideration to such factors. Intuitive deciders, on the other hand, are likely to have some difficulty in accepting a structured approach to career choice and will probably become impatient with the tasks of various stages. With these clients, the counselor will need to be persuasive in "selling" the model and will then need to make all possible adjustments to make a basically foreign style attractive. Dependent decision makers will be the most difficult to deal with, since passivity and dependency are the direct opposites of the characteristics clients need to complete the tasks usually involved in making a personally satisfying career choice. With dependent clients, therefore, the process of career counseling might go quite slowly, giving them time to learn how to become more active and self-sufficient, and leaving room in counseling to address personal issues related to career decision making.

The purpose of career counseling is not to change clients' methods of making decisions from one style to another; however, the process of moving through a rational model for deciding will inevitably have an impact on decision-making style. Some clients will greatly modify their original style, some will make little or no changes, and others will simply learn a new style to add to their repertoire. A pleasing side effect of career counseling occurs when a client understands his or her own style well enough to choose to discard or add attitudes or behaviors, depending on their negative or positive contribution to effective personal decision making.

Phillips and associates (1985) investigated the validity of Harren's Assessment of Career Decision Making (ACDM), a self-report instrument to measure the three styles. They confirmed its validity as a diagnostic instrument but cautioned that client self-reports might not accurately represent actual client behavior. Whether counselors wish to use such an instrument to assess client decision-making styles is a matter of personal preference. In many cases, clinical judgment during the assessment stages and evaluation of the client's performance of and attitude toward career counseling tasks will be sufficient to indicate what kind of decision-making style the client has and the extent to which it might cause problems.

Minority Populations. For members of certain population groups (for example, women, nonwhites, older adults, disabled persons, ex-prisoners), choosing a career and implementing that choice can be complicated by both internal and external constraints. Those who have had direct or vicarious experience with discrimination might well feel anxiety about their career prospects and even a lack of self-confidence; as a result, they might set their sights lower than necessary or tend to become easily discouraged. When the time comes to apply and interview for jobs, they might well find that employers do stereotype them, that there are indeed few jobs available, that they receive many negative responses, or that they are expected to work for unreasonably low salaries or take on inappropriate work tasks. Although we cannot here consider the potential difficulties of each subpopulation, we offer several guidelines and will illustrate the application of these suggestions throughout the text.

First, do not assume that a particular client either has or will have a problem simply because he or she is black, old, female, disabled, or the like. Many people in minority groups (who collectively outnumber the rest of the population) experience few or no difficulties in achieving their career goals, and unnecessary focus on minority status can be discouraging and a waste of time.

On the other hand, you must be realistic. A second guideline is, therefore, to take time at each step in career counseling to establish whether or not problems exist and then intervene appropriately. Do clients have constraining cognitions, such as "No one hires people my age" or "The best I could expect would be a minor position in the back office"? Are clients generating few alternatives because they underestimate their potential or are limiting their options on the basis of assumptions about their status? When preparing for interviews, do clients need assistance in handling difficult questions about their situation or experience? In other words, your counseling techniques and interventions will be individualized for minority clients, just as they would be for all clients.

This type of individualization requires a knowledge base. The third guideline, therefore, is that you be as informed as possible, but at the same time aware of the limits to your own knowledge. While you cannot be an expert on every type of client, it is certainly possible to consult people in the community who have the necessary information. You can also help clients to contact others who have been in the same situation, in order to discover pitfalls and ways to handle them. If you have a large number of clients from one population, group rather than individual counseling might be helpful because of the opportunity for shared information and mutual support.

A final guideline is that you make every effort to be sensitive to the impact on both you and client of differences between you. The greater the gap, whether in life experiences, values, goals, attitudes toward work, or any other area, the more room there is for lack of communication and rapport. This danger underscores the need for a collaborative and experimental approach, in which each step of the model is presented, implemented, and continually adjusted in a way that corresponds to the unique background and personal characteristics of the client.

Individualizing Counseling. Counselors using a structured decision-making model need to be vigilant against a tendency to apply every step of the model to every client. Sometimes clients already have the necessary self-knowledge and skills and have even assembled and researched reasonable options, and they simply do not realize that they are now in a position to make a choice. In these relatively rare cases, the counselor's job is finished when the client has been helped to the realization that he or she is ready to choose and move on. In other (also quite rare) cases, clients are almost completely lacking in skills and knowledge and may have severe impediments to choice or to the process of choosing. For these clients, the actual career choice can be the last link in a long counseling chain. More commonly, clients enter counseling with gaps in their readiness and ability to decide, and the counselor's work is to identify the gaps and help the client fill them in.

The need for flexibility when applying the decision-making model can be illustrated with the people whose stories started this chapter. In the case of Michael Aronsen, the editor, we guess that it would take little time and effort in counseling to discover what he wants out of work and to gather occupational information. It is also likely that he is already an effective decision maker and is capable of writing a résumé and conducting himself well at interviews. In all probability, the most difficult counseling work will be directed toward helping Michael discover new life goals and then take the risk of pursuing them. After twenty years in the family business, he may have more than a few doubts about his ability to learn and compete in an entirely new field, and counseling time may be spent more on psychological than on career concerns.

Doris, who dislikes her work as a cashier, has no need to explore career goals. She and a close friend have always had a dream of running a small independent tailoring business. She has no fears about the quality of her products, having received positive feedback from friends who are successful tailors and buyers for large retail clothing stores. Doris's lack of business experience and information about what will be involved in working for herself tends to make her somewhat naive and impetuous, and the bulk of career counseling in her case is likely to be directed toward information gathering, careful examination of risks, and detailed planning.

Thomas, the packing supervisor, is a typical example of a person whose problems relate directly to the unsuitability of the work environment. Despite his dislike of the supervisory role, Thomas has been given increasingly more responsibility in this area. Failing relationships with several of his younger supervisees have brought him to counseling at the prompting of the plant manager. Thomas's situation is complicated by the fact that he is fifty-six years old, lives in a town with high unemployment, and for family reasons cannot move to a different town. In these circumstances it is unlikely that counseling will focus on helping Thomas to change jobs completely. There are options available, but they might well involve unacceptable risks for Thomas, and the exploration of these options might be brief. Personal counseling can help him learn skills to avoid conflicts with his supervisees or to adjust in other ways to his situation, while career counseling will probably focus on readily accessible options—say, a minor change of position within the company. A bright outcome of career counseling might be for Thomas to decide to pursue an avocation to be completed after his retirement.

These three examples illustrate the need for a flexible and individualized approach to each career client, based on the client's unique pattern of strengths and weaknesses and gaps in skills and information. It is our belief that the successful career counselor takes into account both personal and career issues without allowing the structure of the model to take precedence over the needs of the individual. Logical and systematic as the model may be, it is not rigid and can and should be adapted to individual needs. Thus, career counselors are faced with a complex dual task. On the one hand, they need an understanding of and sensitivity to the marketplace and economic reality, a network of community contacts, and a constant updating of sources of information. On the other hand, they need to remain responsive to how the client is reacting emotionally, to any psychological mechanisms being activated in the client by the search for a career, and to the impact of counseling on the client's psychosocial environment. Without this holistic and individualized process, information important to the development and selection of options may be overlooked, or the client may come to view counseling as impersonal or irrelevant. It takes considerable clinical skill to integrate the client's psychological needs and the requirements of a rational decision-making model without sacrificing one for the other. Yet the flexibility to make this integration is needed if career counseling is to be successful.

❧ 2 ❧

Assessing Client Needs and Establishing Counseling Goals

By the end of the initial assessment stage, which usually lasts two to three sessions, two objectives should be reached: (1) both client and counselor should be clear about what the client wants from career counseling and about the extent of likely success, and (2) the client should be actively involved in counseling and should understand the amount of time and effort likely to be needed in reaching his or her goals.

With some clients, these objectives can be achieved rapidly, even within one session. Consider the example of Joanne, a high school teacher suffering from burnout. Because she had seen a counselor on several occasions over the last ten years and was familiar with the counseling process, and because she was clear that she needed to stop teaching and find a less stressful career, Joanne understood the time and effort likely to be required for her to reach her goal and was actively involved in the counseling process by the end of the initial session.

With other clients the time required for the initial assessment stage can be much longer, for several reasons. Some clients are confused about what they want or are not in the habit of thinking in terms of goals. Others are in a state of mental distress, such as depression or anxiety, that needs to be alleviated first. Still others may come from a complex background or situation that needs time to sort out.

This chapter describes five steps in the initial assessment process: providing a disclosure statement, identifying problems, collecting background information, setting counseling goals, and assigning homework. These steps will not necessarily be accomplished in the order presented but need to be completed before leaving the initial assessment stage.

Disclosure Statement

The first task is to give the client adequate information for making an informed choice about whether to proceed with counseling (American Personnel and Guidance Association, 1981; American Psychological Association, 1981). The purpose of this procedure is to protect clients by providing them with the data necessary for making intelligent decisions regarding the use of a particular practitioner's services. For most clients, the therapeutic situation is a new one; consequently, they are unclear about what is expected of them, what they can expect from the therapist, and what their rights are as clients. Not uncommonly, clients fail to realize that they have any rights, and because they are vulnerable and sometimes desperate for help, they may unquestioningly accept whatever their counselor tells them.

To avoid misunderstanding, provide the client with information about (1) counseling itself, including its goals, procedures, risks, limitations, likely outcomes, and cost; (2) the qualifications and experience of the counselor; and (3) other sources of help.

It is particularly important to explain the process of career counseling, as it involves a certain commitment of time and the performance of activities that might be unfamiliar, tedious, or frustrating to the client. Some clients appreciate a brief explanation of your philosophy of counseling and your beliefs about how people change, but the minimum information to provide is a description of what will happen in counseling—what you will do and what you expect of the client. Identify any techniques other than talking that you might use, such as testing or homework. There is some evidence that clients experience greater benefits from counseling if they are prepared in advance for the role they will be expected to play in the counseling situation (Mayerson, 1984).

Any possible risks should be discussed with the client. For example, counseling may increase psychological awareness to a point that might cause pain and anxiety or produce changes that could cause disruption and turmoil in a person's life. A prospective client might elect not to begin counseling rather than risk this kind of trouble. Consider Sheila, a happily married woman who had not worked for twenty-five years and who consulted a counselor because she wanted to return to work. When the counselor brought up the possibility that her working might disrupt her marriage, Sheila decided she would prefer not to take that risk.

Counselors are expected to keep their counseling relationships confidential, and yet there are limits on that confidentiality that are not under the control of the counselor. These limits should be explained to clients at the outset of counseling, before the client has an opportunity to talk about private material. If counseling is being paid for by the client's medical insurance, the insurance company may require that the counselor's notes be reviewed. If payment is being made by the client's employer, a report detailing what occurred in counseling may be required. In a group counseling situation, the counselor can request but not guarantee that the group members not discuss what goes on in counseling outside the session. Many counselors routinely consult with their colleagues about their counseling cases to get different perspectives and fresh viewpoints. Finally, if a client discloses an intention to harm himself or herself or others, the counselor must report it, and in many jurisdictions, any person, including a counselor, who has reason to suspect child abuse is required by law to report that suspicion to the appropriate authorities.

Disclosure statements typically include two other types of information: (1) the per session fee the counselor charges and any extra fees, such as for testing or telephone calls, as well as the approximate length of time counseling will take; (2) a description of your education and training and the types of clients and problems you are best qualified to deal with. You should verbally communicate alternative ways that exist to deal with the client's concerns, such as self-help books or free counseling at the local community college.

The counselor can give most of this information to the client verbally, present it by means of a written professional disclosure statement (Hogan, 1979; Gross, 1977; Winborn, 1977), or do both. There is some evidence that clients prefer a combination of verbal and written information (LeGendre, 1978). A sample written disclosure statement is provided in Exhibit 3.

Exhibit 3. Sample Disclosure Statement.

Counseling is conducted in a number of different ways, depending on the counselor. As my client you have the right to know my qualifications, how I work, and what you can expect from me as your counselor.

Credentials and Work Experience

I have a master's degree in counseling from Rockport State University and am licensed in California as a Marriage, Family, and Child Counselor. My training included fieldwork at Rockport State University's Career Development Center and at Valley Community Mental Health Center.

Most of my experience has been with adults. I have worked with persons who have a wide range of problems, including marriage, divorce, family, sexual, anxiety, depression, assertiveness, and career. I work with individuals, couples, and families; I do not usually work directly with children or with young adolescents, although I see them as part of family counseling.

Process of Counseling

When people come to counseling, it is because they want something to be different in their lives. They may want to change their life situations, solve a particular problem, make a decision, or understand what is happening in their lives or in themselves. As a first step in counseling, you and I will explore your feelings and concerns and what changes you want. When we both understand your situation, I will help you devise various ways to get what you want, as far as that is possible. For counseling to be most effective, you must make a commitment of time and energy and take an active part in the process; this may well involve activities you undertake between sessions, such as reading articles, listening to tape recordings, or practicing new skills.

My Responsibilities as a Counselor

I will keep anything that you tell me in strictest confidence unless I have your permission to tell someone. The only exceptions are: (1) I may consult with another professional about your concerns and how I might proceed in order to

Exhibit 3. Sample Disclosure Statement, Cont'd.

---

help you, but I will do so without using your name. You have the right to ask me not to consult with anyone. (2) If you tell me you are going to harm yourself or someone else, I am required by law to do anything I reasonably can to prevent that. (3) Most insurance companies require a diagnosis and some require a progress report. If you intend to bill your insurance company for counseling, you might want to check on their requirements first.

Your Rights as a Client

You have the right to understand my reasons for making suggestions or using particular procedures. I will try to explain clearly, but if you have any questions, please ask them—another of your rights. You also have the right to refuse to do anything I suggest. And you have the right, at any time and for any reason, to decide you do not wish to continue counseling.

Time and Money

Most counseling sessions take place weekly and last 50 minutes. Depending on your concerns, however, sessions may be scheduled more or less frequently. The number of sessions needed varies with each person and problem; after I fully understand your concerns, we will discuss the number of sessions you might need. The agency's standard fee is $50 per session, but we have a sliding scale based on your ability to pay.

John Jones, M.S.
XYZ Counseling Agency

Problem Identification

It is unusual to find a client with a single problem that is clearly isolated from the rest of his or her life. Clients usually have multiple concerns and often enter counseling in a state of crisis and confusion. The boundaries of separate problems are often unclear, and clients, overwhelmed by their situation, tend to judge every problem at the same level of severity, failing to differentiate minor from major concerns. Begin by asking clients to identify all their ongoing concerns. In telling their story to a sympathetic listener, they feel understood and accepted, and the counselor has an opportunity to demonstrate empathy and to establish rapport. By asking about all problems rather than prematurely narrowing the focus, the counselor gains perspective on the client's situation and can begin to make a decision about the type of counseling that might be required. Will it be primarily for career problems, for personal problems, or for both? How much do personal problems affect the career problem, and vice versa?

In some cases, it is evident that, even though work is affected, the primary source of the client's problem is an interpersonal issue or a psychological problem, such as depression, usually assigned to personal counseling. For example, Alan sought counseling because his frequent absences from work had attracted negative attention from his employer and he was under threat of dismissal. He came to counseling believing that what he needed was a career change. Discussion in the first session revealed that Alan was normally a good worker and enjoyed his job, but his marital situation had been deteriorating for several months and his work problems had begun only when his wife first announced that she wanted a divorce. Alan's immediate goal for counseling was to put a stop to his work absences in order to hold on to his job, but the main work of counseling was directed toward his relationship difficulties and did not involve counseling for career choice.

A counselor using effective listening skills and prompting questions will typically have little difficulty in eliciting a comprehensive picture of the client's problems and in categorizing and prioritizing them. The following example will illustrate the process. Bob was referred for counseling by a friend who had been a client of the counselor. He presented himself as moderately depressed and had many complaints. He had difficulty sleeping, he was irritable with his spouse, and his sexual life was unsatisfactory. Six months before, because of cutbacks, he had lost his job as personnel director for a large corporation; he had been living off savings and was now seriously worried about his dwindling resources. His doubt and worry were intensified by the fact that, even before the layoff, he had been dissatisfied with his job and was no longer sure that he wanted to continue in personnel work. He reported that two years previously his wife had had an affair and he had felt humiliated and angry ever since. He was concerned that his persistent lack of interest in sex with anyone, including his spouse, indicated that he was getting old and "past it." In recent months he had been drinking more and had put on about twenty pounds. Although he had two good friends who remained close, he reported feeling unaccustomed envy, as both of them had good jobs. Bob missed his friends from work and particularly the workouts at the company gym. He suffered from vague feelings of anxiety and increasing boredom, and he was making fewer and fewer efforts to find work, despite his wife's nagging and complaints that she had "married a loser." He related well to his children but felt guilty about being a poor role model.

During his initial presentation of these complaints, Bob attributed all his problems to the loss of his job and felt bitter and helpless about his situation. When the counselor asked him to inspect the list of problems, Bob realized that he was dealing with three interconnected but still separable problem areas. First, he recognized a connection between his inactivity, boredom, physical complaints, and increased drinking. He also identified the items that related to his marriage difficulties: sexual concerns, anger, fear of aging, and unattractiveness. Finally, Bob was able to identify problems that seemed to relate more directly to his lack of employment. This categorization of problems helped Bob to realize that his concerns were not all due to unemployment. When it came to setting priorities, he had little hesitation in deciding to work first on employment, recognizing that this was the most urgent need and that, in any case, a new job would probably have a positive impact in other areas of his life. In this case, setting a counseling goal was almost a formality.

Throughout the discussion of problems in the client's life, and indeed throughout this stage of assessment, the counselor can also take note of any problems not formally presented by the client that have the potential for disrupting counseling. Be particularly sensitive to the psychological constraints discussed in Chapter One—namely, anxiety, discouragement, external locus of control, impatience, inflexibility, dependency, lack of persistence, lack of self-confidence, and unwillingness to take risks.

An effective way to gather information about these potentially disruptive factors is to keep a running list of client statements that might indicate problem behaviors and attitudes. Since we are concerned here mainly with career decision making, counselors should note in particular any assertions about work, careers, and decisions, such as "I'd feel like a failure if I quit this job," "My father would be so upset if I didn't go into the army," "I know there's one job out there that's just right for me," "I've never really made decisions; I like to let life just sort of flow," "I know I can do anything if I just try hard enough," "I often make a good start at something, but then it all goes wrong." You will probably wish to postpone sharing this list of possible constraints with the client to avoid distracting him or her from the tasks of the initial assessment stage, although you might wish to use some of the information when helping the client set counseling goals.

Background Information

Because all areas of life tend to be interconnected, it is important to gather some limited preliminary information about the client's current functioning in several areas. For example, you will want to learn about health status (illnesses, medications, and recreational drug use, including alcohol), because such information can indicate possible barriers to career choice or problems to be addressed during or before counseling. A second area to investigate is family and personal relationships and current living situation; such information will indicate the responsibilities the client bears, the extent of social support systems, and the existence of interpersonal stressors. A third area to probe is the ways in which the client is coping with current life situations. Finally, you need to know the client's financial status, as it usually has impact, negative or positive, on the urgency of the problem and the intensity of the client's distress.

In addition to information about current status, the counselor will need some brief historical information to help see the client's vocational concerns in the context of his or her life, rather than in isolation. Elements of that context are the person's work history, upbringing, and family of origin. What models of work did the family provide, what values and expectations about work and careers were conveyed to the client, and to what extent did the client endorse and accept them?

As well as trying to get a well-rounded, though at this stage limited, picture of the client's life, the counselor also attempts to identify strengths, possible constraints, and areas that might later require further exploration. We recommend that as much as possible of the information be gathered outside the actual session, since there are usually other matters the client would rather spend time and money discussing.

An efficient way to collect necessary background information is by means of pencil-and-paper devices such as an intake form, a work history, and a vocationally oriented developmental inventory, all of which can be completed by the client at home. Samples of these forms are provided in Exhibits 4, 5, and 6.

Exhibit 4. Sample Intake Form.

Name: _____ Telephone: _____

Address: _____

Age: _____ Referred by: _____

1. Marital status: Single Married Separated Widowed Divorced

2. How many times have you been married before? _____

3. List members of your present family and family of origin. (If person is deceased, identify education and occupation when living.)

	Name	Age	Education	Occupation
Father				
Mother				
Brothers				
and				
Sisters				
Spouse				
Children				

4. Please give the following information about each person who presently lives with you.

Exhibit 4. Sample Intake Form, Cont'd.

Name	Sex	Age	Relationship to You

5. Describe your education and training, including the highest grade you completed in school.

6. Please describe your occupation.

7. What is your present state of health? Please identify any health problems.

8. What prescription or nonprescription drugs do you take?

9. Have you ever been in counseling or therapy before? When, and for how long? Please describe the results.

10. What are your present concerns or symptoms that lead you to seek counseling at this time?

11. How long have you had these concerns?

12. You may have tried a number of things to cope with your problems. Please describe what you have tried and how helpful your efforts have been.

13. If our work together in counseling is successful, in what ways do you think you or your life might be changed?

Exhibit 5. Sample Employment History.

Account for all time for the past ten years, including military service and periods of unemployment, starting with your present or last position.

(1) Company   From month/year   To month/year

_____

Position or title   Salary

_____

Briefly describe your duties

_____

Reason for leaving

_____

(2) Company   From month/year   To month/year

_____

Position or title   Salary

_____

Briefly describe your duties

_____

Reason for leaving

_____

Exhibit 6. Sample Developmental Work History.

1. Describe your memories of your father's work.

2. Describe your memories of your mother's work.

3. How did your parents feel about their work?

4. Do you have the same work attitudes and behaviors as your parents did?

5. When you were a child, was there anyone whose job interested or impressed you? Why? Did you think of doing that work yourself? Why or why not?

Exhibit 6. Sample Developmental Work History, Cont'd.

6. Describe the first job or work (not a regularly assigned chore) you remember doing as a child. How did you feel about it?

7. Describe other, early experiences of work that stand out in your memory.

8. Before the age of twelve, what sort of a worker were you? How would you describe yourself? How did others view you?

9. Did anyone in your childhood expect or want you to do a certain job when you grew up?

10. What were the family values with reference to work (for example, "always do your best")?

Answers to the questions on these forms should provide you with a capsule picture of the client's life. With some clients—those who are not particularly verbal or who have poor writing skills, for example—it might be preferable to simply ask the questions during the session. Some counselors, preferring not to overwhelm a new client with paperwork, request that clients complete only one or two forms, or portions of one form, and collect the rest of the information during the session. Other counselors send only the intake form to the client, asking that it be completed and returned before the first session, as a means of saving session time for other issues. Yet others prefer to give the forms as homework after the first meeting, believing that clients are more likely to complete the forms satisfactorily if the counselor has had an opportunity to explain how the information might be useful. The method you choose will depend on the client and on the structure and detail of the forms you devise.

We recommend that you develop and continue to use a consistent method for collecting background information. After extensive experience with one method, you will develop internal norms that more easily enable you to notice gaps or anomalies in the information provided by the client. These discrepancies should be investigated in greater depth to round out the picture and identify possible trouble spots. For example, what accounts for the client's employment in very different fields, or for periods of unemployment? How does the client explain and feel about the fact that, in a large family, he is the only one not employed as a professional? Why is there such a large discrepancy between the client's high level of education and consistently low level of work? Although answers to these questions might be irrelevant, they can provide information that has an important bearing on career counseling or can indicate unsuspected assets, skill deficits, areas that might need to be explored in personal counseling, and so on.

Counseling Goals

Because goals can be defined in different ways, let us first present our understanding of the concept. We view a *counseling goal* as an agreement arrived at by client and counselor concerning the outcomes toward which counseling efforts will be directed. An acceptable counseling goal has several characteristics: (1) there is reason to believe that it is attainable by this client; (2) it relates as directly as possible to the client's presenting problem(s); (3) it is within the counselor's competence and value system; (4) it is arrived at collaboratively by mutual discussion; and (5) it is "experimental," meaning that the client and counselor understand that ensuing circumstances or ensuing events or a change of heart can lead to a change in the goal.

It would be difficult to overstate the advantages of working within the context of counseling goals that meet these criteria. On the client's side, the collaborative aspect of goal setting decreases client dependence on the counselor and increases a sense of self-control and commitment to counseling. For the counselor, having a mutually acceptable counseling goal provides a way to evaluate progress, to adjust techniques accordingly, and to know when counseling, or at least a particular phase of counseling, has come to an end. A good counseling goal ensures that counselor and client are not working at cross-purposes and are not wasting time and money by straying too far from what the client wants from counseling. Because all counseling goals are of necessity individualized, there is some assurance that the counselor will personalize techniques, rather than use a standardized approach regardless of the client's needs.

To a large extent, the way has been paved for goal setting by categorizing and prioritizing problems. If the client brings only one concern to counseling, there will be little difficulty in choosing a goal, although the counselor will still need to help the client clarify and assess the feasibility of the goal. When the client has multiple concerns, a mixture of personal and career problems, or severe constraints, goal setting becomes a more complex activity and will require more time. Unless the goal is obvious and is speedily determined, this activity is often left to the start of the second or third session. Sometimes counselors ask clients to devote time at home between sessions to thinking about a possible direction and starting point for counseling. The results of this homework form the basis of the goal-setting activity in the next session.

At times, clinical judgment will indicate that the client is not in a position to pursue a career counseling goal. Brown (1985) maintains that career counseling is appropriate only when the client has reasonably accurate perceptions of self and the environment, is motivated to make a career choice, and has a support system adequate to allow for career changes, or when the main source of the client's problems is the work situation. If, however, the client's work problems originate in other areas of life and would not be alleviated by a new career decision, or if the client lacks the support, skills, psychological traits, or mental stability to successfully undertake career counseling, a personal counseling goal, directed at remedying these deficits, would be more appropriate.

If career counseling is not indicated at this time, explain your reasons for reaching this conclusion. For example, you might explain to a severely depressed client that, because of the effect of depression on energy levels, concentration, and decision making, he or she will make quicker and more satisfying progress in career counseling after the depression has been alleviated to some extent. Clients can usually see the logic behind a valid explanation and either will adopt a personal counseling goal preliminary to a career goal or will decide to set and pursue both types of goals concurrently. On the rare occasions when a client insists, even after your explanations, on what appears to be an inappropriate goal, you have two choices: refer the client, or negotiate a contract to work toward the client's goal for a limited period, after which the goal will be evaluated. Sometimes clients can best be served by personal counseling only or by an alternative form of career counseling, such as bibliotherapy, time with an interactive computer program, or group counseling.

In setting counseling goals, we suggest that you begin by taking the client's list of presenting problems and establishing the general areas where the client desires change—for example, career change, relationship with children, physical health. Together with the client, choose a starting place, asking for example: "You've identified a number of concerns; is there one that stands out as most important?" or "Which of the problems that you've listed do you think we should work on first?"

In many career choice problems, time is an important factor because work determines financial survival for many people and also because time may be needed for training or for the job search itself. Thus, the counselor should also inquire whether there is any particular time by which certain problems must be resolved. If there is no urgency, the counselor should help the client identify an area in which a solution would alleviate the greatest amount of distress, or an area for which success could be achieved with relative ease or speed.

In choosing a starting point, counselor and client need to discuss the time and effort likely to be involved in dealing with each area and the likelihood of the problem being resolved. For example, John has several work-related concerns. Besides being restless and bored in his present job, he has communication difficulties with his co-workers. John and the counselor might well decide to make dealing with the latter problem a first counseling goal, since it can very likely be greatly alleviated in just a few sessions, leaving John more relaxed and able to focus on a possible career change.

Once an area is chosen, the goal should be expressed as specifically as possible. In career counseling, appropriately phrased goals might include the following: "Decide on a volunteer activity that I would find rewarding," "Make a five-year career enhancement plan," "Choose between veterinary and medical school," "Decide on a major," "Find out whether a career in business would suit me," "Make an optional plan for if my health fails me," "Choose a career that fits in with my spouse's career," "Get started in my chosen career," "Do a preliminary exploration of my career options."

Homework

To accustom the client to the idea of weekly homework and thus set up a habit that will be necessary later in counseling, as well as to obtain an initial measure of the client's compliance and level of functioning, assign homework from the first session. In this first stage, the main purpose of homework is to fill in gaps in the preliminary assessment process. The most common assignments, therefore, will be pencil-and-paper instruments such as the work history, intake form, or developmental work history described earlier in this chapter. Clients can also be asked to think about possible counseling goals or, if a goal has already been selected, about possible roadblocks to achieving the goal and possible negative and positive consequences of goal achievement. Generally, clients take homework more seriously if they are asked to bring a concrete product, such as a few notes or sentences resulting from their thinking, to the next session.

As with all interventions, assignments should be tailored to each individual's needs and situation. This can be accomplished by adjusting the number of instruments given, by simplifying them if necessary, and by ensuring that instructions are understood and that the client has the time, motivation, and capability to complete the assignment. It is counterproductive to assign homework that the client might not be able to carry out, as failure can damage the client's confidence and reduce commitment to counseling at this early stage.

Problems and Cautions

Pacing and Timing. A rule of thumb for this first stage is to perform the tasks to the minimum extent that will allow for movement to the next stage. Although it is obvious that many factors have to be considered to accomplish the tasks of this stage, counselors should not lose sight of the fact that if the client clearly has a career counseling concern, it is important to move on to the next stage, so that progress is being made toward a work-related choice. This move can be made even if the goal is not perfectly formulated or the client completely understood. There will be ample opportunity during the self-understanding stage to gather further information about the client and to refine the goal, if necessary.

A second guideline concerns establishment of the counselor-client relationship, which must take precedence over other tasks. Many of the activities of this first stage require that the counselor be directive—in asking questions, making assignments, explaining role expectations, and so on—but it is important that enough time be allowed for the client to feel accepted and to establish a connection with the counselor. A client who feels rigidly structured is unlikely to develop the trust in the counselor that will be required for divulging personal material or taking risks. Competent pacing of this stage—and indeed of all stages of career counseling—requires that the counselor remain sensitive to the client's response to the process. If this stage extends beyond a few sessions, it should be because time is required for the client to feel understood, rather than because the counselor wants to gather more information.

Resistance. In its original usage, the term *resistance* referred to behavior that clients evidenced when trying to prevent the emergence into consciousness of unconscious material. We use *resistance* to refer to the client's failure to complete the tasks of the stage—that is, to provide information, to set goals, or to do assigned homework. We do not assume that the cause of resistance lies necessarily with the client's unconscious psychological mechanisms, since resistance may also be the result of environmental pressures, chance events, and even counselor insensitivity or incompetence.

Whatever the cause, client resistance impedes progress and cannot be ignored. One method for dealing with this problem is to identify the resistance and then enlist the client's aid in analyzing and solving the difficulty. This collaborative approach avoids the adversarial position implied by the word *resistance* and removes any indication on the part of either client or counselor to blame oneself or each other. What follow are several examples of resistance with suggested methods for handling the problems.

Janice failed to complete a record-keeping assignment after the first session, because of lack of time. During the week, her children's illness and an unexpected out-of-town visitor had assumed priority claims on her time and energy. Because Janice still appeared motivated to continue counseling, the counselor assumed that her explanation was valid, and they worked out a method for Janice to complete assignments in a modified way if an emergency situation arose again. In following weeks, she completed assignments with no problem.

Mary Ann also failed to complete a first assignment because of lack of time. When the counselor pointed out that Mary Ann was free to complete assignments or not, she evidenced relief and admitted that she hadn't really wanted to do the assignment because it didn't seem to be relevant to her problems, but she was worried about displeasing the counselor. The ensuing discussion revealed that Mary Ann had agreed to a counseling goal that did not feel appropriate, but she had assumed that the counselor knew best. The counselor explained more clearly Mary Ann's expected role as an active partner in counseling, and they negotiated a new goal.

When Jackson returned with an incomplete assignment, it was because he had been lent a self-help book on choosing a career and had spent his time doing exercises that seemed more interesting to him. Discussion led to the decision that he would continue to work on his own using the book and would return to counseling if he felt unable to continue alone.

A final example of homework resistance is Art, who failed to complete several assignments in a row, although each failure had been discussed and the counselor had tried to modify homework to suit Art's needs. Eventually, the counselor explained that completing assignments would be necessary if progress was to be made. Angrily, Art complained that he was paying the counselor to come up with answers to his problems. He was unable to accept the rationale for playing an active role in the counseling process and refused to continue with counseling.

Resistance can also be demonstrated during the goal-setting process. Mildred found it impossible to concentrate on one topic and continually strayed into long rambling stories about her lifelong problems. Her statement "No one understands how I feel" alerted the counselor to the need to postpone the goal-setting task until Mildred felt that she had unburdened herself of all her concerns and that the counselor really understood her situation.

When Jonathan had a similar difficulty in setting goals, the counselor allowed more time for self-expression, but when he began to perseverate and refused to respond to the counselor's efforts to direct therapy, it became evident that confrontation was needed. After the failure of several gentle attempts to ascertain some changes that Jonathan would like to make in his life, the counselor asked directly: "Do you want to make any changes at all, or do you want things to stay as they are in your life?" Jonathan was unable to answer with a clear yes or no. When asked about his ambivalence, he admitted that he was pessimistic about his ability to make changes and frightened to face new challenges that would probably result from change. What emerged from this discussion were two related, time-limited goals: to explore the likely effects of career change and to examine Jonathan's ability to manage his life, with the understanding that these goals in no way committed Jonathan to actually making a change. Not unexpectedly, this exploration reduced his doubts to the point where he was able to begin career counseling just a few weeks later.

Sometimes resistance is expressed as "Yes, but . . ." because the client believes that the situation is hopeless and nothing will work. In such cases, the client can often be persuaded to try an experiment for a few weeks, to see if change can occur. Interventions designed to produce even minimal improvement will usually overcome the client's initial sense of helplessness, and career counseling can proceed. There is some evidence that fear of failure can lead clients to devalue counseling (Saltoun, 1985), so it is important to provide adequate emotional support and success experiences. Ensuring success often entails setting small weekly goals rather than an overwhelming large one.

Resistance can also be the result of a hidden agenda. Some clients come to counseling with a decision already made. What they are looking for is reassurance that the decision is wise, the permission of an authority figure to pursue a course that possibly entails harm to others, or a stamp of approval that can be used to persuade significant others that the chosen goal is appropriate. For example, despite his family's derision, Tim had decided to go to medical school and wanted to be able to tell his relatives that the counselor said this is the best career for him. Jackie wanted the counselor's endorsement to allay her guilt at deciding to divorce her husband, give him custody of the children, and return to modeling.

You might suspect the existence of a hidden agenda if any of the following occurs: the client brushes off efforts to widen the discussion and continually reverts to one option; the client comes to the first session with a goal already decided; the client is unwilling to discuss any negative aspects of the goal; the client indicates that, once the goal is chosen, counseling has ended.

The counselor's suspicion that a hidden agenda exists should lead to an open discussion. You can ask, for example, "How would your parents (children, spouse) feel about this goal?" or "What effect would pursuing this goal have on your family?" If the client feels respected and supported by an unbiased counselor, the agenda is usually brought into the open, and the client can be invited to discuss whatever issues might be involved, such as rebelliousness, subassertiveness, guilt, or independence.

❧ 3 ❧

Promoting Client Self-Understanding

Unlike personal counseling, in which understanding oneself can be an important end in its own right, career counseling explores self-understanding in the service of discovering what work situations would please the client and fit his or her personality and desired life-style. Because work is inextricably bound up with other aspects of life, the assessment process includes more than simply work, but the focus remains at all times on the client's career-related concerns. It is important to maintain this focus, to avoid the often attractive trap of continuing to assess for self-understanding beyond what is needed to help the client meet the immediate goal. Although it is not the purpose of self-understanding in a career counseling context to effect personality change or increase insight into the client's general personal and interpersonal dynamics, even the relatively circumscribed exploration required for career choice can be surprisingly revealing. Should material emerge during the remainder of the assessment stage that indicates a need for further personal counseling, the current counseling goal might need to be renegotiated.

The time required for completing this stage can vary greatly. For a self-aware, articulate client, one session might be sufficient to complete the interview described in this chapter. However, more time will be needed if, for example, tests take a week or two to return from computer scoring, or the client has been asked to engage in field trips or work experiences. In the interim, it is usually neither necessary nor desirable to devote multiple sessions exclusively to assessment activities. One alternative is to suspend career counseling temporarily, asking the client to maintain contact by means of regularly scheduled telephone calls to report progress. A second option is for the client to keep a log of career-related experiences, presenting you with sections of the log at weekly intervals.

The counselor might also anticipate and address the client's probable future career counseling needs—out of sequence, as it were. Consider the case of seventeen-year-old Karen, sickly for much of her childhood and consequently unable to participate in a wide range of teenage activities, including work outside the home. Not once had she thought of the future, much less a career, until her parents indicated that she would be expected to work when she graduated from high school. Not surprisingly, she could tell her school counselor little about her work preferences, her life-style dreams, or even her current interests. For Karen, therefore, the self-understanding stage included having her try volunteer work in several different jobs over a period of three months. During this time, individual counseling was devoted to Karen's concerns and anxieties about living on her own. She also attended group sessions directed at job search preparation, where she practiced interviewing skills and discussed issues appropriate to her entry into the world of work.

Work-Related Preferences

The major difficulty with the self-understanding stage is not acquiring information but rather organizing it into a form that will be useful for evaluating options and for the job search process. We find it most helpful to summarize the mass of self-understanding material into statements that reflect what the client wants from work in terms of tasks, working conditions, location, and benefits. These statements we refer to collectively as *Work-Related Preferences*.

Both theorizing about and research into the nature of work and of people's interaction with it have produced a consensus that assessment for career choice should include an understanding of the client's interests, abilities, and values. Some authors add personality or temperament to this list (for example, Isaac-son, 1985); others add career maturity (for example, Zunker, 1985); yet others, the work environment (for example, Holland, 1985). Increasingly, career counselors are emphasizing the value and function of work in the client's overall life, rather than view-ing a job or career as somehow separate from other activities, such as family life and leisure (Burck, 1984). This focus on the interaction between life-style and work seems legitimate when one considers that motivation for and commitment to work are likely to be influenced by the value work has for the worker and that the extent to which a person is able to participate in work is often determined by the strength and importance of competing demands from nonwork environments and circumstances.

Given that information about a client's work preferences and life-style is desirable, the central questions become: How much information is needed, and by what methods should it be acquired? The traditional answer to these questions is to ad-minister a battery of pencil-and-paper inventories and exercises, usually assessing abilities, interests, and values, which the coun-selor then analyzes and interprets to the client. This systematic and comprehensive approach can be the most appropriate one in certain circumstances. With a group of clients, for example, it is often more efficient to proceed in a structured manner than to attempt individualization. Certainly with young, naive, or inexperienced clients it can be necessary to assess in detail each aspect of the client's personality, beliefs, hopes, interests, and so on that could impinge on career selection. A further advan-tage of the battery approach is that many of the widely used instruments have been well researched and demonstrate good reliability and validity, thus providing some assurance of high-quality assessment.

There are, however, valid reasons to consider a different approach to career counseling assessment. Many clients, espe-cially older and more experienced ones, know their work-related needs and wishes quite well; for these people, it would be a waste of resources to perform elaborate assessment activities in areas where self-understanding already exists. More cogently, one can argue that assessment at this point—that is, before specific job alternatives are available to consider—takes place in something of a vacuum. It is frustrating to conduct a detailed assessment on a client only to have the client change his or her mind about priorities and even values, or provide new information, once faced with particular career choices. Acquiring occupational information and assembling several viable alternatives can render previous assessments irrelevant, inadequate, or inaccurate as new doors open or close for the client. Furthermore, the use of a battery of instruments is an indirect approach that by its nature is limited in individuality, and it often produces a great deal of information that is difficult to organize in a useful and coherent manner.

In the interests of efficiency and individualization, we therefore recommend that, rather than automatically administering a predetermined battery of general assessment instruments, counselors conduct a semi-structured interview with clients to discover Work-Related Preferences. The interview approach has several advantages: it is direct and personal, it is relatively rapid, it can be adjusted to individual clients, and it results in a concise, portable summary that can be used to evaluate options when they are assembled. The use of a personal interview also allows the assessment process to be self-limiting, since, if the client can provide the information requested during the interview, no other form of assessment will be necessary and the client will be ready to proceed to the stage of assembling options and information. Any gaps in the client's self-knowledge will be immediately apparent during the interview, and the counselor can then select an assessment method designed to fill in the specific gap.

Exhibit 7 contains a list of Work-Related Preferences (WRPs), arranged in four categories, that are of potential interest to clients. Although it is unlikely that all possible variables have been included, these categories and the specifics we will be discussing do cover most aspects of most work situations and should provide a comprehensive picture of what the client wants— a picture representative of interests, values, and life-style preferences. Following is a description of the items in each category of Exhibit 7.

Exhibit 7. Work-Related Preferences.

Work Tasks

1. Routine work
2. Physical work
3. Work with machines, tools, equipment, materials
4. Work with numbers
5. Work with words
6. Work with plants or animals
7. Work with people
8. Work with information or ideas
9. Clerical tasks
10. Creative expression of ideas or feelings

Working Conditions

1. Relationships with people
2. Movement and time
3. Performance conditions
4. Variety
5. Environment

Location

1. Indoors/outdoors
2. Geographical
3. Urban/rural
4. Special preferences or needs

Benefits

1. Salary and fringe benefits
2. Opportunities
3. Job security
4. Fame/status
5. Valued work
6. Challenge or excitement
7. Enjoyable colleagues
8. Portability

Work Tasks. The work tasks category is usually the most important section of the interview because it concerns the skills and activities that consume most of the working day and therefore have the greatest impact on work satisfaction. Most items in this category cover a wide range of activities, many of which may not occur to the client, especially if the person has limited experience. The client should indicate preferences regarding:

1. *Routine work.* Structured and repetitive tasks, such as filing, assembly-line work, data coding. Usually nondemanding and predictable.
2. *Physical work.* Work requiring use of muscles as a primary aspect. Can range from heavy labor to fine craft work.
3. *Work with machines, tools, equipment, materials.* The range of equipment is wide, from microscopes to earthmovers, from surgical instruments to typesetting machines, from computers to cameras.
4. *Work with numbers.* Tallying, collecting, manipulating, using formulas, theorizing mathematically. Jobs can range from accountant to physicist, from computer programmer to statistician, and so on.
5. *Work with words.* Writing, editing, translating, verbal or written work, reading, critiquing, and so on.
6. *Work with plants or animals.* Work that may involve nurturing, healing, researching, experimenting, and so on.
7. *Work with people.* Teaching, supervising, selling, persuading, negotiating, leading, protecting, advocating, performing, entertaining, helping with spiritual, mental, or physical welfare.
8. *Work with information or ideas.* Collating, analyzing, collecting, discovering, explaining, theorizing, problem solving, and so on.
9. *Clerical tasks.* Proofreading, copying, filing, sorting, and so on.
10. *Creative expression of ideas or feelings.* Music, dance, drama, poetry—all the arts.

Working Conditions. For many people, working conditions are as important as the work tasks themselves because they address the psychological aspects of work, such as independence, self-image, security, and interpersonal relationships. The client should indicate preferences regarding:

1. *Relationships with people.* This item includes contacts with both co-workers and the public. Does the client prefer to

work with many co-workers, or with just one or two? Does the person prefer working alone, in a small group, or as part of a large team? Does the client like egalitarian, democratic working relationships with those in positions of greater or less authority, or does he or she prefer an authoritarian structure, with clear-cut hierarchical distinctions? Is there any group or type of person whom the client strongly prefers to work with or to avoid, such as children, the elderly, the needy? What sort of contact does the person want with the public and in what settings—that is, will the contact be intermittent or constant, one on one or in groups, casual or formal? Does the client like cooperative or competitive relationships with colleagues? Relationships that are friendly, formal, relaxed, orderly, or spontaneous? What sort of feedback does the client prefer, from whom, and in what form—that is, immediate or delayed, written or verbal, from colleagues or authority figures or from the task itself?

2. *Movement and time.* Does the client prefer to stay in one location, such as an office, all day, or move from one setting to another? What about work that requires crosstown travel or work located in different buildings? How does the client feel about work that requires out-of-town travel and absence from home overnight? How often would such travel be acceptable? What about working on weekends or in the evenings?

3. *Performance conditions.* How much control does the client want over work tasks and the manner in which they are to be performed? How much input does the client want into planning and policy? What sort of supervision does the client prefer? Does autonomy extend to salary—that is, would it be acceptable to the client to be paid only for the work he or she actually produces, or to be responsible for generating business for others? Does the client want autonomy over all aspects of work, including setting his or her own working hours? What degree of certainty does the client want to have at work as to clarity of boundaries for tasks, roles, and responsibilities, amount of advance planning and information so that it is clear what to expect, and degree of risk taking required? How much responsibility does the

client want, and of what kind: responsibility to meet goals, to make others perform, to reach standards? What degree of flexibility or structure does the client like in both the hierarchy of the workplace and the assignment of tasks?

4. *Variety.* How much variety does the client want in terms of tasks performed and people worked with? What about relocation to other departments or other areas of the country? How predictable should working hours and vacations be?

5. *Environment.* In what sort of atmosphere does the client prefer to work: calm, relaxed, quiet, or bustling, exciting, noisy? What are the client's preferences for the physical plant? How large or how small? Is esthetic appearance important?

Location. Life-style preferences and environmental constraints dictate many of the client's choices in this category. Health problems, for example, can require a particular climate or access to special medical facilities. A spouse who is unable or unwilling to relocate can limit choices. Children might have special needs or talents that can be nurtured only in one or two parts of the country. The client should indicate preferences regarding:

1. Indoors or outdoors.
2. Geographical location: country, region, state.
3. City, town (how large), rural area (what type).
4. Special preferences or needs, such as an allergy-free climate, near particular recreation areas, in a school district having special classes for learning-disabled students.

Benefits. This category deals with all those benefits, subtle or not, that are additional to the rewards of working at something one enjoys. When the tasks of a job are limited in their appeal and stimulation—for example, most assembly-line work—the other benefits of work gain greatly in importance. Because most people prefer to have as many benefits as possible and are therefore likely to endorse most items on the list, it is more useful to have the client rank order the following items rather than simply indicate preferences:

1. Salary range and specific fringe benefits (medical, retirement, bonuses, stock options, and so on).
2. Opportunities: to advance, to learn different skills, to meet famous people, to prepare for alternative work, and so on.
3. Job security.
4. Fame and status: as a leader, an expert, a pioneer, a member of a prestigious organization.
5. Work that is thought by the client to be important, useful, ethical, of benefit to society. Contributing to an important cause, setting a good example.
6. Feeling needed, challenged, appreciated, stimulated.
7. Enjoyable colleagues. This could mean enjoyable as social companions outside work or as pleasurable working companions because of their qualities of cooperation, stimulation, intelligence, and so on.
8. Portability. A field of work that is in such high demand that a person could move to almost any part of the country and be fairly certain of obtaining a job.

Process for Obtaining Work-Related Preferences

The sample methods presented in this section are part of a process that will lead to a meaningful summary of the client's WRPs. The six steps of this process are to analyze work experience, discuss preference categories, assess ability, assess lifestyle context, prioritize WRPs, and complete summary form.

Analyze Work Experience. The client has already completed a work history as part of background information. Preferably before the interview (in the interest of time), but perhaps during the session in the case of clients who have difficulty with written assignments, ask for a list of the various tasks the client performed in each job. If the client has held many jobs, narrow the field by asking for tasks performed in the jobs held longest or liked best.

The next step is to elicit which of the tasks the client liked and disliked and the reasons for these attitudes. To illustrate the depth and specificity needed, we provide the following sequence of questions that one counselor used to probe for increasing detail while asking a client about five years of summer employment as a youth camp counselor. The focus was on the client's dislikes, but the same questions would relate as well to likes:

1. How did you like that kind of work? (Ask open-ended question, but specific to work)
2. Tell me what your tasks might be on any day. (Elicit details)
3. Which of these did you dislike most? (Narrow focus)
4. Why did you dislike it? Was there anything about the task that you did enjoy? What might have made the task more enjoyable? Why do you think that would have made a difference? (Analyze item)
5. What other tasks did you dislike? (Expand focus)
6. Of all these tasks, which would you most like to have to do for a living? Least like to do? (Request evaluation, comparison, prioritization)
7. How could you tell that you disliked those tasks? Do you think you have changed at all since then, in a way that might alter your feelings about those tasks? (Ask for verification)

The work history can also be used to look for patterns that might indicate stable interests and preferences. For example, suppose you are asking the client about preferences relating to working conditions and learn that the client likes to work in a well-ordered, highly structured environment. You might turn to the work history and ask which jobs met that criterion, how important that aspect of work was compared with others, what the advantages and disadvantages of that aspect were, and so on. The point is that information anchored in real-life situations and experiences is likely to be more detailed and more reliable than information derived as part of a general conversation with no specific references.

The information gathered in the process of analyzing past work experiences should be organized under the four WRP categories: tasks, working conditions, location, and benefits. It does not matter whether you or the client records the information as long as both of you have a copy.

Discuss Preference Categories. Using Exhibit 7, proceed through the list of WRPs, eliciting information from the client about areas not already covered as a result of the analysis of work history. The order in which the categories are discussed is not important, nor is it a matter of concern to complete one before proceeding to another.

Clearly, not all items will apply to every client, and common sense and knowledge of the client should guide the choice of items to focus on. However, no item should be omitted; each one takes little time to mention, and it is better to err on the side of going beyond the client's interests rather than on the side of restricting them because of prejudgments about what you believe to be appropriate work for your client. Allie, for example, was fashionably dressed and coiffed and had worked for twelve years in sales-related positions. The counselor decided to omit questions concerning tools and machinery, judging that Allie would have no interest in these areas. As Allie was leaving the session, a chance comment about woodworking class alerted the counselor to return to the rejected category, which turned out to be of serious interest to the client.

In discussing the WRPs, it is important to use sufficient details and examples to ensure that both counselor and client have the same understanding of the more complex items. While "shift work" might cause no confusion, for example, "responsibility" can take many forms and needs to be defined.

It is also important to arrive at the core interest underlying a client's preference rather than accept a superficial statement. John, for instance, at thirty-two years of age with limited education and inadequate social skills, had worked mainly in low-level, minimum responsibility clerical positions. He told the counselor that what he would like to do is be in charge of a big operation, managing a big staff and large sums of money— "like an IBM executive," John explained. Although it was extremely unlikely that John would ever come close to the position he wanted, the counselor took his wishes seriously and asked for elaboration:

Counselor: If you got a job like that, what do you think you would enjoy most about it?

John: People would think I was important; they'd pay attention to me.

Counselor: And what would you like most about that?

John: If you're a big shot, you don't have to follow the same rules as the rest.

Counselor: Any rules in particular that you would avoid if you were a big shot?

Further exploration along these lines elicited the information that what John valued most was a position in which he could be in charge of his own time. His biggest objection to previous jobs had been having to punch a time clock or have someone else monitor the length of his breaks. In John's eyes, only top management was free of such regimentation, a notion that was the main factor accounting for his interest in a management position.

As a second example, consider two women who stated that it was important for them to be in a job where they could work alone. In response to such questions as "What sort of work do you like to do alone?" "For how long?" "Where?" and "Why do you prefer this?" two very different pictures emerged. Phyllis liked to work in a separate office because she was easily distracted by chatter and clatter. She also worked slowly and carefully and hated to be hurried to complete work, preferring to be given the day's assignment so that she could proceed at her own pace and use break and lunch time to catch up if she decided. For Grace, on the other hand, working alone meant not having to interact with co-workers. In the past she had had considerable difficulty with work relationships, the exploration of which emerged as a secondary career counseling goal. In reality, Grace was quite gregarious and would much rather work on a project where responsibility was shared with others. Only her past interpersonal problems had led her to say that she preferred to work alone.

In the case of three other clients, the phrase "I want to be my own boss" turned out to have three different core interests: being able to control every aspect of the operation; being free to take risks without endangering others; and being free of any authority figure. In all three cases, the clients agreed that there were drawbacks to being one's own boss and that they would be happy to obtain a position that satisfied their core interest, regardless of whether they owned and operated the business. In other words, the first client would have been content as sole manager of a single department within a large organization, the second in an entrepreneurial firm that encouraged initiative, and the third in a democratically run organization. These examples illustrate the need to elicit specific answers from clients, who often tend to make vague or global statements.

Because people are quite naturally influenced by the opinions and values of others, it is important to check that what the client states is, in fact, his or her own considered preference, rather than a perhaps reluctant acquiescence to someone else's expectations or demands. Ask for evidence that the client has thought through the preference with questions such as "How do you know that you like working on a team?" or "What experiences have you had where you enjoyed working with your hands?" If such questions produce vague or incomplete answers, explore what the client enjoys about the stated preference by such requests as "Tell me what you like most about using your imagination."

It is also important to ascertain whether the client's view of a situation is reasonably accurate. Paul, for example, was convinced that his dream of moving to Alaska would be shared by his teenage sons. Asked for evidence, he admitted that his belief was based on the fact that two years previously they had all seen the movie *Never Cry Wolf* and had talked about how exciting it would be to live in that part of the country. Knowing how quickly teenagers change their minds, the counselor asked Paul to discuss with his sons a possible move to the north. He was dismayed to find that they both strongly preferred to remain at their present schools, with familiar friends—a preference that influenced Paul's own wishes.

Although the WRP items all concern interests and values related to the work situation, questions need not be confined to the client's work experiences, especially if the client has had few experiences or expresses a desire for something different from previous work. Any activity at which the client has spent time—

including hobbies, sports, vacation choices, social activities, volunteer work, and tasks involved in parenting and household management—can indicate preferences. For example, a displaced homemaker with little employment experience might feel unable to say whether she prefers regular or irregular hours. Ask about how she plans and organizes her time as a homemaker, whether meals are eaten at regular times, and how she feels if her schedule is broken; the answers are likely to reveal her preferences. The case of Brent provides another example. He was a university professor tired of the pressure to publish but with no interest in a related professional field or in any form of work that involved sales or business. It seemed that he was unable to think of anything else that interested him apart from the work with which he was now disillusioned. The counselor asked about hobbies, but he had had none for years. Eventually, a discussion of childhood activities elicited the information that Brent's father had been a master carpenter, and Brent had thoroughly enjoyed helping out in the workshop his father owned. The passage of time and his focus on the academic world had all but erased the memory of an interest and a skill that proved important for Brent's second career choice.

If the client states a preference but is unable to explain what is enjoyable about it or to provide examples of past enjoyment, further investigation might be called for, especially if the interest is salient. Elliott, for instance, was a twenty-two-year-old business major who expressed an interest in working with numbers. Because he was apparently unhappy with his chosen major, the counselor decided to analyze his interest in greater detail. Questioning revealed that Elliott was not excited by discovering the solutions to number problems or by knowing for certain when he was right; nor was he particularly reassured by the security and reliability of numbers, and in fact he was not interested in any of those aspects of numbers that excite people who usually express this preference. Eventually, Elliott and the counselor traced his interest in numbers to the fact that his first-grade teacher had placed heavy emphasis on basic arithmetic and had rewarded him for the neatness of his numbers. His parents, delighted with his apparent skill, had told him that he would be more successful than anyone in the family if he focused on the business field, and their compliant son never questioned his supposed love for numbers. This kind of analysis can be time consuming and should be postponed until after all the interview questions have been asked. By then, you will have a clearer picture of the client's needs for further assessment and will be in a better position to decide the importance of any single item.

Assess Ability. Because many aspects of work relate to ability as well as interest, abilities should be briefly evaluated as you proceed with the interview. Suppose, for example, that Doris maintains that she has an interest in a leadership role. You have ascertained that Doris does indeed enjoy leading but is not sure how well she performs. While Doris relates incidents as evidence of her interest, you can ask such things as "When the camp leader fell sick and left you in charge, why do you think you were the one chosen? How did things work out that week? What did others say about the kind of job you did?"

In a society that places emphasis on all forms of achievement, one's ability, talents, and personal characteristics can become a source of negative or unrealistic attitudes. Listen, therefore, for low self-esteem, which often presents itself as: "I'd really like to, but . . . " The but is followed by any number of self-limiting statements, such as "I'm not smart enough," "I could never look right," "I would never pass the exam," "Girls can't do that sort of job," or "I've never been good at writing." The extent to which these assertions are true might need exploration later. For now, note privately these negative views and ask the client to focus on preferences without trying to evaluate ability. The time to focus on the client's ability is at the stage of investigating specific job options with known requirements.

It can be reassuring to clients with little confidence in their academic ability to be told that in many, if not most, jobs, verbal and mathematical aptitudes are not the most important factors in performing or keeping the position. Motivation, work habits, and especially the ability to relate to others often carry more weight. The client can also be told that an academic degree, if that is the issue, can be acquired at almost any age, should it be necessary.

Although standardized tests of ability are widely available, it is unlikely that they will be used by counselors outside of an academic or military setting, as the vast majority of career counseling clients will already have sufficient school and college records to indicate their ability.

It is obvious that not every one of the client's statements about interests and preferences can possibly be analyzed in detail. Most of what the client says can be accepted at face value or verified with one quick question, such as "Have you tried that before?" If the client's face lights up with enthusiasm when discussing a long-standing interest, it is hardly necessary to seek further confirmation of enjoyment. In general, items to explore in more depth are those subject to multiple interpretations or those for which the client's terminology is so vague that you do not have a clear picture of what is meant (for example, "manage," "create," "something worthwhile").

When requesting clarification of the client's statements, take care to avoid any impression that you are doubting the client's truthfulness or trying to correct the client's use of a particular word or phrase. Many people find the process of operationalizing quite difficult and can become upset if they think they appear stupid, especially in front of a person such as a counselor, who represents an authority figure to many clients. In order to avoid an air of interrogation, promote a strong collaborative relationship, show interest in the uniqueness of the client's experiences, and provide adequate explanations of the need for specificity. Many of the examples presented in this chapter can be used to illustrate to clients not only the differences among people but also the significance of those differences in the context of career choice.

Exhibit 8 provides an extensive example of counselor's notes on WRPs after completion of the steps described thus far. For contrast, we have included two sets of responses, labeled "satisfactory" and "unsatisfactory." The latter label does not indicate that the response is intrinsically worthless, only that it does not provide the type of information that will be useful in discovering and evaluating alternatives. As can be seen from Exhibit 8, unsatisfactory responses tend to occur when the client is self-derogatory, is concerned about ability and not interest, gives the opinions of others rather than of self, philosophizes about work rather than giving a personal preference, can think only of negative aspects, gives responses that do not relate to the category, considers only one limited aspect of a task, thinks in terms of specific jobs rather than about the task or category, or gives vague and skimpy answers.

Exhibit 8. Counselor Notes on Work-Related Preferences.

Work Tasks

1. Routine work
    Satisfactory responses: I like to be organized, and I enjoy putting everything in its place, but only so I can achieve the end result of efficient organization. I get bored very easily when I have to do the same thing over and over. I've done work like that and hated it—no challenge at all.
    Unsatisfactory responses: I like routine in my life. I hate to be bored. I think you have to accept a certain amount of routine.
2. Physical work
    Satisfactory responses: I like to work in the garden when the weather is nice, but I get pleasure not so much from actually using my muscles as from the fact that it looks so pretty when I've finished, and the day is so lovely. I do paint for a hobby and I enjoy fixing things around the house, but I know I wouldn't like physical work to be a major part of my job. I think muscles are a useful way to get something done, but at work I prefer to use my mind.
    Unsatisfactory responses: I'd never want to be a manual laborer, they don't earn enough. I couldn't do physical work because I have a bad back.
3. Work with machines, tools, equipment, and materials
    Satisfactory responses: I hate anything dirty, noisy, or that could get dangerously out of control, but I like being able to do a better job by using the right tool, for example, in woodworking; I also like knowing which is the right tool to use because it gives me a sense of competence. I wouldn't mind a job where I used tools or machines for part of the time—say, a computer—but I think I'd feel a bit cut off from people if I just worked with things in this group.
    Unsatisfactory responses: Machinery and I just don't get along. My husband says I'm no good with tools. Aren't those just lower-class jobs?
4. Work with numbers
    Satisfactory responses: I really enjoy the way numbers can be used to express a great deal of information succinctly, and I like being efficient in things like balancing my checkbook and working out taxes; I think that's because I like to feel that my life is in my control, not because I really want to work with numbers. I never do mathematical type puzzles and I usually skip

Exhibit 8. Counselor Notes on Work-Related Preferences, Cont'd.

over the numbers section in research reports to the discussion section. I'm quite good with numbers so I wouldn't mind if they were a small part of my work.

Unsatisfactory responses: I think that sort of work is best left to men because no one likes a woman who's good at math. I'd feel life had passed me by if I just sat there adding all day, like a loser.

5. Work with words

Satisfactory response: My favorites are writing and editing; I wouldn't like more mechanical activities, such as translating scientific articles, and I don't like to do imaginative writing, such as writing plays.

Unsatisfactory responses: I've always loved anything at all to do with words. Words are the most important tool we have for communication. I wish everyone realized how careful you have to be with not only the content but also the manner of your speech.

6. Work with plants or animals

Satisfactory responses: I enjoy training my German shepherd but I can't stand to see animals hurt or abused or caged, so I wouldn't want to work with them at all. I don't seem to have much of a green thumb, and my interest in plants is really limited to the seed packets for my garden.

Unsatisfactory responses: I've never tried it, so how would I know? I love it if the weather is really nice.

7. Work with people

Satisfactory responses: If I can use humor to get my point across better, then I like to be entertaining, but I would hate to entertain just for the fun of it. I like to help people, but not with physical problems, because I don't like to see pain and poverty and terrible living conditions. I really enjoy helping people solve interpersonal problems, but I don't like to have to discipline people or be responsible for how they do their work. I really only like to help people who want to be helped. I like to teach, but I hate to sell or try to persuade people to my point of view.

Unsatisfactory responses: There's no way to avoid working with people, in any job. I like people a lot and would like to work with them. People have always been an important part of my life.

8. Work with information or ideas

Satisfactory responses: I enjoy putting ideas together, explaining things to people, presenting information clearly, comparing and contrasting theories, and thinking up new ways to do things. I like applying theory in practical ways, for example in working out plans and developing strategies.

Unsatisfactory responses: I think science is boring. If it means working with computers, I wouldn't want it. I don't have the education to be a professor.

9. Clerical tasks

Satisfactory responses: I find these tasks boring, although I like to do them well when I have to do them, because I like to see that my finished product is complete and attractive and I like to be organized.

Unsatisfactory responses: I failed typing in school. There's no future in being a secretary.

10. Creative expression of ideas or feelings

Satisfactory responses: I love to look at paintings and like to paint as a hobby,

Exhibit 8. Counselor Notes on Work-Related Preferences, Cont'd.

but I don't have any interest in doing this as part of my work. The only place I like to use my imagination at work is in thinking up new and interesting ways to present ideas, or new ways to solve problems and perform tasks. *Unsatisfactory responses:* That's a good line of work to be in if you make it big. I've always wondered if I had the talent for that sort of thing. I used to fail art regularly at school.

Working Conditions

1. Relationships with people
   Satisfactory responses: I'd like colleagues with whom I could collaborate, maybe work on a project together. I would want to meet the public in some sort of teaching or helping capacity, probably one at a time or in small groups. I'd like to be around bright, well-motivated people at work; stodgy "We tried it before and it didn't work" types are a real bore. I like a mixture of ages and sexes to work with—a real melting pot.
   Unsatisfactory responses: I can get along with just about anyone. You can't tell until you get into the situation whether you will like the people.

2. Movement and time
   Satisfactory responses: I much prefer not to sit at one desk all day, but I wouldn't like to have to work out of two or three different offices—that would be too scattered. I'm fairly free of responsibilities to others, so weekend or evening work would be fine occasionally.
   Unsatisfactory responses: I can't really say—it would depend. If your salary is reasonable, you can't expect to keep 9-to-5 hours.

3. Performance conditions
   Satisfactory responses: This may not be possible, but I work best and enjoy myself most when I have 100 percent control over my work tasks. I like to take one project and see it through from start to finish before I get involved in something else. I get much more done when I get to decide my working hours, which I like to keep pretty irregular, since I hate punching a clock. I absolutely refuse to do shift work. I would get very nervous if I thought I had to generate my own salary—I prefer to leave financial and policy matters to others.
   Unsatisfactory responses: I think I might like being my own boss. I've only ever worked for undemocratic employers. I wouldn't want someone else getting paid for my work.

4. Variety
   Satisfactory responses: I'd like some variety but not too much—probably a job with three or four different aspects to it. I don't like to change colleagues often—it takes too long to get to know people.
   Unsatisfactory responses: I'm open for anything. I don't see you have a choice about relocation.

5. Environment
   Satisfactory responses: It's very important to me to work in an attractive place, clean, tastefully decorated. I like a relaxed unconventional atmosphere where people get excited about ideas.
   Unsatisfactory responses: People are people; you'll meet some good ones and some bad ones. It's the top management that's responsible for the atmosphere at work.

Exhibit 8. Counselor Notes on Work-Related Preferences, Cont'd.

Location

Satisfactory responses: I would like a temperate climate, in or near a fairly large sophisticated city with a good cultural life. I definitely don't want the deep South or anywhere poverty-stricken. Keeping fit is important to me, so I'd like to work within pleasant walking distance of my home.

Unsatisfactory responses: I haven't liked anywhere I've lived yet, so I'm not hopeful. You have to go where the jobs are.

Benefits

Because this category requires rank ordering of specific items, all answers will be satisfactory.

Assess Life-style Context. Before going on to step two (prioritizing the client's preferences), conduct a brief exploration of the context into which the new career choice will have to fit, since the reality of this context will certainly influence and be influenced by the choice. Although you do not want to unnecessarily or prematurely thwart ambitions or dash hopes, clients are generally better off if they can learn and accept that constraints, both in the marketplace and in their own lives, exist and will limit choices, that ideal jobs are rare and therefore some values and interests almost always have to be satisfied outside the work situation, and that any career choice will affect and be affected by important people in their lives.

It is not unusual for clients, enthusiastic about their own career plans, to overlook or dismiss the reactions of others, even though these reactions can form some of the most difficult environmental constraints. Suppose, for example, that a woman with several small children wishes to return to school, an executive with a generous salary wishes to take early retirement in order to write poetry, or an only child with an ailing and widowed parent wants to work for a corporation based in Europe. In each case, others are likely to suffer losses as a result of your client's career change. Because of such potential effects, it is important to know ahead of time what sort of opposition others will put up, what value conflicts the client might feel, and what the client's history has been in dealing with either internal or external conflict.

Life-style information can be elicited by means of several focused questions. First, consider the client's present life-style:

"Give me a picture of your life at present. What parts of your life do you enjoy, and what parts do you dislike? Who are the most important people in your life, and how do they contribute to both your enjoyment and your difficulties? How important is work to you, and how big a part do you think it should play in your life?" Second, discuss the client's hopes for the future, within realistic parameters: "Which aspects of your present life, whether enjoyable or not, will stay with you, regardless of what work you do? Which aspects of your present life do you hope will be changed by a change in work—if not immediately, at least within a few years? What dreams would you like to have come true in the next ten to fifteen years?"

General questions such as these should provide information about what part work plays in the client's life, what environmental constraints may exist, and how much the client is expecting from work. Note areas that might need further exploration—for instance, a belief that a new career or job will automatically solve all the client's present problems ("Once there's more money coming in, my wife will feel better about our marriage"), a tendency to minimize serious difficulties ("I know I have three small children, but I'll love working so much, it will be no trouble to take care of them"), or what seems to you to be unrealistic self-appraisal ("There's really nothing I dislike about any work situation. I've been successful at anything I've ever been given to do"). This discussion of the real-life context into which any career decision will have to fit need not take a great deal of time, especially as earlier exploration—during goal setting, for example—may have elicited most of the desired information.

Prioritize Work-Related Preferences. To establish what is most important to the client, and also to condense the great amount of material acquired so far, prioritization is essential. Ask the client to look over the entire list of possibilities in each category and select three to five top-priority preferences or interests, then rank them using a simple system, such as a rank of 1 for something considered essential, 2 for strongly desired, and 3 for desirable but less important than items in the first two ranks. Next, the client should select three to five items in each category that are definitely to be avoided and also rank them.

This preliminary summary will often lead to corrections, withdrawals, or additions. In the interest of the client's full self-awareness, be prepared to ask the reasons for a particular rank when the rank does not seem to fit with what the counselor knows of the client or with what has been said earlier. Charlie's wife, for example, wanted him to have a secure job with regular hours and paychecks, and he ranked these items as number 1. However, Charlie himself had frequently expressed an interest in a position where he could take risks, be spontaneous, and meet challenges head on. When he ranked these items as third, the counselor pointed out the possible conflict between the two sets of wishes, not in an effort to change Charlie's mind but in order to ensure that he understood the implications of his ranking decisions.

Depending on the client's needs, it might be advisable to prioritize items in terms of time. Parents, for example, often restrict their own wishes in order to accommodate what they consider to be their children's needs. Thus, a man might be interested in a position that provides stability and security for the next decade but also provides the opportunity to branch out and take risks later when he feels his responsibility for raising children is over.

By this point, you may well have noticed some inconsistencies among a client's various interests and preferences. For example, how likely is it that Ricardo will find a job with a high level of decision and policy making in a competitive environment yet that still leaves all his weekends and evenings free for sports activities? Alternatively, if Molly obtains work that carries almost no responsibility and consists of performing clear-cut routine activities on the instructions of others, is it likely that she will also satisfy her desire for excitement and variety at work? And how will Sonya reconcile her desire for a job where she can travel and meet new people with the fact that she likes an orderly, predictable routine and time to spend with her family? Other typical career-related values conflicts that arise include: pleasing oneself versus pleasing others, personal ambition versus expected cultural or gender roles, and desire for success or prominence versus desire for an unstressed existence.

Because it is difficult to address these conflicts and inconsistencies without a specific job or career option as a reference point, we recommend deferring discussion of such conflicts until after the client has made a list of several job options that might be appropriate. There are sound reasons for this approach. For one, when they are faced with a specific career possibility, clients often find that their priorities change, and incompatibilities in their wishes simply disappear. For another, an essential feature of career choice counseling is that the client is planning to engage in a new and different relationship with the working world. This very newness will require the client to take risks and to behave in unfamiliar ways, but as yet you have had no opportunity to assess directly how your client handles change and the prospect of risk. However thorough the assessment process, clients often respond unpredictably when faced with reality in the form of a specific career option. There is a large difference between saying "I would like a job where I can help people who are troubled" and spending a day observing a juvenile court psychologist and asking oneself constantly, "Would I really like to spend my time this way?"

For some clients, problems that arose during the assessment stage resolve themselves in contact with the reality of the work world; just the sense of making steady progress toward a goal can be therapeutic, increasing enthusiasm and self-confidence. For other people, unexpected new problems arise or old ones intensify to the point where it is clear that further progress is not possible until the problems are addressed.

Complete the Work-Related Preferences Summary Form. As a final step, either counselor or client should transfer the prioritized items onto a summary sheet. Examples of ways to organize the material are presented in Exhibits 9 and 10. The material can be organized differently should client needs dictate; what is important is that the summary be brief, clear, and evaluated for accuracy by the client.

Exhibit 9. Sample Work-Related Preferences Summary Form.

Category	Definite Preference	Definite No or Prefer to Avoid
Work tasks	1. 2. 3.	1. 2. 3.
Working conditions	1. 2. 3.	1. 2. 3.
Location	1. 2. 3.	1. 2. 3.
Benefits	1. 2. 3.	1. 2. 3.

Exhibit 10. Work-Related Preferences Summary.

Would Like to Have Work Involving:

(1 = essential; 2 = strongly preferred; 3 = gravy)
Frequent high-energy contact with large variety of people (1)
Selling, persuading, making deals, negotiating (1)
Using words, maybe public speaking (1)
Planning visual and audio presentations of material (2)
Opportunity to increase salary by own efforts (2)
Freedom to innovate (2)
Travel opportunities, preferably international (3)
Interaction with lively, energetic, competitive, self-assured people (1)
Being challenged, put on my mettle (1)
Being part of a network of successful people (3)
Being part of a prestigious organization (3)
Life in a modern dynamic setting; large lively city (3)
Responsibility for own achievements (2)

To Be Avoided:

(1 = refuse to consider; 2 = avoid if possible; 3 = accept if I must)
Work dealing with weapons (1)
Confinement to office or desk (1)
Academic research (1)
Scheduled hours (2)
Routine tasks (1)
Rigid deadlines (3)
Collecting data (1)
Organizing and analyzing data (3)
Political infighting at work (3)

The WRP summary represents the best current knowledge of what the client wants from work, but it should not be
regarded as final. In the process of acquiring new skills or information and having new experiences, a client may undergo
changes in interests, values, and self-concept. Although it is
unlikely that the changes will be extensive, even small differences
can be important. Marie's first summary sheet indicated fairly
limited and circumscribed interests and hopes. When she began
considering specific options, she realized the extent to which she
had been living life according to her husband's wishes and standards and found the courage to make a far more dramatic career
move than she had originally hoped for. A revised summary
sheet indicated a wider range of interests and greater ambition
than previously. For example, she originally rated having regular
work hours as number 1, because she wanted to be home to
make her husband's evening meal. She later reduced the rating
to a 3 when she saw that regular hours were incompatible with
the work she was really interested in. Clients should be encouraged, therefore, to review and update the summary sheet whenever necessary, rather than regarding it as the final word. Any
such updates should, of course, be discussed with the counselor.

Homework

Homework activities throughout this stage can be quite
varied and will be assigned for any of three reasons: (1) to save
session time; (2) to give the client opportunity or a different setting in which to ponder a topic in depth; and (3) to acquire experiences that are available only outside the office. As always,
the amount of paperwork should be adjusted to the client's time,
motivation, and interest. Not all clients will need homework,
especially if it takes no more than one or two sessions to arrive
at summary statements of what the client wants from work.

Work History. Although it is generally easy for the counselor to elicit sufficient detail about the client's work history during a regular session, some clients are able to satisfactorily begin
the analysis of the work history by themselves, using a form
such as Exhibit 11. For a more extensive analysis, clients could

Exhibit 11. Work History Analysis.

Using your employment history as a guide, please list each task involved in every job you have had under "Description of Task." If you have had few salaried jobs, list tasks involved in other activities, such as volunteer work and school activities. When you have listed all the separate tasks you can recall, move on to the next two columns, identifying for each task what you liked about the experience and what you disliked about the experience.

Description of Task	What I Liked About the Experience	What I Disliked About the Experience
Example: YWCA Activities Coordinator		
Designing costumes	Working with fabric in wild colors. I was the boss; I had the final word. Excitement of the kids.	Noisy workroom. Insufficient funds for the supplies I wanted.

be asked to analyze each job they have held in terms of the following questions:

1. What did you like or dislike about any aspect of the job?
2. What skills did you need on the job? What new skills did you learn from the job? How well did you perform the various tasks?
3. What one or two changes might have made the job either more or less enjoyable?
4. What did your friends and family think about the job, and how did their opinions affect you?
5. What were your relationships with your superiors and colleagues at work? What did they say about you as a worker?
6. How did the job affect your life outside work?

This exercise can be helpful not only in saving time but also as an indicator of the extent to which the client is able to draw conclusions from past experiences, and therefore of the amount of work that might be required before it will be possible to proceed to the next stage. However, you need to be cautious in assigning this homework. If the client is unable to complete the analysis with the requisite specificity, you will have to cover the same ground again in session, with the possible danger of making the client feel that homework is unimportant or that he or she has failed to carry out the assignment well. Either of these attitudes could have a negative effect on the counseling relationship or on the client's enthusiasm. Ideally, this homework should be given only to highly verbal clients who have shown evidence of the ability to be objective and to analyze information.

Work Awareness. When clients lack work experience in general or are unfamiliar with a field that interests them, they should be encouraged to gain such experience, preferably as directly as possible. This may mean volunteer or part-time work, either in one field or in several different areas. Clients can also *job shadow,* that is, spend a period of time (at least a day) simply following someone around on the job. Next to actual experience, this is perhaps the best way to get the flavor of a particular type of work and work environment. A less direct way of increasing knowledge of the work world is to interview people about their work. The least direct method, but still of value, is to read about jobs. For example, a woman interested in business might read *The Managerial Woman* by Hennig and Jardim (1976).

The purpose of these activities is to increase work awareness in order to increase understanding of one's own work preferences and interests, rather than to evaluate a particular job. Sometimes inexperienced clients are more concerned about the work atmosphere and environment rather than the specific tasks of the job. They should be instructed, therefore, to evaluate each awareness experience from an emotional and personal point of view: "If I worked here, what sorts of things would frustrate me? Give me satisfaction? How would I fit in with the people here? If my day went like this person's day, how would I feel at the end of it? Who is in charge in this office, and how does he or she use authority?" If your client has any specific concerns, devise appropriate evaluation questions. Encourage your client to make systematic evaluations, preferably in written form, during or immediately after each experience. The immediacy captures the greatest emotional impact, and the written form provides cumulative material that can be inspected later for patterns or inconsistencies.

Significant Others. Even clients who require no further assessment than is provided by the interview can find it helpful to verify their self-understanding with others who know them well. Using a copy of their preliminary answers to the categories in Exhibit 7, they can interview friends and relatives, asking: "Does this sound like me, from what you know of me?" Clients should also be encouraged to share their career counseling experiences with those who will be most affected by their decisions. This process has the advantage of avoiding surprises to either party, since the client is aware of and can take into account others' reactions, while those others will not find themselves faced, after a long period of silence, with an unexpected and perhaps unpalatable fait accompli. Furthermore, those who will have to live with the client's eventual decision are likely to be more supportive if they have been allowed to have some input into the decision.

Problems and Cautions

It is always difficult to decide when enough information has been gathered. Our major criterion is simple: All things being equal, it is time to move on when the client has completed a Work-Related Preferences Summary Form, such as that in Exhibit 9 or 10, in sufficient detail that the counselor has a personalized picture of what the specific client wants, rather than a document so vague or sketchy that it could apply to many different people. Further assessment is required if: your best efforts during the WRP interview still result in large gaps in information, the client seems to have unusually limited interests, or environmental constraints or psychological problems (such as depression) become too pressing to be ignored. Frequently, these problems will become apparent early in the interview, which can then be suspended until the necessary intervention or assessment has been completed.

Concerns About Ability. In general, it is better to delay a discussion of the client's abilities until job alternatives are under discussion. Sometimes, however, it is obvious that earlier intervention is appropriate. Brian, for example, had never grad-

uated from high school but realized that whatever field he decided to enter, he would need his G.E.D. Helga also knew that
for the level of work that interested her, and for her own satisfaction as well, she would need to complete the last semester
of her bachelor's degree, interrupted some years earlier by marriage and her husband's posting abroad. Both these clients took
immediate steps to remedy their educational deficits without
waiting for specific job options to be under consideration.

Concerns About Preferred Life-Style. When a client cannot
come up with a preferred life-style, except in vague or unrealistic
"movie-style" terms, or if expressed preferences do not seem
to fit the client very well, further assessment is called for. How
the client currently allocates resources of time, money, and
energy can indicate a great deal about preferences. The only
caution is to avoid the trap of thinking that the fact that the
client has remained in one situation for a long time means that
there is something attractive about the situation, something the
client would like to carry into the future. It could be that the
client has stayed because of a values conflict, a fear of change,
or a sense of hopelessness and powerlessness.

In investigating current life-style, consider the client's likes
and dislikes, the extent to which change is possible, and the
reasons for lack of change thus far. For example, George spent
no time on sports activities although he professed an interest
in outdoor recreation, such as canoeing and hiking. Because
George had never actively pursued these sports, despite having
the necessary resources to do so, the counselor questioned the
extent and nature of his interest. It turned out that George's
interest in the outdoors had been recently acquired, together
with an enthusiasm for a healthier diet and the start of an exercise program. As a result of discussions with his counselor,
George joined the Sierra Club, began hiking, and discovered
that the interest was indeed there.

To assess clients' current or preferred life-style, you might
ask them to keep a daily calendar or journal to list what they
spend their time, money, and energy on. You can later work
with clients to analyze what activities they have put their heart
into and whether this is how they really want to live. You

might also ask about the various places clients have lived, what they have liked and disliked about each, and which parts of their life-style they would like to keep.

Environmental Constraints. Environmental constraints—that is, constraints that are outside the client—include the lack of necessary resources, such as time, money, or qualifications; the needs or opposing wishes of important others; and societal barriers, such as age, gender, and race.

Any environmental constraints usually emerge during the structured interview or even earlier, and further assessment is needed only if you believe the client to be underestimating the severity or refusing to acknowledge the existence of a constraint. It is true, of course, that many constraints can be easily removed and that others can be worked around, but it is important for the client to have a realistic picture of what might be ahead.

Intervention to remove or cope with all constraints is not usually necessary until a specific job option is under consideration and the extent of the constraints becomes more obvious. However, work on constraints imposed by other people can be started immediately. Ask the client to list all those who will be affected by any proposed career change and then to identify what each person stands to gain or lose from the change. Ask the client to predict from past experience how each person will respond to losses. Armed with this information, you can plan with the client how to handle the situation. A typical plan is for the client to discuss career options with the other person, explaining the reasons for wanting a particular career decision and asking for the other's support. Various methods of broaching the subject can be discussed and role played in the counseling session.

Few or Negative Interests. Sometimes further assessment of interests seems warranted because the client turns out to have few job-related interests, a limited amount of enthusiasm for any interests, or strong feelings only about what is disliked rather than what is appealing. In career counseling, the lack of interests can be a problem because the client and counselor have little information to guide the process of searching for options.

Limited interests can result from lack of experience. A

person might have had few jobs or might have always worked in similar job environments, performing similar tasks. Such a client can be asked to gain firsthand experience of different types of work, as suggested in the homework section. Cliff, for example, had worked for twenty years as a custom jeweler in a small downtown store in a large southwestern city. An unsteadiness in his hands put an end to his career, but he had had no other work experience since his teens, when he had worked as a delivery boy. A partial disability pension gave him time to explore other possibilities, and, after doing volunteer work at the local hospital, he discovered in himself an unexpected interest and accompanying ability in organizing and improving volunteer services. In Cliff's case, what began as a search for wider interests ended career counseling, as he was hired into a permanent position within six months of beginning volunteer work.

When the client's low interest levels seem to extend beyond work and are reported as uncharacteristic of the client, check for symptoms of general depression, a health problem of some kind, a substance abuse problem, or a life-style conducive to low energy (poor diet, inadequate sleep or housing conditions, no exercise, and so on). Any of these problems should be discussed with the client, with a view to assessing the potential impact on career counseling and career changes and to possibly adjusting the counseling goal.

An important method of assessing interests is by means of vocational interest tests. These tests are commonly used for two purposes: to increase self-awareness, and (the purpose discussed here) to expand the list of career options by acquainting the client with suitable occupations that he or she might not otherwise have considered. Inventories may also be used at this stage of career counseling for those clients who need extra help in identifying their work-related preferences.

Most interest inventories are designed to measure a person's interests in different fields of work; however, some also provide an assessment of interests in educational fields of study. Although some counselors still use a "test 'em and tell 'em" approach in which they give the client an interest inventory and then advise the client to enter whatever occupation comes up highest on the test, this is an improper use of vocational interest tests, as a single test can list only a small proportion of the many occupations available; furthermore, the test relates only to a person's interests and not to the many other factors that must be considered in selecting a vocation. Used properly, interest inventories can not only identify interests the client may not be aware of but also confirm the client's stated interests and identify discrepancies between abilities and interests. Here we consider four frequently used interest inventories that can be used with upper-level high school students, college-age individuals, or older persons.

The Strong Campbell Interest Inventory (SCII) (Campbell, 1977), which is a combination of the male and female versions of the Strong Vocational Interest Blanks, is the best known and most frequently used interest inventory and has a long history of research and development. Research studies on earlier forms provide powerful evidence of test validity. The more recent revisions (1974 and 1981) have attempted to eliminate sexist terminology as well as culture-bound and dated items.

The SCII contains 325 items concerning occupations, school subjects, activities, amusements, types of people, and personal characteristics. The interpretation format includes 6 General Occupational Themes (Realistic, Investigative, Artistic, Social, Enterprising, Conventional) based on Holland's (1973) typology; 23 Basic Interest Scales; 162 Occupational Scales; and Administrative Indices and 2 special scales.

The Basic Interest Scales assess the strength and consistency of specific interest areas, such as agriculture, social service, or sales. The Occupational Scales were empirically developed by identifying those items that distinguish people in specific occupational groups from people in other occupational groups. They measure the degree of similarity between the client's responses and those made by men and women in the various occupations. Most of the Occupational Scales have keys for both men and women, although they will not always appear under the same general theme.

The Administrative Indices are validity checks, designed

to detect carelessness and test-taking response sets. The total responses (TR) score indicates how many of the 325 items were answered; if TR drops below 305, the counselor should check to see why. Items on the Infrequent Response Index are those that receive the same response from most people; only a negative number indicates a validity problem.

The two special scales, Academic Orientation and Introversion-Extraversion, were empirically developed against nonoccupational criteria. The Academic Orientation Scale is not a measure of ability but an indication of people's degree of comfort in academic environments, interest in theoretical subjects, and likelihood of continuing their education beyond high school. People who leave college without graduating average a score of about 40, those who never enter average about 30, those who earn B.A. degrees about 50, M.A.'s about 55, and Ph.D.'s about 60. The Introversion-Extraversion Scale, developed from the responses of students identified as introverts or extraverts on the MMPI, does not measure interpersonal skill but reflects the person's interest in working alone or with people. People who prefer to work alone typically score 55 or above, whereas those who like being the center of attention and who enjoy working with others score in the extraverted direction, 45 or below.

The SCII is best used with people who are considering occupations involving college preparation. It can be completed in about 30 minutes but can be scored only by computer scoring centers. The counselor will need to plan for a week or more turn-around time before results are available.

One of the newest instruments, the Jackson Vocational Interest Survey (JVIS) (Jackson, 1977), uses a forced-choice format in which the client is asked to indicate a preference in each of 289 pairs of statements. It contains thirty-four scales covering twenty-six "work roles" and eight "work styles." The work roles are job-related activities; some of these roles are closely associated with a particular occupation, such as medicine or law, whereas others cut across many occupations. The work styles refer to kinds of behaviors expected in certain working environments, such as planfulness, independence, or leadership.

The JVIS was designed to be equally applicable to both sexes. Norms were derived from large samples of college and high school students in the United States and Canada. Because the JVIS is relatively new, follow-up studies are still unavailable; it must therefore be used with caution until more data are available.

The instrument can be completed in 40 to 60 minutes, and a definite advantage is that the answer sheet can be hand scored in about 5 minutes without the need of stencils. Consequently, counselor and client can have results immediately. A computer-scored form is also available that provides additional data not present on the hand-scored form.

The Kuder Occupational Interest Survey, Form DD (Kuder, 1966, 1979), was first published in 1966 and was revised in 1979. It is useful for clients who are not interested in professional fields that require graduate school but who are interested either in entering the work world directly from high school or in going to college or obtaining other training beyond high school. Descriptions of activities are presented in triads, and the client is asked to indicate the most and least liked items in the triads. There are seventy-seven occupational scales and twenty-nine college major scales for men and fifty-seven occupational scales and twenty-seven college major scales for women. It takes between 30 and 40 minutes to complete the inventory, which can be scored only by computer.

The protocols of interest inventories identify specific occupations that might be of interest to the client. At this stage of career counseling, the counselor can use these suggested occupations to help the client identify work-related activities that might be of interest. Exhibit 12 presents a structured method of identifying such activities, to be used with the SCII.

The Self Directed Search (SDS), originally published in 1970 and revised in 1977, is a self-assessment device developed by John Holland and based on his typology (Holland, 1977b). In a test booklet, clients provide information regarding their occupational daydreams, their competencies, their attitudes toward specific occupations, and their self-estimates of their abilities.

Exhibit 12. Interest Summary Sheet.

Part I

"Similar" or "Very similar" scores on occupational scales	What is it about you that makes you similar to people in these occupations?
Example: Farmer	Like to work outdoors. Like to work alone. Primarily concerned with objects rather than interactions with people. Like to be my own boss.

1.

2.

3.

4.

5.

Part II

"Dissimilar" or "Very dissimilar" scores on occupational scales	What is it about you that makes you unlike people in these occupations?
Example: Nurse	Don't like to take orders. Don't like structured, routine activity. Can't stand to see people in pain.

1.

2.

Exhibit 12. Interest Summary Sheet, Cont'd.

3.

4.

5.

6.

Raw scores are converted into a three-letter summary code reflecting a composite of three occupational types/environments.

The client self-scores the instrument and is then provided with the three-letter code that reflects his or her choices in terms of Holland's occupational typology and with an explanation of what the summary code means. The SDS booklet then directs the client to the Occupations Finder (Holland, 1977a), a booklet containing the 500 most common occupations in the United States, organized around Holland's six work environments. The SDS Form E was developed for individuals with limited reading skill. Most people can mark and score the SDS in 40 to 50 minutes.

These and other interest inventories have their place with different clients. The counselor might want to use the SCII with a bright, highly motivated upper-level high school student or adult for whom college or university training is fairly certain and graduate training a possibility. The Kuder DD might be a good choice for a client who would prefer less extensive training beyond high school. The counselor might choose to use the JVIS when time is important and it is unwise to wait the ten days to two weeks for a computer-scored protocol. The SDS might be the test of choice when the counselor judges it beneficial for the client to work alone.

Counselors must meet certain requirements if they are to use tests ethically (American Psychological Association, 1974). These basic user qualifications include a general knowledge of measurement principles and of the limitations of test interpretations; knowledge of testing principles; and an understanding of the concept of measurement error. Test users are expected to have an elementary knowledge of the literature relating to the test they are using, to be fully trained to competently administer the test and interpret an obtained test score, and to be accurate in scoring the test.

Although aptitude tests need not be used often in career counseling, when they are used, the results should be interpreted as an estimate of performance under a given set of circumstances rather than as permanent or absolute characteristics of the client. Test results should be interpreted with reference to sets of norms appropriate for the individual tested. For example, high school students who want to attend college should be told what their Scholastic Aptitude Test results indicate about their standing relative to those in or entering universities. Special caution is needed when interpreting test results for members of minority groups whose characteristics may not correspond closely to those of the normed population.

Counselors are responsible not only to have knowledge about testing in general and about the particular tests they are using but also to do the research and thinking necessary to conduct a thorough and useful test report session. Being a skillful test reporter requires understanding clients' self-views and what it will likely mean to them to find they have interests in areas that they had not thought of or that they have tested ability that is lower than they wanted or higher than they expected. Counselor preparation for test-reporting sessions should involve analyzing the test protocol in relation to what is already known about the client and anticipating the client's reactions.

It is important that the counselor not view test reporting as a mechanical task. Many counselors tend to treat test results in a mechanical, perfunctory manner—an approach they would never use with those parts of counseling that deal with feelings and needs. Although test results, which are reported in numbers or brief descriptions, are factual and objective, they often have great meaning to and elicit strong feelings from clients. Test results can represent a complete divergence from the way clients see themselves or a confirmation of a long-held self-image; results can mean encouragement that they can accomplish what they had hoped to, or can engender deeply felt disappointment that they cannot be what they want to be. Because of potential strong feelings, the client should be given ample time to react to and discuss each test finding. Throughout the discussion of the test results, the counselor needs to watch for signs of discomfort in the client by paying close attention to comments, body language, and facial expression.

It is important to provide appropriate introductory and explanatory information before giving the client actual test results, as once the profile is in the client's hands he or she is unlikely to attend well to this sort of information.

At the outset of the test-reporting session, the counselor should review with the client the purpose of taking the tests, reminding the client that the objective was to develop a more complete and accurate self-understanding and to gather additional information on things he or she might like to do. The counselor should also point out to the client that an interest inventory does not measure abilities, but *interests,* and that its purpose is not to identify specific job alternatives but to identify interests and brainstorm ideas.

Both clinical experience and research evidence indicate that clients have a tendency to accept uncritically a test report about themselves (Goldman, 1971). They are apt to view tests as magical instruments that read minds in some mystical way and to expect that they will discover hidden talents and find out things about themselves that they didn't know before. By pointing out to the client that tests are not all-powerful mind readers, you may be able to squelch the tendency toward uncritical faith in test results.

The counselor should also explain that no test is infallible, that there is a margin for error in all tests, and that the test results must, therefore, be approached with caution since, in a small percentage of cases they are, in fact, wrong. Consequently, the best procedure is to examine each result and consider carefully whether it fits into the total pattern of what clients already know about themselves. Clients should be encouraged to view with an open mind those interests that the test indicates are high and not to be too upset if the test reports they are not interested in something that they already know they like. Most important is to make certain the client understands that even though most test results list potential occupations, this does not mean that the client should pursue the careers mentioned.

Most clients will know little about tests, and some may have misconceptions, unrealistic expectations, or invalid assumptions. The counselor should take a few minutes to explain to clients briefly and simply about the tests they have taken—what they measure, how they were developed, on what group(s) they were normed, and what is known about their validity. Technical terms (percentile, stanine, standard score, norm group) should be avoided if at all possible and defined if not possible.

Rather than sitting passively listening while the counselor explains the test results, the client should actively participate in the process of examining the information the test provides. Interpretation of test results should be a collaborative effort in which counselor and client work together to tease meaning out of the test scores, draw inferences, and generate hypotheses. As each test result is discussed, the counselor can help the client understand its meaning by relating to it what they already know about the client from other sources, such as comments the client has made about himself or herself in earlier sessions, information from personal data forms, or observations made by the counselor.

Clients should be given the time and opportunity to express their attitudes and feelings about the test results, to indicate what the results mean to them, and to raise any concerns they might have. Discussing test information sometimes leads to the identification of data that need further investigation. Counselor and client can then plan together how they might explore the area.

Another clinically useful method of identifying and organizing interests was adapted from the Tyler Vocational Card Sort (Tyler, 1961) by Dolliver (1967) and later by S. K. Gilmore (personal communication, 1971). As a homework assignment between sessions, Gilmore, for example, gives clients the following kind of instructions for completing an individualized card sort: "On a separate 3 × 5 card, write every occupation, interest, work activity, or work setting which might be of interest to a person such as yourself. Don't eliminate an occupation because you wouldn't really want to do it or another item because you don't like all aspects of it. Include any item that you might find interesting. For example, you might not choose to be a madam, yet you might find some aspects of the job interesting, such as supervising other people, so you would include Madam as an item on one of the cards. Ignore concerns of ability and don't let practical considerations influence you. Include as many cards as you can; somewhere between 25 and 75 would be ideal."

When the client arrives at the next session with the stack of cards, have him or her sit at a large table (or on the floor) to sort the cards. Give the client the following instructions: "Break your stack of cards into smaller groups that for some reason go together in your mind. Place those you would choose for one reason in one group, those you would choose for another reason in a second group, and so on. There are no rules about the number of groups you should come out with or about the number of cards in each group."

Following the sorting into subgroups, the client is asked to label each group—"What would you call this group?" or "Tell me what it is that each group represents"—and the counselor records each label or explanation. The counselor continues the inquiry until certain he or she understands the distinctions the client makes. The client is also given an opportunity to elaborate on earlier responses.

Because the card-sort technique focuses on the criteria the client uses to evaluate work and related activities and settings, it can be a fruitful method of adding information to the WRP inventory.

Constraining Beliefs. A constraining belief can also be responsible for a person having few interests. Clients sometimes prejudge what they might be capable of or what is appropriate for them and narrow their interests to fit their cognitive restrictions. Clients who are members of minority or disadvantaged groups tend to be especially prone to such constraints. One way to detect constraining beliefs that limit the expression of interests is to observe the client during the interview, attending to any nonverbal signs that precede negative answers. For example, a wistful or interested look that is immediately followed by a sigh or a head shake might indicate an interest that has been rejected by a negative thought. A look of fear, a long pause, an unnecessary emphasis to the "Oh, no, I could never do that!" could also be indicative of internal constraints, which might be assessed in the following way:

Counselor: Lori, how do you think you would enjoy a job where you helped people who were in some sort of trouble?

Lori: (face brightens, then falls) No, I don't really think I'd like that.

Counselor: When I asked you that question, you first looked interested, but then looked sad, and said you weren't interested. What were you thinking to make you feel sad?

Lori was unable to identify her thoughts, so the counselor continued: "I'd like you to try an experiment. I will ask you the same question again, and this time I'd like you to smile, just as you did before, and then, without any pause at all, say to me: 'Yes, that sounds really interesting.' "

After Lori did this, the counselor asked for a repeat performance, but this time in the original manner, with the sad face and the pause.

Counselor: This second time, what did you have to think about or to remember in order to erase the interest and get back the sad feeling?

Lori: I remembered when I used to try to help my little sister with her homework, but my mother said I wasn't good enough at my own work to help other people.

Another simple technique for eliciting negative cognitions is to point out a pattern or an inconsistency and ask for an explanation. Nancy, at thirty-nine, was tired of the working hours and conditions as a nurse. During the structured interview, however, she consistently reported interests and wishes that seemed to relate strongly to the profession of nursing. The counselor pointed this out and asked Nancy to explain. Immediately Nancy responded, ''But that's all I know how to do.'' Nancy held the belief that one is only supposed to be interested in work for which the ability has already been developed. When the counselor guided Nancy to remember times when she had first had an interest and only later gathered the experience and practice that produced ability, she recognized that interest is often the fuel that motivates learning and was able to identify many interests besides the ones she had satisfied in her nursing career.

During the self-understanding stage, handle only those negative cognitions that severely restrain the client from identifying interests and preferences. Although self-assessment activities can also reveal clients' negative attitudes toward work or their own abilities as workers, it is not usually necessary to attempt to change these attitudes at this stage, as they are typically triggered in full force only when the client is face to face with a specific option; until this happens, you will not know which cognitions are the most dysfunctional and require intervention. There is, too, the possibility that the self-assessment activities, especially if they involve actual work experience, will serve to modify a client's negative self-talk.

Unrealistic Self-Assessment. In some cases, a client's self-assessment will seem somewhat unrealistic, either overestimating or underestimating abilities and talents. Unrealistic self-assessment poses a problem because, in entering the work world, the client is approaching an established and highly structured environment that is more likely to demand conformity from the client than to yield to individual idiosyncrasies. In simplest terms, reality is defined by the standards required by the workplace, not by the client's erroneous beliefs about the quality of his or her contribution. If the client has a seriously distorted self-view, there is a chance that he or she will pursue unsuitable goals or will prematurely exclude options. Again, however, as with abilities and many negative cognitions, intervention, should it prove necessary, will be more immediate and powerful at a later stage when the client is considering specific options. Because for now the concern is to heighten rather than reduce enthusiasm, intervention to correct unrealistic self-assessment should be omitted—unless, of course, the problem is so severe that it requires treatment as a separate counseling problem.

❦ 4 ❦

Developing and Refining
Appropriate
Career Alternatives

This chapter addresses the stage of career counseling during which the client will conduct research into the world of work and into several specific occupations, with two purposes: (1) generating a list of career possibilities and (2) learning about the options on that list. In the following stage (described in Chapter Five), these possibilities will be evaluated, and the client will choose from among them.

Several complications arise during these two stages. For one, the activities of the stages overlap and intertwine, often involving considerable backtracking, thus demanding considerable alertness and flexibility from the counselor. For another, these stages can be difficult from the psychological point of view, as the client is being asked to take a new role in the career counseling process, practicing unfamiliar skills, taking risks, and making a commitment—all of which tend to activate any underlying anxieties and doubts. A third difficulty arises from the fact that the client's activities and decisions during these stages have an immediate and potentially threatening impact on significant others, whose reactions must therefore be taken into account. In fact, so many interdependent difficulties can arise during these two stages that we will devote Chapters Four and Five to a presentation of the process as it should go if no serious problems arise and Chapter Six to a discussion of various problems that can indeed occur.

99

As is so often the case, there is no way to predict how much time the client will need to complete these processes. The time needed will depend largely on how much information must be acquired and the methods used to acquire it. It is during this stage that you will need to be flexible in session scheduling, since the standard one hour per week regimen might well be inappropriate to the client's needs. Much of the activity of this stage takes place in the community, and the client is likely to need frequent check-ins, in the form of telephone calls or abbreviated sessions, either in addition to or in replacement of regular sessions.

During these stages of generating and choosing among options, there is a drastic change in task performance, with the client taking on the majority of the work, both in gathering and evaluating information. After the work of the assessment stages, many clients expect that you, as counselor, will be able to take the information gathered thus far and translate it into the perfect career choice. This would obviously be satisfactory for the client because it would provide an immediate choice, and one bearing the mark of some presumed authority. To prepare clients for their responsibility in carrying out the activities of these next stages, you will first need to disillusion them of the idea that making a career choice is simply a matter of matching information to job. They will need to be told, probably not for the first or last time, that there is rarely a perfect place for each person and that choosing a career or job requires weighing many different factors, making trade-offs and compromises, and eventually arriving at a good approximation of a pleasing choice. Because it is the client who will have to live with the choice, it must obviously be made by the client, not the counselor. While clients might be disappointed to hear that their career search is not yet ended, most can see the rationale behind their own heavy involvement in evaluating options.

For years, career counselors have been criticized, with some justification, for steering clients toward or away from certain occupations, such as directing women and blacks into traditional, stereotyped careers (Fitzgerald and Crites, 1980). Before beginning to work with the client in these two stages, in which specific careers will be investigated, you need to become aware of your own biases in this area. If, for example, your parents both worked in professions and most of your current friends and acquaintances are professionals, it is possible that you would be biased toward this type of career, especially for clients from backgrounds similar to yours. Awareness of such bias can help you keep from unconsciously presenting information or leading discussions in such a way as to persuade clients in any particular direction.

What to Do and Why

The first of the major tasks at this stage, gathering occupational information, includes acquiring general information about the world of work as well as specific information about occupations. The knowledge gained forms the data base for later evaluation of alternatives and also serves to correct clients' misconceptions about work. Many clients have inaccurate, insufficient, or stereotyped knowledge about jobs and job settings, about the requirements of jobs in terms of personality traits, ability, or academic qualifications, about the tasks performed and the rewards offered. These misconceptions must be removed if the client is to make a reality-based choice.

The major difficulty for both counselor and client when it comes to occupational information is the overwhelming nature of the subject. To do an excellent job of career counseling at this stage, the counselor should ideally be a labor market expert, with complete access to the latest information and a clear understanding of the latest career trends. Unfortunately, rapid changes in the work world and in the economy, coupled with increasingly efficient and complex methods of storing and retrieving vast amounts of information, have made it functionally impossible for anyone to keep up to date, except perhaps those few counselors whose sole activity is career counseling and research. Counselors with limited experience of or perhaps limited interest in career counseling are unlikely to be able to perform as expert providers of occupational information. This situation does not mean, however, that career counseling need be confined to such experts. For one thing, career information experts might be unavailable to the client. For another, counselors without this particular expertise are well able to guide the client through all other stages of career counseling. The issue, therefore, becomes one of how to provide the client with enough career information to satisfy ethical demands on the counselor's competence while staying within realistic bounds.

Clients often have difficulty understanding why they have to do the legwork of hunting down information—why you cannot simply provide what they need to know. You need to explain the evanescent nature of career information, the immense volume of material available from multiple sources, and the virtual impossibility of keeping current. To avoid losing your credibility at this point, be certain that you can speak authoritatively about several sources you know well and that you convey to the client the fact that in this particular area, your expertise lies in being able to direct the client to the best sources rather than in possessing the information yourself. Because much of the client's information gathering will be in the form of personal contacts and direct experience of work situations, you can further explain that a valuable part of information about careers and workplaces is the client's own personal impressions, which must be obtained firsthand.

The second major task at this stage, generating alternatives, requires first a widening of choices to include as many options as possible, whether they appear feasible or not, and then a narrowing of those options until a select few are marked for detailed evaluation in the next stage. This process will not necessarily be performed in a neat, lockstep fashion. As new information is acquired, alternatives can be added to or deleted from the list; a new alternative sparks the need for new information. It is not usually possible, therefore, to complete one of the steps and then move on to the next. The extensiveness of each step will also vary with clients. For example, a person who is trying to decide among engineering subspecialties at college already has a list of alternatives—that is, those specialties offered by various colleges—and that task will be quickly completed. For some clients, particularly those with little or no work experience, it will be important to become familiar with the world of work in general before trying to gather alternatives. There are others whose habits of thinking lead them to learn little from general experiences; for these people, gaining familiarity with work is best accomplished by obtaining information about specific alternatives.

A difficulty during this process is to encourage the client to cast a wide net without making value judgments and thus beginning the elimination process prematurely. Once the options are narrowed to a select few (step three), the problem is to help the client remain open to new possibilities. As a matter of practicality, only the options on the short list are researched with any thoroughness.

As a preliminary to the task of generating alternatives, you will find it valuable to introduce the client to a simple scheme for organizing the world of work. This scheme will not only allow the client to envision new possibilities but also will provide the first opportunity for the client to see where he or she might fit in the working world. An organizational scheme also provides an orientation to the way in which much printed career information is arranged and therefore will reduce clients' confusion and sense of unfamiliarity when they first use the material. However, not all clients need to know how jobs can be classified, especially those who are interested in a career in only one field or who are already familiar with the world of work.

Sample Process

Exhibit 13 illustrates a typical four-step method of progressing through the tasks of this stage.

Step One: Present Occupational Classification

The first step describing the classification and organization of careers is of importance chiefly for clients who fail to realize, for example, the similarities between administrative tasks in a drug company and in a large opera house, or the fact that skills from one field can often transfer to another apparently

Exhibit 13. Tasks Involved in Gathering
Occupational Information and Generating Alternatives.

Start
> Client has no or an insufficient number of options and no or inadequate career information.

Step One (optional)
> Provide the client with an occupational classification scheme.

Step Two
> With the client, generate an extensive list of career alternatives.

Step Three
> With the client, reduce the list to the two to five best alternatives.

Step Four
> Instruct the client to gather information about each alternative on the reduced list (from step three).

End
> The client has a short list of options with adequate information about each and is now ready to evaluate these options.

---

quite different field. Many clients tend to see only the most obvious aspects of a particular field or setting. Thus, "hospital" brings to mind doctors, nurses, and possibly some of the more visible support staff but rarely positions in filming, public relations, electronics, psychology, and so on that exist in a large medical establishment.

Many different classification schemes have been proposed, each with its own merits. The simplest is that of the *Dictionary of Occupational Titles* (DOT) (U.S. Department of Labor, 1977), which divides the focus of work into data, people, and things. Prediger (1981) expanded this scheme by adding ideas as a fourth category and forming a vertical axis (ideas–things) and a horizontal axis (people–data). Within each quadrant so formed, Prediger placed twenty-five occupational clusters, further subdivided into job families. Another familiar classification scheme is Holland's (1985) hexagon of realistic, investigative, artistic, social, enterprising, and conventional categories, which correspond to work environments. Other schemes are based on commonly accepted clusters—such as industrial, office, construction, transportation, scientific, mechanics, health, social sciences, social service, design, and communications occupations—or on different types of industry, as in the *Occupational Outlook Handbook* (U.S. Department of Labor, 1984).

Many such schemes have been developed by people whose main interest is in the process of classification itself or in the possibility of research applications. As a result, the methods of classification often become exhaustive and complicated, providing a wealth of information that is likely to be overwhelming to a client who needs a simple overview or road map. Often, all that is needed is to explain, briefly, the organizational scheme used in the particular career information source with which you are most familiar and which you intend to use most with that client. Alternatively, you might choose a scheme that most closely fits the client's needs and situation.

The interest shown by the client and the questions asked will serve as a guide to how much education your client needs before proceeding. Tom, for example, having spent much of his two adult decades in prison, had limited and often inaccurate information about how the ''straight'' world ran. When the counselor showed him the table of contents of the *Occupational Outlook Handbook,* it became apparent that Tom did not understand much of the terminology (technician, technologist, agent, researcher, wright) and had little sense of the hierarchy of many jobs or the relationship of that hierarchy to skills and educational level. Once he received the necessary information, he was ready to proceed with the next step.

Another counselor, with a preference for using the *Dictionary of Occupational Titles* as a major source of career information, provided clients with a written summary of the first- and second-level occupational clusters in this book, together with three examples from the main text. Each digit of the code was explained for the examples, so that clients could appreciate the kind of information that it was possible to extract from the DOT. For example, the data–people–things classification used as part of the DOT code helped one client put his Work-Related Preferences into perspective and gave him a simple scheme for viewing job alternatives.

Perhaps the most important aspect of work classification schemes concerns not the client but the counselor. Many clients can proceed satisfactorily with little appreciation of the complex organization of the world of work, but the counselor cannot. Such appreciation is essential if you are to be efficient in pointing clients in new directions and helping them translate their interests and skills into specific jobs. We suggest, therefore, that you become familiar with a limited number of schemes that, in combination, have these characteristics: (1) they are similar to or easily translate to the schemes in the most widely used sources of occupational information (discussed below); (2) they allow for easy translation of interest inventory results to specific jobs; and (3) they are fairly comprehensive. For an extensive review of such schemes, the reader should consult Isaacson (1985).

Step Two: Generate Alternatives

The aim of step two is to create a list that embraces the greatest feasible number of alternatives—even those that at first glance seem of limited or peripheral interest. Obviously, you would not retain, even on this first list, such complete impossibilities as jobs requiring, say, perfect eyesight when your client wears bifocals, but if there is any hint at all that a job might be feasible and of interest to the client, it should be included on the list.

Before beginning to identify alternatives, you and the client need to decide on which criteria to use, since it is impossible to make a list based on no criteria at all. There are many criteria to consider when generating a list of alternatives, and the ones selected will depend on the individual client. For clients with limited, clear-cut interests that take precedence over all other considerations, the sole criterion for generating options will be how much each option fits those interests. For other clients, it may be necessary to apply more than one criterion. For example, Isaac had a firm belief that a father should invest a great deal of time in his children until they leave home. Since he had three youngsters under the age of eight and was looking for a career to span the next twenty years, it would have been a waste of time for him to consider options that required frequent travel away from home or many extended work days.

The number and rigidity of criteria chosen to guide the

process of generating alternatives must be carefully tuned to each individual client. Theoretically, the use of only one criterion, such as interests, could lead to an unwieldy list containing numerous highly unsuitable options. In reality, however, clients (especially those inclined to take a negative view of their own potential or opportunities) are more likely to create too short a list, overlooking or prematurely rejecting possibilities. The client should be encouraged, therefore, to employ, at least in the beginning, as few criteria as possible for the selection of alternatives.

Emphasize also the importance of holding off on evaluation of the options until later. Before the client begins to make the list, the process of and rationale behind the generation of alternatives should be carefully explained, together with instructions to err on the side of liberality rather than conservatism. One client, determined not to continue with any more education, was persuaded by the counselor not to use this as a criterion when widening the list of options. When he realized later that all his most desirable options required graduate work, he changed his mind about avoiding further schooling. By this point, clients have invested considerable resources in career counseling and can usually be persuaded not to waste these investments by hasty or careless efforts.

Help the client explore options by the use of more than one method, so as to tap different sources of ideas. Some suggested methods for generating alternatives include:

From Personal Sources

1. Childhood dreams
2. Stimulus questions
3. Environmental models
4. Brainstorming
5. Work-related preferences

From Commercial Sources

6. Interest inventories
7. Matched lists
8. Specialized literature

In order to produce a long list of options covering as wide an area as possible, we prefer to begin with methods that elicit idiosyncratic responses unconnected to interest inventories or published information. There is a simple rationale for this approach. Many clients have a naive faith, despite counselor disclaimers, in the magic of psychological tests or printed material and tend to make two mistakes when they see test results indicating, for example, that they have an interest in librarianship. The first error is to believe that this piece of test information carries more weight than their own ideas; the second is to stop looking for other alternatives or to limit their ideas to careers or jobs related closely to what they believe is their destined career. Because you want to avoid producing such inflexibility in your client at this early stage, begin the list of possible job alternatives with personal material the client already has.

Childhood dreams are often good sources of alternatives. As a child, what did your client dream of doing upon reaching adulthood? Why was the job or career not pursued? Does the client show even a hint of interest in that career now? If the interest was age-typical (such as fireman at age three) or fleeting or of no current interest, it can be ignored, but it can probably be included on the list if it was a somewhat unusual interest, persisted over time, or aroused intense feelings. The greatest advantage of including remote possibilities on the list is their capacity for stimulating other ideas. Take the example of Lynette, who for about eight years of her childhood longed to marry a farmer and live in the country. As an adult she claimed to find the country aversive. Even so, farming was put on the list and led to consideration of several more viable alternatives having to do with care of animals.

For many clients, directed use of the imagination can provide access to hidden desires. Directions should, of course, be tailored to the client's needs and situation and can take the form of a written exercise or a verbal report. You might ask, for example: "What job would you like if you were *not* married?" "Suppose you found out that you had only ten years to live; what work would you do?" "If you were told that you *had* to work for a large school district (for one of the country's top ac-

counting firms, in an isolated community in Nebraska, etc.),
what would you choose as your job?'' ''If you were a different
sex (age, personality, etc.), what would you do with your working life?'' ''Suppose you *had* to develop a cottage industry (*had*
to be a freelance worker, could *only* work part-time); what would
you do?''

Your selection of stimulus situations or questions should
be guided by what you know of the client, but be cautious that
you do not limit the client too narrowly, especially at the start
of the process of generating alternatives. In particular, avoid
using prompts to the imagination that are confined to your own
experience of work or to areas that you believe would be appropriate for the client. Some of the best questions will be in
areas where the client appears to have cognitive constraints. If,
for example, the client has a tendency to say, ''I'm not confident enough,'' you might ask, ''What would you want to do
if you had all the confidence in the world?''

Clients can also gather alternatives by looking at what
others in their environment do. For example, instruct the client
to purchase a newspaper with an extensive Help Wanted section and to circle every want ad that has any appeal at all,
regardless of pay, job requirements, or any other consideration.
Each of these jobs should be added to the list. If the client watches
television, he or she could be asked to make a list of, say, ten
jobs that are portrayed in the course of an evening that the client
might have some interest in. The client should be told to focus
on the characteristics of the job rather than on aspects that are
not necessarily correlated with the job, such as the personalities
of the job performer or the relationships among the cast members
(not every newsroom resembles the one depicted on the ''Mary
Tyler Moore Show''). You might also ask the client to list the
jobs of every relative and acquaintance and choose ten that might
be appealing. If the client is attracted to a particular setting,
such as a hospital, it can be profitable to arrange for a site visit,
where the client gathers information, either by observation or
by discussion with personnel, about the many different types
of work performed in that setting. The client can then be asked
to identify the ten jobs that have some appeal.

Brainstorming is another time-honored technique for generating alternatives. Instruct the client in the most important rules of brainstorming—that is, to allow the imagination free range and to write down every idea, no matter how silly or impossible it might seem. Any evaluation of the ideas must be avoided at this point. This activity can be conducted profitably with people who know the client well, such as friends and relatives. However, brainstorming should not be undertaken with any person who might attempt to dominate or persuade the client or who might be viewed as having an authoritative voice, since this would have the effect of limiting the client's freedom to imagine. A high school senior, for example, might ask his girlfriend, his trusted grandfather, or his favorite teacher a question such as "What job do you think I'd be best at, or enjoy most?" but he should not ask an authoritarian father who has definite ideas on what is right for his son.

Although the client's Work-Related Preferences will be most important in the evaluation stage, they can also be a source of alternatives, especially once the client has seen the fit between his or her work-related preferences and the world of work. It can be helpful to the client's objectivity to ask about the WRP in the third person; for example, "What sort of a job would you think of if your buddy at work said these were the things he was interested in?"

It will be liberating, and therefore more productive, if you can make this part of the stage as lighthearted and playful as possible, attempting to engage the child and the dreamer inside the adult. Because the purpose of these activities is to list alternatives and not to do an intensive investigation of particular jobs, there is no need for much written detail. But if the client has a serious interest in a particular position or setting and is likely to need more information later, it may be worth killing two birds with one stone to have the person take time to conduct a more intensive investigation of the situation.

After some of the less formalized methods have been used to help the client gather alternatives, considerable use can be made of written and structured materials. One major value of interest inventories is their ability to generate alternatives for the client. Tests such as Holland's Self Directed Search and the SCII have the added advantage of translating the client's interests directly into DOT codes, saving guesses as to how interests might translate into actual jobs. High-interest occupations can also lead to other possibilities in the same field or requiring similar skills. There are also published materials in the form of lists of interests that match different fields and levels of work. Mencke and Hummel (1984), for example, present 500 occupations classified according to interests served, skills required, career field, and DOT code. Campus and public libraries generally have available books and pamphlets on such topics as careers in education, what to do with a liberal arts degree, jobs in computers, dangerous jobs, and work overseas. None of these sources can be comprehensive, but if the client researches enough different sources, most bases will be covered.

No one can say how long the list of alternatives should be before beginning the narrowing process. When the client is especially talented and has a wide range of interests, the list might contain numerous possibilities. On the other hand, when the client has severe constraints the list might be too short to reduce further, and all alternatives will be evaluated in depth. It is generally quite apparent when the stream of ideas has dried up, and in any case, options that come to mind later can always be added.

Throughout the process of generating alternatives, the client should be encouraged to read over the list occasionally and to reflect on the positive aspects of each option. This activity should have the effect of making the most outrageous options familiar to the client so that they will not be rejected just because they feel strange. The focus on the positive will, one hopes, reduce the tendency of most clients to see only the negative side and to prematurely reject options that might be feasible.

Step Three: Narrow the List

Once the list of alternatives has been compiled, it is time to narrow the choices down, for the simple reason that detailed examination of options takes time, and the client probably neither needs nor wishes to spend unnecessary hours examining the less fruitful alternatives. There are several methods for narrowing choices. The client might separate the items into categories representing the most desirable options, the least desirable, and those in between, using any criterion that is important to the client. If this method still leaves an unwieldly number in the "most desirable" category, the client can reduce the list by adding other criteria. If all options in the "most desirable" category are equally attractive, another possibility is to select any five, or five that come from different career fields, or the five most dissimilar. The remaining options can be considered later. In fact, since even the most promising options might be rejected during the detailed evaluation process, the rest of the items in all categories should be retained as a pool from which further options could be chosen later.

The only alternatives that should be permanently discarded at this point are (1) those involving immovable constraints, such as location in a part of the country incompatible with the client's health or the requirement of skills that would be clearly unattainable for the client, or (2) those that arouse a definite negative reaction in the client once there has been time to think about them. For example, Ray had originally added soldier to his list, as a result of looking at his childhood dreams. The appeal of travel, adventure, and camaraderie remained, but Ray's adult experiences in the peace movement had left him with a strong antipathy toward the military establishment, which precluded any possibility of work with the armed forces.

When the client cannot separate the alternatives into categories, it is sufficient to simply ask for a short list of the three to five that the client would prefer to start with, based on some criterion that is important to the client, such as status or financial rewards. Sometimes, clients narrow their options in consultation with family members who will be affected by the ultimate choice. This method has advantages, but you need to check that the client is not being influenced away from appealing options before he or she has had the opportunity to examine those options in detail.

Whatever method is chosen for narrowing, it should take little time, since its main purpose is convenience. In fact, even after the choices have been narrowed, the client should be encouraged to continue to keep an open mind for further alternatives to add to the larger list and to select more options for evaluation.

Step Four: Gather Information on Each Option

Occupational information is any information about a job, including facts such as work tasks, work settings, training requirements, and wages. Occupational information also includes information that cannot be obtained from printed materials but that may be important, such as whether taking the job would require relocating to a new region of the country and how the client's spouse feels about the occupation.

Sources of Occupational Information

Occupational information can be obtained from a variety of sources, including printed media, audiovisual materials, prepackaged systems, interviews with experts, personal experiences, and informal information. We will discuss each source, beginning with those that least involve the client and moving along to those that most involve the client.

Printed Media. Printed information on occupations is in abundant supply and not difficult to come by, as it is available in public libraries, high school media centers, career resource centers, state employment services, and so on. Each issue of the *Vocational Guidance Quarterly* includes a list of recently published career materials. The United States Department of Labor (USDL) generates and publishes a vast amount of career-related information that is used primarily by a number of federal and state agencies for research, job placement, and career counseling programs. Many of the USDL career-related materials are free, while others can be purchased for a minimal fee. Two of the best-known and most often used references published by the USDL are the *Dictionary of Occupational Titles* and the *Occupational Outlook Handbook* (OOH).

The DOT is an encyclopedia of job descriptions, its fourth edition (1977) providing detailed technical descriptions of approximately 20,000 occupations. The DOT uses a nine-digit coding system, with each digit having a different meaning (such as which of 97 occupational divisions the occupation fits). The DOT is a good resource for descriptions of occupations not found in the OOH and allows for comparisons between the assessed characteristics of the individual and the various requirements of jobs. However, many career counselors find the technical style used to describe occupations boring and the complexity of accessing the information and the voluminous amount of information too difficult to manage for practical use (Zunker, 1985).

The OOH, revised every two years, is the most current, accurate, and detailed occupational information resource available. It provides information on over 850 occupations, including a description of the work and working conditions, places of employment, training and qualifications, and earnings and a projected employment outlook. The occupations are organized into 13 clusters of related jobs, an organization that enables a reader to review, in a selected field of interest, a variety of jobs whose training and skill requirements are at varying levels. Despite its value, the OOH is limited in the number of occupations it considers. Thus, it may be necessary to use the DOT for descriptions of occupations not included in the OOH.

Other useful printed materials include books devoted to listing internships, summer and part-time job opportunities, and volunteer and travel experience opportunities. (For an excellent discussion and annotated list, see Mencke and Hummel, 1984.) One book that may be especially interesting to clients is *Working* by Studs Terkel (1972), because it describes over 125 people, their jobs, and how they feel about their jobs. Although limited in scope, it is fascinating reading because its descriptions are personalized, giving readers a flavor of each occupation and a sense of some of the intangible rewards and stresses inherent in some kinds of work. Other materials that can be helpful to clients in researching options include information on postsecondary education and training and financial aid for students, and local job information published by the state employment service.

The advantages of printed information are that it is in abundant supply, much of it readily available at the nearest library, and it takes less time to access than many other types of information. Its disadvantages are that it goes out of date quickly, that most of it does not give the flavor of the occupation, that it is not appropriate for clients who do not read well, and that it often bores the client.

Audiovisual Materials. A different sort of information source is audiovisual materials. University or college career centers sometimes maintain audio tape files of major fields of study, and high schools often have video or audio tapes that portray various occupations. Audiovisual materials are more "alive" and give more of a taste of the occupation than do printed materials, but they provide limited information, can be cumbersome to use (requiring that the appropriate machinery be available), and retain their accuracy no longer than printed materials. They also tend to be expensive and are more aversive when dated than are printed materials.

Prepackaged Systems. There are also a variety of prepackaged systems that, although not exclusively devoted to career information, take the client from beginning to end of the career counseling process. The client can use them either for the entire career choice process or for selected parts of the process. Career planning guidebooks are one type of prepackaged system, of which there are many excellent examples (see Figler, 1979a; Gainer and Stark, 1979; Loniello, Sugimoto, and Jackson, 1984; Radin, 1983). These guidebooks take the client through every phase of the career planning process, from self-understanding to job search techniques. The advantage of such programs is that the client can proceed at his or her own pace. The disadvantage is that if the person works entirely alone, there will be little attention paid to his or her needs, no counselor to monitor the client's reactions and internal dialogue. The client might make premature decisions, and no counselor will be there to recognize the decision as premature.

Another type of prepackaged system is computerized

career planning software programs, such as SIGI PLUS (System for Interactive Guidance and Instruction), published by the Educational Testing Service, and DISCOVER, published by American College Testing. Both programs include self-assessment exercises, personalized lists of occupations based on the user's values, interests, skills, and level of education, and information about careers and the preparation each requires. SIGI PLUS also allows users to estimate their chances of completing the education or training required for a particular occupation, offers information on practical concerns such as financing education, and helps weigh the potential rewards and chances of success of various career options. In addition, SIGI allows for localizing information—that is, the career center can plug in local job information. DISCOVER, unlike SIGI, has a memory, which can recall a client's information from one session to the next.

Computerized career planning systems have been around since the mid 1960s, and their application is bound to increase. A counselor who is not now using such a system would be well advised to keep an eye out for new developments in this area, since increased use might well reduce costs to a point where this approach is within reach of anyone with a personal computer. The biggest disadvantage of career software programs is lack of access. Because the cost of leasing such programs is high enough to eliminate them as options for most individual practitioners, you and your client would have to be near one of the 400 or so colleges or universities that lease them, and to have the necessary qualifications to use them (such as student status). In addition, it takes approximately four hours to complete either SIGI or DISCOVER, which might be an added constraint for some clients. On the other hand, an advantage of computer programs for career counseling is that for young people (high school) they are fun to use, whereas books and audiovisual materials often are not.

If prepackaged career planning programs, either printed manuals or computer software, are used, it is important for the counselor to keep current on what the client's thoughts and feelings are about the material by debriefing each segment of the system with the client. For example, you and your client could go through a self-help book together, discussing each part, with some exercises being assigned as homework.

Interviews with Experts. Mencke and Hummel (1984) believe that the best way to obtain information about careers is to talk to people who actually work in the occupation one is considering. They send University of Arizona students in their career planning course to downtown Tucson with the task of going to the top floor of any office building and requesting a five-minute interview with the president of the organization, usually without an appointment. By interviewing the president, the person with the broadest possible perspective on the organization, students hear firsthand about the challenges, advantages, and problems of that organization and thereby learn how that organization might fit into the career they are exploring. There are other benefits to be gained from this exercise. The students rapidly overcome their shyness at approaching strangers and authority figures to ask for information, learn how to negotiate their way around secretarial staff (part of whose job is to protect the president from that sort of invasion), and lose their awe of people with exalted titles or multiple degrees. In essence, the exercise provides, in addition to information, a desensitization to interviewing that will be valuable when clients are job seeking.

Company presidents are not the only persons worth interviewing. Anyone who works at a particular job is, in fact, an expert on that job. To obtain a broad view, it is a good idea for clients to interview several people who are working in each of the occupations they are considering. Clients might contact friends and family as a starting point for names of people to interview and could ask each interviewee for names of others who might also be willing to be interviewed. In addition, many schools (high schools, colleges, universities) maintain reference files of local people who have agreed to talk with students about their work.

The advantage of personal interviews with experts as a source of occupational information is that the workers have firsthand experience of a job—how it feels, what it demands, its frustrations and satisfactions, and how it influences their lives. They are in the best possible position to provide the most valid information. There are, unfortunately, some drawbacks to the expert interview. There is always the possibility that the particular person the client is interviewing is not representative of other workers in the field or that the worker will either attempt to recruit the client, mentioning only the best aspects of the position, or emphasize how difficult or demanding the job is. These difficulties might be overcome if the counselor telephones the possible contact person in advance and makes a clear statement of what would be most helpful for the client to hear. The counselor should also work with the client to identify the best questions to ask in order to elicit the most complete and unbiased information.

Personal Experiences: Observation and Participation. Personal experience with an occupation is, in most cases, the best method of gathering information. Some workers might be willing to show the client around the office/organization or to allow a client to "job shadow"—that is, follow the worker around for a day or two in order to learn what the job entails. Even more information can be obtained if the client can arrange to actually work in the setting that she or he is considering. Part-time or summer work can often be obtained, and internships for college students can often be arranged (see Mencke and Hummel, 1984). If these options are not possible, volunteering often is; many businesses are willing to allow people to volunteer their time, and doing so gives the client an excellent firsthand experience of the job. Isaacson (1985) warns that the experience needs to be continued long enough (three to four weeks) and long enough each day (several hours) to provide a realistic sample of work. The advantage of such opportunities is that they provide a firsthand experience for those clients who have had little exposure to world of work. Disadvantages are that they are often difficult to obtain and that they take a good deal of time. Internships may not be a good option for people who are unable to take time off from their present position. And because many internships are not paid, they can realistically be considered only when earning money is not of immediate concern, as for a home-maker thinking about entering the workforce or a college student whose parents are willing to support a summer's internship.

Informal Information. Informal, or grapevine, information is occupational information that is unwritten and that often modifies or contradicts official statements and published information (Overs, 1967). Examples of this type of information might be that XYZ business works every possible angle to avoid hiring women, that the boss at QRS plays favorites and people do not get raises unless they are on his good list, or that JKL doesn't pay as much as its competitors but looks after its employees in a more humane fashion. Although such information will be of most importance at the time of job searches, clients should be encouraged to notice any information of this type in case they need it later. Sources of such information include present and former clients, professional contacts, newspapers, and observations gathered in field visits (Reardon, 1984).

A more thorough discussion of the sources of career information can be found in books devoted entirely to the subject (for example, Hoppock, 1976; Isaacson, 1977; Norris, Hatch, Engeles, and Winborn, 1979). In addition, the counselor might consult *Where to Start: An Annotated Career Planning Bibliography* (Rockcastle, 1985), a regularly updated resource that describes publications on career materials.

Evaluating Occupational Information

Because a great deal of available occupational information is, for one reason or another, not very helpful to clients (Brooks, 1984; Reardon, 1984; Srebalus, Marinelli, and Messing, 1982), the counselor should be involved in evaluating it before the client relies too heavily on it. Although information published by the USDL, such as the OOH and the DOT, can be counted on to be unbiased, other printed information is often inaccurate, presenting only positive information or information that is out of date.

To evaluate printed occupational information, look through

the material to note the date; if it is more than three years old, it might present an outdated picture of the particular work in question. If the author seems to be trying to sell you on the occupation, mentioning only advantages and no disadvantages, the literature is not accurate. Also check to see whether the reading level is appropriate for client and whether the material is free from sexual, racial, social, ethnic, age, or religious bias that might adversely affect your client. The most thorough method of evaluating printed or filmed information is to use the guidelines for preparation and evaluation of career information published by the National Vocational Guidance Association (1980).

Labor market trends, although useful to consider in career planning, should be used with caution. Trends do not last forever, and the person who decides to major in chemical engineering at the outset of his or her college career may find, for example, that upon graduation the market is not as rich with engineering jobs as it had been five years earlier. In addition, trends are averages and may not apply to the one client sitting across from the counselor. For example, the information that in future years there will be a lowered demand for museum curators means only that in general there will be fewer jobs than there have been in the past, not necessarily that a particular client should not prepare for a career as a museum curator. The client might be exceptionally well trained, have contacts, be willing to relocate, have outstanding job search skills, be unusually persevering in job hunting, make a memorable and positive first impression, or be very lucky. Information about career trends should be regarded as simply that, a piece of information to be included with all the others when evaluating a particular option.

Some career counselors maintain a list of people in various occupations and at various levels who are willing to talk to clients about what they do in their jobs. If you first interview these people yourself you will be able to ascertain the extent to which they are representative of their field and the likelihood of their information being accurate. When it is the client who has identified people to interview for information about occupations, you and client together should evaluate the results, focusing especially on how accurate, biased, or representative the information is.

Because not every counselor can be a labor market expert, one way around this dilemma is to locate an information specialist and arrange to work with that person. Perhaps there is a community college nearby with a career center staffed by a knowledgeable career librarian who would be willing to work with you and your client if you both traveled to the center, or with your client alone. In the latter case, you need to spend time establishing a working relationship with the librarian to ensure that the client will obtain the type of information and service you think would be most helpful. If it is not possible to find a career information expert and you are all the client has to rely on for expertise, you should, at the very least, be familiar with one or two of the standard information resources such as the OOH and DOT; in addition, you should know what information is available, where it is located, and how to go about finding it.

Process for Working with Occupational Information

Assuming that you have already evaluated the occupational information, there are only two major tasks to be accomplished at this stage: teaching the client information-gathering skills, and discussing the gathered information with the client. When it comes time to gather occupational information, it is the client who should do the gathering, not the counselor. Certainly, if there is a copy of the OOH in your office, it is not necessary to send the client to the library to get the same information, nor is it necessary, or even advisable, for the client to identify his or her own experts to interview. Nevertheless, for clients to become maximally involved in the process, it is they who must do the legwork of seeking and acquiring occupational information.

Your task is to teach your clients the most efficient method of obtaining the most useful information. If it is printed information they are after, most clients will already have the requisite library skills, and in most cases you need only point them in the direction of the most helpful librarian and most likely places to begin hunting. On the other hand, most clients can benefit from instruction on how to interview people for information.

Left to their own devices, they are apt to ask questions that can be answered by readily available materials—the OOH for example. You can maximize the value of information interviews by, in collaboration with the client, developing good questions to ask—life-style questions that cannot be answered by printed materials—and by planning the interview in advance (see Exhibit 14).

Exhibit 14. Interviewing for Information.

Name _____ Official title _____

Date interviewed _____ Employer _____

Years in present position _____

1. How much do you like the job?

2. What are your activities and responsibilities on the job?

3. How does a typical day go?

4. What do you like best about your job? Why?

5. What do you like least about your job? Why?

6. How and by whom are work decisions made that affect you?

7. How much influence do you have over decisions that affect you?

8. Does your work affect your social life? How?

Exhibit 14. Interviewing for Information, Cont'd.

9. What do you find most difficult about your job?

10. What about the job would you change if you could?

11. What sort of person do you have to be to be really good at this job?

12. How did you decide to enter this field?

13. What steps did you take to enter this field?

14. Where do you expect to go from here?

15. Is there any specific advice you would give someone entering this field?

16. Other (questions related to special interests or concerns)

17. Can you suggest names of other people I might speak with in this field?

When the client returns with either printed information or the results of an interview with someone who works in the field in question, the task is to go over the information that has been obtained with the client. In this discussion, you must make certain first that information on both negative and positive aspects of the job is represented. If one of these aspects has been omitted in printed information, the client might have read only promotional literature and should be steered toward less biased material or sent out to interview someone who works in the field. If the omission has occurred because an interviewed person included only one side of the picture, the omission should be pointed out to the client. You might then instruct the client to try to complete the picture, perhaps by returning to the same person armed with additional, specific questions, or perhaps by interviewing a second person in the same field.

Your second task in discussing the obtained information with the client is to help the client explore the personal meaning of the information, allowing ample opportunity for the expression of attitudes and feelings. The portion of career counseling that deals with occupational information might seem to be a cognitive activity, unlikely to call forth many feelings in the client. But as Tyler (1969) pointed out, "The girl who has been seriously considering social work . . . [may be very disappointed] when she discovers what very low salaries many social workers receive, [and] the would-be psychiatrist may suffer a rude shock when he finds out that a complete medical course is required before specialization in psychiatry can begin." The client might very well find out information that dashes dreams or hopes, and the expression of his or her feelings is important at this stage of counseling. However, these options should not be discarded, even if information found has been disappointing, because doing so would represent premature evaluation on the basis of only one criterion.

∽✿ 5 ✿∾

Helping Clients Choose Among Career Alternatives

The stage of choosing among alternatives is a turning point in career counseling. Thus far, the client has selected and investigated several potential career options and has narrowed the list to a favored few. In this stage, the client will evaluate these options in order to arrive at a final choice. As it becomes apparent that the time for action is close, the client is suddenly gripped by an intensity, an urgency, that can be both exciting and frightening. However active the client has been to this point, no decisions have been called for; but now the client must make an active choice, which implies commitment to change and a much riskier kind of involvement. For many clients, therefore, it is the psychological rather than the technical aspects of decision making that cause problems and that will receive much of the counselor's attention at this stage. Special difficulties will be addressed in Chapter 6.

This can also be a difficult time for the counselor who, by now, very likely has considerable investment in having the client make a choice, and make a good one. Unlike other types of counseling, career counseling carries with it the burden that evaluation of success is, to the client at least, simple and obvious. If the client ends up with an attractive job, counseling is judged as successful; if not, the client is inclined to see counseling, and you by association, as having failed.

125

The major temptation to be avoided at this stage is guiding the client toward an option you favor. Because the client, not you, must live with the choice and all its consequences, the decision must be made as freely as possible. From the start of this stage, therefore, help ensure freedom of choice by verbalizing it with phrases such as "This has to be your decision," "You are the one who has to live with this, not I," and "I can't make this decision for you."

There are four tasks for the client to accomplish at this stage: preparing to make a choice, evaluating options, making a choice among the options, and coming to terms with the choice. Sometimes the task of choosing among alternatives is inappropriate or unnecessary, in which case a different sort of decision will have to be made, such as to put the choice on hold for a time or to choose a path of action that will leave doors open to several different options.

To increase the likelihood of making a good decision, the counselor needs to be sure that the client is both ready and able to make a choice. Readiness involves sufficiency of information, while ability involves cognitions that could restrict choice or events outside the client's control that need to occur before the client is free to choose.

Making a choice is an act that often happens without any outside help, and the client may come to a decision without intervention on your part. Most clients, however, need help integrating the rational and emotional aspects of the data they have gathered. By now they have been investigating options for some time and have no doubt formed emotional impressions that can be quite confusing, especially if the situation is complicated by the pressure to make a decision both immediately and wisely. This is a good time for clients to disengage from gut reactions and engage in a systematic evaluation process that will encourage objectivity and will tend to ensure that nothing important has been overlooked. Simply having gone through such a process can be reassuring later, when the client can fight doubt and hesitation by thinking: "I know I looked at every aspect of my decision carefully, and as far as I could tell, this was the best choice for me at the time."

Coming to terms with the choice is an essential part of the decision-making process. Rarely does a choice have only overwhelming advantages and no drawbacks, and rarely does a client simply make the choice and proceed with plans without a backward glance. Part of the counselor's job at this stage is to help the client handle, on cognitive, emotional, and practical levels, the imperfect aspects of the choice, particularly if all the options are fairly equal or if the final choice has severe disadvantages. There are many reasons for last-minute cold feet, such as disapproval by significant others, a sudden loss of self-confidence, or a turn for the worse in the economy; whatever the cause, the discomfort must be dealt with until the client reaches a point of commitment to the choice sufficient to allow progress to the next stage. If doubts are not resolved, there is a strong likelihood that the client will sabotage or fail to carry out plans to reach the goal.

Assessing Readiness

Several psychological, social, and procedural factors need to be considered in gauging the client's readiness to make a decision.

It is not unusual for a client's goals and preferences to change over time or as a result of new information, and events may have occurred to change the time frame discussed at the start of counseling. Before proceeding to evaluate options, therefore, it is good for both of you to be clear about what sort of decision has to be made, meeting what desired outcomes, and by when.

Investigate whether any other issues in the client's life should take precedence over a career decision. For example, if Katherine is struggling with the question of whether to have another child, she should probably settle that issue first, as it is likely to have an impact on her career decision. Similarly, if a client is facing the decision of whether to get a divorce, that choice should take precedence, since such a serious change in life-style might well have consequences that would affect the client's career plans. Discover, therefore, what other decisions the client has pending that might need to be addressed first. Of course, there is no reason to postpone career counseling if the client is willing to make two choices, one to fit each eventuality. In Katherine's case, this would mean one career to fit the life-style of a new mother and a second one more appropriate to her current situation as the mother of a ten-year-old.

Sometimes the client cannot make a career choice until outside events have occurred or until others have made their own decisions. Until she learns how the proposed reorganization at her current company affects her, Alice will not be in a position to decide whether to continue her efforts to climb the corporate ladder or to go into business for herself. Joe is psychologically ready to choose among three options, two of which require overseas training, but his wife has just had a serious car accident, so until he knows what sort of medical care she will need he does not feel he can leave the country. Jane is considering options that would involve a return to school, but her husband has just told her that he is also thinking about further schooling, which Jane and he agree would take precedence over her education. Until he decides, Jane cannot.

A final element in decision readiness is intrapersonal factors. Sometimes a client is not ready to make a decision until a particular personal problem has been dealt with. Although not all personal problems must be solved before a person can make a career choice, it is important to address those that directly affect career. Stan, for example, loved to tutor math on a one-to-one basis and believed that he would enjoy classroom teaching, too. Unfortunately, he was so shy that he failed to see how he could ever speak in front of a group and was therefore leaning toward becoming an accountant, even though he found that a much less attractive option than teaching. In Stan's case, it made sense to deal with his shyness first, so that he would be able to make a free choice.

It is sometimes difficult for clients to delay making a choice when the factors that indicate a need for delay are internal, such as immaturity or psychological blocks. Some clients might well go ahead and exercise their right to make a decision despite your reservations. If you believe that a client is not ready to decide, the most you can do is suggest a delay, explain the reasons as carefully and tactfully as possible, point out the benefits the delay could have for the client, and enumerate the possible costs of a premature choice. If the client insists on proceeding, decide whether you can be supportive and help minimize problems or must refuse further help, on ethical grounds that you cannot provide adequate service, and refer the client.

One of the easiest ways to ensure that all aspects of readiness are covered is to use a checklist, such as the one presented in Exhibit 15.

Exhibit 15. Readiness Checklist.

All of the following questions are to be answered in the affirmative before proceeding:

1. Has the counseling goal been updated, if necessary?
2. Has the list of work-related preferences been updated if necessary?
3. Do you know the time frame for the decision?
4. Do you have a list of no more than five well-researched alternatives for evaluation?
5. Is the client free to make a decision on these grounds:
   a. Client has no other major decisions to make that will affect career choice.
   b. Client is not waiting for some event to occur that is outside his or her control but that would affect the choice made.
   c. Client does not need to deal with some intrapersonal issue before making a career choice.

Evaluating Options

There are several ways to evaluate options, ranging from the simple to the complex, and the choice of method will depend largely on the client. The easiest method, which still takes time and requires patience, is the most preferable for clients who are generally impatient, impulsive, or averse to meticulous work, or for clients for whom the decision is not likely to be difficult. The more complex methods can be kept as a backup, either for decisions that cannot be made in a simpler way or for clients who express an interest in learning a more exact method of decision making. The basic approach of all methods is to help the client look at each option in turn and to formulate the best possible answers to the following questions:

> Of what benefit would this choice be to me?
>
> What price would I have to pay in order to have this choice?
>
> How likely is it that I could actually get this choice, given my constraints and assets?
>
> How does this option compare with the others?

In the following pages we present five exercises designed to help clients evaluate their options. Exhibits illustrate the use of each exercise. It is not important to follow any particular method slavishly, only to ensure that the client has not overlooked any foreseeable impact that a particular choice might have on his or her life. There is no particular order to the exercises (except where one specifically depends on information from another), and they should be selected, omitted, or modified as needed for individual clients. At a minimum, we suggest that clients complete some version of the exercises on desired outcomes and on the pros and cons. In almost all cases, it will be advisable for you to show the client how to set up the paperwork for the exercises and explain or model the amount of detail and thoroughness required.

Because the exercises are quite straightforward, it is possible for clients to complete them both rapidly and superficially, an approach that will usually negate the effectiveness of the exercises. Encourage clients to take their efforts seriously by reminding them of the importance of making a good decision. If you doubt the client's ability to do an exercise thoroughly, it would be better to spend session time on it than to have the person complete it for homework. Ultimately, the client will gain greater benefit from one exercise done well than from several done poorly.

If the client has done an excellent job of researching the various options, completing the exercises can go smoothly. Sometimes, however, information is lacking and must be gathered before the client can proceed. It is wise to alert clients to the fact that making the choice among options can be time consuming and might require some backtracking.

Desired Outcome Exercise. The purpose of the desired outcome exercise is to check each option against the client's list of Work-Related Preferences (WRPs), which has been developed and updated throughout the previous stages of counseling. Exhibit 16 is an example of a form that could be used for this exercise. Scores have been filled in for a hypothetical client.

Exhibit 16. Desired Outcome Exercise.

How likely is each option to provide the desired outcome?
3 = very likely, 2 = somewhat likely, 1 = unlikely

Desired Outcomes	*Options*		
	Law	Politics	Advertising
Status	3	2	1
Money	3	2	3
Autonomy	3	2	1
Use creativity	1	2	3
Power	3	3	1
Total	13	11	9

After explaining the purpose of the exercise, set up the form by heading the columns with the options under consideration and by listing on the left-hand side the client's top five to seven preferences (in order, if they have been prioritized). The example in Exhibit 16 is set up for three options, but obviously this number could be altered. Ask the client to take one option at a time and estimate the likelihood of that option providing the desired outcome. The client can use the scale suggested (3 = very likely, and so on) or a percentage ("There is *x* percent chance of this option providing me with the degree of status, amount of money, and so on that I would like"). The information to make the estimates should be available as a result of the client's research into each option.

When the page is completed, the client can see at a glance how the options compare. Totals at the bottoms of the columns make the comparisons more dramatic. When options seem equal on the basis of the client's top priorities, it can be worthwhile to repeat the exercise using the client's next group of WRPs— that is, preferences that would be enjoyable but are not considered essential or of overwhelming importance. Sometimes these secondary preferences tip the balance when comparing otherwise equal options. Be careful, however, not to let clients forget that, however attractive the lesser advantages of a job are, it is their top priorities that count most.

Keep in mind that the desired outcomes are as the client defines them. Paul and Art, for example, are both interested in power as a desired outcome. Paul defines power as influence over people's tastes and selection of goods and therefore estimates that advertising is his best option for achieving power. Art, on the other hand, believes that law will give him the most power because he defines power as the ability to have far-reaching influence on people's freedoms. If you suspect that the client is using terms in a general rather than a personal sense, refer back to the WRPs, not only to the summary but also to the extensive detailed notes taken while eliciting the WRPs.

Pros and Cons Exercise. The pros and cons exercise is designed to consider the long- and short-term advantages and disadvantages of each option. After explaining the purpose of the exercise, determine with the client the time limits for short and long term, such as "in the next six months," or "by my fortieth birthday." Set up the exercise sheet by marking out quadrants designating the pros and cons both short and long term (see Exhibit 17), with the option under consideration written at the top. The client may fill in quadrants in any order but should try to leave no quadrant empty, as it is unlikely that any option will have no disadvantages or advantages either short or long term.

Unless the client makes a decision the first time this exercise is tried, it is worth repeating several times, with increasing detail. For example, the client might fill in the form once in rough detail, then complete other exercises or consult other sources in order to gather more information, return to flesh out

Exhibit 17. Pros and Cons Exercise.

OPTION: Air force		
	Pros	*Cons*
Short Term	Travel.	Little freedom or
	May get to fly.	autonomy.
	Free education.	Have to leave Amy.
Long Term	Retire early enough	Many moves hard on
	to start new career.	family.
	Many challenges in	Might become a
	developing field.	military "type."

the form, and finally spend a session in your office attempting to fill in any gaps. In order not to overlook any possible consequences of the option, clients should use their WRPs, exercises such as future forecast, their imagination, the experience of those who have chosen the option, the impressions of other people who know them—in fact, any source of information.

The pros and cons exercise should be repeated for each option, using a separate sheet for each. When all the sheets are finished, discuss them with the client, asking about any change in attitude toward the options or any concerns the client has. If the client can rank order the options at this point, the choice is virtually made. If you need to summarize or highlight the information more clearly, there are several methods. For example, the client can be asked to weight each consequence by assigning a number to indicate its importance and then to total the numbers in various ways, depending on which quadrants the client is more concerned about avoiding or achieving. Younger people might assign a lower weight to short-term cons, feeling that they have more time available to reach long-term benefits. A man whose wife has served notice that she will file for divorce unless there is rapid improvement in their financial situation might certainly weight short-term consequences, both positive and negative, more heavily than ones that are in the distant future.

Balance Sheeting Exercise. The balance sheeting exercise represents a more structured method for helping the client focus on the areas and people that will be affected most by the choice of a particular option. Explain the purpose of the exercise and identify with the client several (usually about five to eight) categories of prime importance. For example, a housewife considering a return to school might want to estimate the pros and cons for her husband, her children, her own health, the family finances, and her social life. To perform the exercise, the client should list such categories on the left side of a sheet of paper and for each option fill in the positive and negative consequences for the categories, as in Exhibit 18. When all the options have been treated in this way, they can be compared and discussed.

Exhibit 18. Balance Sheeting Exercise.

Option: Return to school

Effect on	Negatives	Positives
Husband	He'll hate sharing chores.	He says he wants us to be more equal.
Children	No one home after school.	They'll learn some independence.
Health	May get overtired.	Won't get depressed the way I do now.
Finances	Will strain family budget.	Will bring in greater income in the long run.
Social life	May lose contact with my housebound friends.	Will meet new people.
Self-confidence	Depends on whether I do well.	

The client may then wish to plan some way to circumvent some of the disadvantages and make adjustments accordingly on the balance sheet. As with the pros and cons exercise, the consequences on the balance sheet can be weighted for importance, to aid in making a choice among the options.

Probability Estimation Exercise. The consequences that a client thinks of sometimes represent distortions of reality, because of the client's undue pessimism or optimism or unrealistic self-assessment. This exercise is designed to help the client estimate how likely it is that the anticipated consequences will, in fact, occur. If you or your client have concerns about whether the client will be able to reach the desired goal, an assessment of that probability should also be included in this exercise.

Using a form similar to that in Exhibit 19, take one option at a time and identify with the client the major consequences, both positive and negative, that are important to the

Exhibit 19. Probability Estimation Exercise.

Option: Mechanic in my brother's garage

Consequence	Probability of Occurrence
Sara would object to the dirt.	15%
I'd make good money.	75%
I'd go no higher.	100%
My friends would look up to me.	15%
Dad would be disappointed.	50%
I'd have fun with my brother.	85%

client. After a discussion of the probability that each consequence will occur, the client should assign a percentage to each. Estimates should be based on the most accurate information that can be gathered. Facts, such as salary amounts, should be checked as close to the source as possible. Estimates for such subjective matters as the probability of enjoying a job should be based on firsthand recent experience as much as possible. When the consequence involves someone else's opinion ("Dad would be disappointed"), the client should talk to that person before arriving at a final estimate.

The process should be repeated for all options the client is considering and the results discussed. The client might determine that the probability of a negative consequence is so low that it can be ignored or that the chance of achieving a positive consequence is so poor that the option should be discarded. A not unexpected reaction is the "sour grapes" response of "Well, that's not so important anyway.'' This may be true, because client priorities do change, but if you know that, throughout the process of career counseling, a particular work preference has seemed very important, do not allow the client to dismiss it without discussion and time to reflect. Chuck, for example, repeatedly expressed interest in having an occupation in which he could spend his time outdoors. When he considered the possibility of being able to own and run his own farm, he concluded that, at his age, with his existing credentials and financial resources, there was a low probability that he would reach his goal within an acceptable time frame. In frustration, he wanted to throw out all his other options relating to the outdoors and go to work in the local missile manufacturing plant. His counselor acknowledged that this plan was a possibility but insisted that Chuck submit it to the same sort of evaluation that he had given to other options. As a result of this process, Chuck realized that, while assembly-line work would satisfy some of his preferences, it would not provide him with the outdoor contact that was so important to him. The exercise also gave him time to recover from his disappointment over farming. He returned to his love of the outdoors, generated more options in line with his interests, and eventually found a feasible and acceptable compromise in a position as traveling salesman and demonstrator of agricultural equipment.

When clients try to estimate their likelihood of obtaining a particular job or of beginning a career, they sometimes need additional information about their own abilities or about the marketplace. For some people, past performance, either in academic matters or in tasks requiring a specific skill or talent, is an adequate predictor of future performance, and it will be apparent from school records and the client's history that the ability is there to meet the needs of the desired option. In addition, almost all universities and graduate schools, as well as many companies, have entry examinations of some kind.

It is quite common for clients to hesitate and doubt their ability when they realize that they have to meet qualifying standards. The quickest way to overcome this hesitation is to have clients find out what abilities are required and to ascertain areas where practice or tutoring might be needed. They could, for example, take sample tests of the Graduate Record Examination. Many clients who do so are disappointed by their first performance, and you will need to reassure them by pointing out their unfamiliarity with the test and perhaps their lack of practice at academic examinations. If they have other abilities that would make them suitable for the job, they should not give up the option because of poor test results but should prepare instead to make extra efforts to overcome this barrier. (More complex problems related to the client's ability are addressed in Chapter Six.)

Assessing the marketplace can be difficult if the client is interested in an unusual or obscure option. For common jobs or careers in the professional or business world, the information is accessible in the form of annual government reports about demand for certain positions and about the numbers and types of businesses that are established or go bankrupt in a year. Individual professions and businesses also publish regular status and forecast reports. For recently developed positions or ones outside the mainstream, clients will need to be more creative in seeking the information they need and should recognize that what they learn might be biased and inaccurate. The best sources of information will be people actually in the field, who should be interviewed regarding their own difficulties in entering the job, their knowledge of an increase or decrease in openings, any personal changes they have experienced (for example, in amount of time they work), income or revenue, and clientele. An important question to ask those already succeeding in the field is what factors differentiate those who succeed from those who fail.

Future Forecast Exercise. The future forecast exercise is a more imaginative way to consider possible consequences of an option, especially at different points in the future. This exercise is a guided fantasy and requires debriefing; thus, it needs to be conducted in session, with the client sitting relaxed, eyes closed. Begin as follows:

The option you are considering is to become a
——. You already know a great deal about what
that entails, so I'd like you to let your mind move
forward into the future five years, when you will
be——years old. I will ask you some questions
to guide your imagination, and want you to paint
a picture for yourself of how your life will be if you
adopt this choice. Don't tell me any of your thoughts
until the end of the fantasy; for now just let your
imagination flow.

Then read the questions from the future forecast question list in Exhibit 20, being careful to allow sufficient time for
the client to create the fantasy. When the questions are finished,

Exhibit 20. Future Forecast Question List.

(Add or delete questions according to what you know of your client's most important values and interests.)

Work

1.   How do you spend your time at work?
2.   What does the workplace look like?
3.   How do you spend time with co-workers?
4.   What sort of people are they?
5.   What is your position, and what prospects are there for advancement?
6.   Do you take work home with you?
7.   Who is your boss, and how are you treated by him or her?
8.   What is your salary and what perks do you have?

Living Environment

1.   Where do you live—city, town, farm? House, apartment?
2.   What is your place like? How is it decorated?
3.   What sort of a neighborhood is it? As you look out your window, what can
     you see and hear?
4.   What do you own in the way of clothes, transportation, and so on?
5.   Who lives with you, and how do you spend your time together?

Social Life and Recreation

1.   Who are your friends? How do you spend time with them?
2.   What sports do you enjoy?
3.   What hobbies do you spend time on?
4.   How do you spend your vacations?

client should be asked to describe his or her forecast. Debriefing is done by asking whether the client received any surprises
or felt a change in attitude toward the option. Help the client
achieve some objectivity by pointing out any discrepancies, such
as a fantasy that includes an activity or preference not previously
mentioned. The fantasy should also be checked against the
client's WRPs, looking especially for contradictions or missing
elements. For example: "On your WRP list, you say that having time for your family is very important, but I noticed that
in your fantasy you were away from home a lot. Does this mean
that you have changed your mind about how you want to relate
to your family?"

There are many useful variations of the future forecast.
To gain a clearer picture of the pros and cons of adopting a
choice, you might make a list of what the client reports, putting items in two columns, one for negative and one for positive
consequences. This tactic will enable you to graphically demonstrate any imbalance—that is, a focus exclusively on one aspect
of an option. Another variation is to repeat the fantasy using
the same option but for different future points of time. If the
client wants to be a surgeon, five years in the future would put
her still in training. While this would certainly give her a realistic
picture of what might lie ahead if she takes this route, you might
need to move ten or even fifteen years ahead before the client
can begin to picture some of the real benefits (or drawbacks)
of this particular career.

The future forecast exercise can have the beneficial effect of correcting unrealistic self-assessment. Eighteen-year-old
Adolpho, whose parents and two sisters worked in social service occupations, had adopted the family value that helping
others is a worthwhile task. Although he appeared quite shy and
had no history of enjoying activities directly helping people, he
became defensive and anxious when the counselor tried to encourage him to widen his options, and he proceeded to assemble a list of occupations such as social worker and probation
officer that required intense involvement with others. During
the future forecast fantasy, his most imaginative efforts were
devoted to his life away from work, a life with just a few close

friends and a great many solitary activities, generally of a scientific nature. When the counselor pointed out this emphasis, Adolpho recognized that, in fantasy, his social service work was a duty he felt he owed the world, one that would allow him to pursue his real interests with a quiet conscience. Once the counselor suggested that it might be possible to satisfy conscience and preference, he was able to redefine helping others as any job that would be of value to others, even indirectly, and explored such previously rejected options as medical research.

Another common result of the future forecast exercise, especially for people who have little experience of the economic aspects of survival, is the realization that the desired fantasy life-style will not be supported by the option under consideration and that some adjustment will be necessary. With young people in particular, it can be enlightening to have them price the various aspects of their fantasy, such as rent, car, vacation, clothes, and entertainment, and to compare the total with their expected salary. The discrepancy often produces a more sober but more realistic look at options.

Making the Choice

In the final analysis, the only instruction you can give clients regarding the actual making of a choice is: "Decide." In some cases, the choice will be obvious and deciding will be easy. But when there is no obvious or good option, people use very different methods to decide. Some go home, sleep on it, and make the choice that feels best the next morning. Others prefer to present information to family and friends and act on others' advice. Many people believe that they have an internal guiding light that will point them to the correct decision if they simply relax and let the answer come. All these methods are probably fairly equal, as long as the client is well informed about the options and has evaluated them carefully.

As a final exercise before making a choice, you can help the client summarize and compare the options under consideration so that relevant information can be seen at a glance. Such summarizing can be done with the ranking by multiple criteria exercise

Exhibit 21. Ranking by Multiple Criteria Exercise.

Criteria	Options		
	Radiology	Pediatrics	Family Medicine
Greatest appeal	3	2	1
Mike's opinion	3	1	2
Best schedule	1	2	3
Fewest negatives	3	1	2
Total	10	6	8

shown in Exhibit 21. Explain the purpose of the exercise and then identify with the client several criteria by which to rank order the options. These criteria should be whatever the client feels are most important in terms of making a decision. Some suggestions:

How attracted I am by the option.
How my spouse feels about the option.
The number of long-term consequences.
The number of short-term consequences.
The probability of my being successful.
The speed with which I could reach the top.

These criteria should be listed on the left-hand side of the page, and the options across the top. Have the client rank order the options according to each criterion, assigning a 1 to the option that best meets that criterion, 2 to the option that next best meets it, and so on. When all options have been ranked for all criteria, ranks can be totaled, with the lowest total representing the option that appears best.

When you have done all that you can do to help the client evaluate and compare options, put the weight of deciding firmly on the client's shoulders and refuse to help in this task. In fact, even if the client voices a decision in your office, it is unwise to consider it final until he or she has reached the same conclusion at least twenty-four hours later in a different setting. Should the client be unable to reach a decision, even after a reasonable amount of time for reflection, we refer you to the suggestions for solutions discussed in Chapter Six.

Accepting the Choice

Once the choice is made, the client should live it out in fantasy for a few days. Thus, several times a day, the client should pause for purposeful daydreaming, thinking, for example, "If I were a paramedic right now, I'd be going to . . . , planning . . . , remembering . . . , worrying about . . . , and my kids would be . . . , and my spouse would be . . . , and we'd be living . . . , and this weekend . . . " This exercise serves several purposes. It allows the client to become more accustomed to and therefore more accepting of the choice, it increases enthusiasm for moving toward the goal, and it strengthens commitment to the choice should others cast doubts. If the choice is indeed a poor one, this exercise will often reveal the problems with the decision and the need for reappraisal. The exercise is made more powerful if the client, after living with the choice in fantasy, then publicly "owns" the choice by telling others about it and dealing with subsequent feedback.

Sometimes the choice is so obvious, the goal so desirable, and the steps required to reach the goal so clear that the client can proceed alone. Usually, however, things are not so simple and you need to look out for normal "cold feet" issues that can arise even when it seems that the best choice has been made. In the days immediately following the decision, keep in close contact with the client to assess what impact the decision is having. Clients may experience a variety of positive reactions, including relief and the loss of anxiety. Negative reactions can also be expected, including depression, loss of confidence, desire to stay with a safe situation, doubt about the wisdom of the choice, and problems with the reactions of others. Normally, these responses dissipate in a few days and do not constitute a problem unless they become extreme. Provide support by focusing the client's attention on benefits to be gained from the career choice and on existing strengths and skills. Do not overlook the importance of your own attitude as a means of support. If you are excited by the possibilities opening up for clients, your enthusiasm will warm many a pair of cold feet.

Alternative Choices

For some clients, this stage involves either no choice at all or a different kind of choice. Some young people, in high school or in their early college years, for example, might be eager to make a choice but should be discouraged from doing so. Perhaps they lack sufficient experience of the world or opportunities to discover their own interests and talents; perhaps they seem intent on looking only at those options that would signify defiance of their parents, or they show interest only in careers that their friends or admired siblings are pursuing, regardless of their own interests. In general, these early years are better spent in wider exploration of career possibilities, allowing interests to crystallize. The goal of career counseling at this point is to assemble several viable alternatives, deliberately not choosing among them but instead devoting time and energy to developing a plan to pursue all of them, or at least to close no doors to an option that might be chosen later. For such young people, the most appropriate next step might be to visit the school academic advisor to decide on the requisite courses and course sequence.

Clients who are awaiting an event beyond their control might wish to make two choices to accommodate different eventualities or might decide to establish a time when they will be ready to choose. Sometimes the very discussion of separate career paths can help the client with a related decision. Paula's career decision, for example, was complicated by the fact that her daughter was considering divorce and a return to the family home with a three-month-old baby. Paula was not at all clear about whether to encourage her daughter's return or to insist that she take care of herself in a more independent fashion. In the process of considering career options that would be affected by the presence of two more people in the house and ones that would allow her the freedom and autonomy she was accustomed to, Paula realized with increasing clarity that she would prefer to provide financial help but have her daughter live elsewhere. Thus, one decision helped resolve the other.

Blake's career decision was somewhat different. He had been struggling for some time to get into law school, believing that a law career would satisfy his values, interests, and preferred life-style. Unfortunately, he seemed to lack the necessary academic ability. Despite excellent work habits and attitude, he had consistently, throughout school, performed at no better than average levels, especially with verbal material. Blake insisted that tests and reports did not represent his true ability and presented considerable evidence of his persistence and ability to overcome obstacles, but he admitted that he was concerned about the passage of time and wanted help deciding whether to go to law school. In this case, what required careful evaluation was not only the advantage of law as a profession but also the price Blake might have to pay to achieve that goal. He admitted that his constant studying and worrying about academic failure had eroded his social life and self-confidence. He talked to law students at varying stages to learn about the competitiveness and pressure of law school and thus assembled a realistic picture of what his life might be like for the next few years. Blake still insisted that law was his dream but recognized that he seemed to be stymied for the time being. Eventually, he decided to work for two years before resuming efforts to apply to law school. This would give him a break from academic problems, allow him to increase his savings, give him more experience of the world, probably increase his self-confidence, and allow him to let go of his ambition without too great a sense of loss, should he decide to forgo the law. In this way, Blake postponed a final decision in a way that allowed him to still feel in control of his life.

6

Overcoming Roadblocks and Solving Problems

Although the actual tasks the client is asked to perform during the selection stages of generating options and choosing among them are not particularly complex or confusing, they can present considerable difficulties to many clients, and often what seems like a straightforward process becomes a series of steps forward and backward. Without claiming to include all possible problems that can arise during these stages, we have identified many of the most common problems that can occur and in this chapter present some ideas for handling these difficulties. Some of the concerns, such as unrealistic self-assessment, arise from previous stages; others, such as opposition from other people, are occasioned by elements in the client's environment; and many are the result of the client's own negative cognitions or behavior deficits.

Although it is easy to recognize when the client is having a problem, it may be more difficult discerning the reason for the particular problem, a discernment that is essential, since your intervention will obviously change according to the presumed cause of the problem. Exhibit 22 lists some common client behaviors and reactions that will alert you to the existence of a problem. The right-hand column contains several possible reasons for each problem. You may encounter others.

As long as the focus of your work together remains on career rather than personal counseling, concern yourself only with problems that affect the process or outcome of generating

Exhibit 22. Some Difficulties of the Selection Stages.

Problem	Possible Causes
1. Client fails to do adequate research.	• Fear of interviewing for information. • Confusion about roles.
2. Client generates few or no options.	• Premature rejection of options. • Constraints that limit options.
3. Options or choice appear inappropriate.	• Unrealistic self-assessment or expectations. • Inaccurate WRP.
4. Client resists tasks necessary to the stage.	• Low frustration level. • Discouraging information.
5. Client is unable to make a choice.	• Fear of adverse effect on others and of their disapproval. • Unwillingness to risk. • No option excellent. • Equipotentiality.
6. Client is dissatisfied with choice.	• Doubts as to wisdom of choice. • Feeling of anticlimax.

and researching alternatives and choosing among them. Thus, you may know that a client is anxious when interviewing for information, but if the anxiety does not prevent completion of the interviews or result in poor quality information, there will be no need to embark on interventions designed to reduce the anxiety, since it does not appear to be inhibiting in these circumstances.

The timing of interventions for problems in the selection stages will be dictated by common sense. Thorough preparation of clients for the tasks and roles of these stages will prevent some difficulties, but generally you should not anticipate problems and intervene too early. For example, a client might suffer intense anxiety during the first two or three interviews that she or he conducts for information but quickly gain confidence after that. Allow your client, therefore, a little time to become accustomed to the tasks and also allow for daily mood fluctuations and personal style before you assume there is a difficulty requiring intervention. Keith, for example, became enraged and frustrated when he had problems in finding information he needed. In his daily telephone progress reports to the counselor, he ranted and fumed. However, his emotional reaction never stopped him from going ahead with his task, and the counselor realized that for Keith annoyance was a motivator, empowering him with energy for the pursuit of information and, incidentally, overwhelming any nervousness he might have felt when trying to gain the cooperation of others. When a behavior or attitude seems to be becoming entrenched or seems to be getting worse, the best approach is to tell the client what you have noticed and to ask whether there is a problem that you both need to address.

Cognitive Techniques

Because many client difficulties have a cognitive component, a major intervention is likely to be some form of cognitive therapy. The following approach, based on the theory and research of Beck and his associates (1979), is particularly effective in tackling negative cognitions connected to career counseling because of its emphasis on reality testing. Although Albert Ellis's rational-emotive therapy (Ellis, 1962) is a similar approach to dysfunctional thinking, Beck's model lends itself more easily to individualization.

According to Beck, seriously upsetting negative emotions that continue to exert a deleterious effect on functioning are almost invariably associated with erroneous ways of thinking. Although most of Beck's work has been in the area of depression, the same process can be seen at work in career choice. It is quite natural, for example, for the notion of failure to occur to people planning to change to a new and challenging career, and the thought "What if I really make a mess of this?" might arouse momentary unease or doubt. It is the way in which people answer this question in their own minds that produces a positive or negative emotional reaction. If they say to themselves, "Oh, well, I can only try my best; I have been successful at other things before and have no reason to expect failure here," the moment of discomfort will pass and equanimity will be restored. If, however, the thought is "That would be terrible; I couldn't stand a failure at this point in life," clients are likely to panic, and the unpleasant moment will be both intensified and prolonged.

Not all problematic thoughts in career counseling are the result of erroneous thinking processes; some derive instead from a values conflict. Because maladaptive thinking and conflicts in values result in similar emotional upset for the client and can be handled in a similar manner, they will be treated together here, without differentiation.

The majority of negative cognitions that occur during career counseling fall into one of three categories. First, the person may hold expectations for performance that can result in self-condemnation, anxiety, and guilt—for example, "I should not make mistakes," "I ought to be able to please everyone," "I ought to be able to do this quicker and better than other people," "I ought to be able to handle job and family perfectly," "I mustn't make a fool of myself." A second category of negative cognitions involves viewing oneself and one's roles in ways that, at least in the context of career choice, can make for confusion, self-limitation, and self-depreciation—for example, "I'm too stupid," "I always fail," "I have no right to be selfish," "I must be a mother first," "I've never tried it so I won't be able to do it," "I wouldn't feel like a man if I did that sort of work." The third category concerns expectations of other people or of life itself, such as "It's not fair," "It won't work anyway so why try?" "Other people will disapprove of my choice," "Other people should be of more help to me," "This shouldn't be so hard or take so long," "Once I've made a choice, I won't ever have to decide again on a career." Thoughts such as these lead almost inevitably to anger, resentment, self-pity, or discouragement. Note that in the case of many of these cognitions, the problem lies not in the statement itself but in the unstated portion that is being added mentally. "Other people will disapprove of my choice" is no more than a statement of fact. It becomes upsetting only when one adds a coda such as "and that would be unbearable" or "I'd fall to pieces if that happened." Similarly, "It's not fair" may well be an accurate observation of how life often is. The trouble arises when one adds "and it is *supposed* to be fair, so I feel cheated and abused when it is not."

Cognitive therapy comprises a wide range of complex therapeutic skills, which will not be discussed here in depth. Many clients can, however, be helped toward a resolution of conflicts and a new view of themselves and their situation if you guide them through the following process, adapted from work with depressed clients (Yost, Beutler, Corbishley, and Allender, 1986):

1. Ascertain what the client is feeling. If possible, anchor this feeling to a specific situation, as doing so usually enables the client to more readily obtain access to thoughts and feelings.

2. Ascertain the thoughts, beliefs, attitudes that are associated with the feeling. Generally, avoid expressing the idea that thoughts "cause" feelings, since this is not necessarily the most accurate way to describe the relationship between cognitions and emotions and can lead to argumentative sidetracks with clients. To help clients who have difficulty identifying their thoughts, ask such questions as "What would you have to think or to tell yourself or to believe or to picture in your mind, in order to make that feeling stronger?" "If you wanted to feel that way right this minute, what would have to go through your mind?"

3. Summarize the client's thoughts into one or two sentences that you believe capture the essence of the belief or attitude, and check with the client that you have understood it correctly. These sentences constitute the client's "old" way of thinking, which needs to be changed.

4. Intervene to help the client examine the thought in the light of reality and rationality. Interventions will often be in two parts, the first a cognitive evaluation of the "old" thought, usually leading to the formulation of a "new" cognition, and the second an experiment designed to test the validity of the "old" or the "new" thought. Interventions are often in the form of questions, to lead the client to come up with his or her own solutions, rather than to have you provide the "correct" answer. The following questions address most of the common types of erroneous thinking:

a. Is your belief in fact true? What is your evidence? (Ask the client to gather evidence that would be convincing.)

b. If you have no actual evidence, is there any other possible explanation for what you believe, one that might be less distressing? (Ask the client to check out different explanations in vivo.)

c. Is this really as bad as it seems, in the light of other terrible things that could happen?

d. How likely is it that the consequences you dread would occur? (Ask the client to check with others, people who have facts or experience in the area, for likelihood of occurrence.)

e. How reasonable are your expectations or your standards for judging performance? If you are applying especially difficult or high standards or rules to yourself, what is your reason for regarding yourself as better than others?

5. Assign homework to test the validity of beliefs or ideas. Suggestions in parentheses above might be followed; other methods will doubtless come to mind or can be found in recommended reading materials.

An example will illustrate this five-step cognitive therapy process. Anne was excited by the interesting career alternatives she was discovering. During counseling, however, she recalled an incident when she had been sitting by her six-year-old's bed, reading a goodnight story, and suddenly felt a surge of guilt and anxiety (step one). She identified many thoughts that seemed to "go with" these feelings (step two), which the counselor eventually summarized as "So your belief is that a good mother puts her children first and that you will be a bad mother if you take up an exciting career that steals time, attention, and energy away from your kids" (step three). Anne agreed that that was the bottom line of what was making her feel so upset. The cognitive evaluations of this belief centered around questions a, d, and e in step four. That is, what evidence did she have for believing that working mothers are bad mothers, how likely was it that her kids would end up as juvenile delinquents or on drugs as a result of her working, and why did she apply rules for maternal behavior to herself that she said she did not apply to all of her friends or even to her own mother? In vivo interventions involved research at the library on working mothers and their children, discussions with Anne's own mother about guilt feelings she might have had on going to work, and the establishment of criteria for good motherhood that would allow Anne to take a job.

Readers who are interested in further investigation of cognitive therapy techniques are invited to consult Meichenbaum (1977), Foreyt and Rathjen (1978), Kendall and Hollon (1979), Freeman (1983), Emery, Hollon, and Bedrosian (1981), and Sank and Shaffer (1984), as well as the journals devoted to cognitive therapy, such as *Cognitive Therapy and Research.*

Specific Problems and Solutions

In addition to cognitive techniques, there are many other ways to approach problems that arise during the selection stages. In general, concerns will be handled with less pain and greater speed if you use several techniques, attacking a problem from many sides, rather than relying on the efficacy of a single approach. The suggestions provided in the remainder of this chapter as we address each of the problems listed in Exhibit 22 are intended as a stimulus to inventiveness rather than as definitive answers.

Incomplete Information

With adequate preparation for their active role in the selection stages of career counseling, most clients adjust well to the increased burden of solo work. Some, however, still retain the belief that the counselor should be the one to do all the work, especially the work of gathering information, either because they expect their fee to include this service or because they generally do not expect to take much charge of their lives and activities. In both cases, counseling should be stopped until the issue is settled. Refer clients to the information statement given to them at the start of counseling and remind them of the section explaining the role required of a career counseling client. If necessary, repeat your rationale for having clients perform the various tasks and clarify your role in order to reassure them that they are, indeed, receiving something from you. Because the counselor has been encouraging active collaboration in the counseling process from the start, even the most passive clients will by now have a backlog of successful efforts at participation and self-direction, and you can encourage them to take pride in their increasing independence and competence.

It is also important to adjust expectations to reasonable levels, building up the client's strength and self-confidence by easy stages, offering more assistance at first and withdrawing it according to the client's developing capacity to perform the necessary tasks. There is no reason, for example, why a passive and dependent client could not begin the process of gathering information with the help of a friend or relative, although it will obviously be in the client's best interests to be weaned from this support eventually, since the client will not be able to take a friend into an actual job interview.

A common reason for client failure to obtain information is fear of interviewing. Sometimes cognitive techniques will be needed to deal with beliefs such as "I don't have the right to take up their time" or "I'll look stupid (and that would be awful)." Clients may also need to be informed of their rights in various situations. For example, clients who are not familiar with the world of books can become intimidated by the atmosphere of a large library and need to be reminded that librarians are paid to assist the public and patrons have the right to ask for that help. If clients lack the skills to conduct interviews for information—such as making requests of strangers, bypassing secretaries when necessary, or explaining themselves clearly—they can learn these skills through such techniques as instruction, modeling, and role playing. Timid clients might also be encouraged to join an assertiveness training group. To further decrease anxiety, provide graded task assignments; that is, have the client begin with short, simple activities that are almost guaranteed to be successful and therefore act as confidence boosters. If such techniques still leave the client uncomfortably anxious after considerable practice, more direct methods to control anxiety might be needed, such as anxiety management training (Suinn, 1972) of self-instruction training (Meichenbaum, 1977).

Too Few Alternatives

Although there is no ideal number of options, it is to the client's advantage to cast a wide net, as undesirable fish can always be thrown back later. Sometimes, however, clients appear unable to generate more than a scant handful of ideas, far too few to represent what might be appropriate for and of interest to them.

The first approach with clients who are unable to generate many alternatives is to check that they are indeed following the process as efficiently as possible. Some clients, especially those with limited experience and knowledge of the world of work, might need to begin with a list that has no relationship to their interests and narrow it down, just in order to have a starting place. Ask these "stuck" clients to write down, for example, every different job performed by their relatives, or their neighbors, or their church members. Lists could also be generated from the OOH or the DOT. Any source is acceptable as long as it provides a starting list of, say, thirty to fifty different jobs. Then ask the client to select the ten least aversive jobs on the list, or to eliminate no more than 50 percent, and discuss what the client found attractive about each one and how it relates to the list of Work-Related Preferences. The client can next be asked to do minimal research on each of the selections (for example, read the description in the OOH), with the requirement that for each one researched another must be added. This technique can be particularly helpful with high school students, who are typically unaware of the wide range of possibilities available to them or who might have difficulty getting started on the task of generating alternatives.

When it is clear that the client can follow the process but is still arriving at no alternatives, you need to discover the grounds upon which the client is rejecting options. In a relatively few cases, the client's criteria for rejection are unimpeachable because they represent constraints that cannot be overcome. It is fact, not imagination, that a person over a certain age often has fewer options than a younger person of equivalent talent and education. And despite progress in recent decades and equal opportunity laws, women and members of minority groups may still find their horizons limited. For practical reasons, there are some jobs that the sick or physically impaired cannot do; for example, a person requiring frequent medical attention with the use of expensive equipment is probably unable to consider careers that involve much travel or relocation in impoverished and isolated rural areas. Clients with private constraints related to family wishes and responsibilities can also find their options limited. Even in these cases, however, encourage clients to include apparently impossible options, as they might lead to ideas that are feasible.

When it comes to the narrowing stage, be sure that these clients gather information that is as accurate and up to date as possible about the problem area. In general, for example, medical schools do not take applicants who are over forty years old. This does not mean that all medical schools in all countries adhere rigidly to this rule 100 percent of the time, however, and this option should be retained for more thorough evaluation if it seems to fit the client's needs or interests. It is important to remember that only one good choice is needed by the end of the whole process, and the fact that there are few options does not automatically mean that they are poor ones. The client may indeed end up with few options, but the concern at this point is that the client not reject alternatives prematurely and unnecessarily.

Far more frequently, you will find that clients are prematurely evaluating options on the basis of criteria that are not necessarily valid, such as instant emotional reactions, opinions offered by friends, or unfounded assumptions. Joan, for example, rejected anything to do with the field of education on the grounds that she did not like children, Mark rejected business because he did not want to end up like his father, and Grace was attracted by some aspects of dentistry but struck it from her list because she did not want to spend her days with her hands in someone's mouth. For clients such as these, you need to explain again the purpose of gathering a large number of options that will not be evaluated until a later time. In addition, it is usually helpful to provide examples, preferably from life, of the possible negative consequences of rejecting options before the narrowing and evaluating stage.

Sometimes your explanations are not convincing, and another approach is needed. Abram, for example, claimed that it was a waste of time to include options "that I'd never go near in five lifetimes." As a compromise, the counselor asked him to keep two lists, one of "real" possibilities and one of options that he would definitely not consider, even though they had some appeal for him. This seemed to satisfy Abram's need to be practical and serious, without eliminating his creativity and free spirit. When the time came to narrow his list, he recognized that almost every option on his "impossible" list involved considerable risk, whereas all the options on his "real" list were safe and respectable. The contrast led to a valuable discussion about the apparent conflict in his wishes and resulted in a much more exciting list of "real" alternatives.

Inappropriate Options

When clients first get into the mood of gathering alternatives, they often add what appear to be wild and impossible options to their lists. This is part of the brainstorming process and should be encouraged. Sometimes when the initial brainstorming is over, however, it becomes apparent that the majority of the client's options are still inappropriate in some way. You may recognize, for example, that the options all require a level of ability that appears to be unrealistic for the client. Or they may require a personality style at odds with what you have seen in this person. At other times, the alternatives seem to fit a life-style quite different from the one the client seems to prefer. And sometimes the ideas on the client's list appear to bear no relationship to the WRPs.

This is an extremely sensitive area because of the potential for conflict between the client's right to freedom of choice and the counselor's responsibility to provide expert opinion. Although this issue, essentially an ethical one, arises in all types of counseling, it takes on a unique aspect in career counseling because you are being consulted as a person who presumably has more concrete information about the world of work and the process of choosing a career than the client has. As an expert, you are also expected to have the organizational ability and objectivity to integrate information about the client and notice discrepancies between, for example, preferred life-style and career ambitions. At the same time, you are subject to biases and prejudices, capable of making mistakes, and, in any case, quite unable to predict a client's future performance in a particular job. Should you find yourself in the difficult situation of believing that your client's chosen options (or final choice) are inappropriate, we offer some suggestions and strategies that may help in choosing an approach satisfactory to both you and your client.

First ensure that your reservations are based on analysis of the situation and the client and do not result from your own biases or negative experiences. If you were once miserable as a schoolteacher, you might not be objective with a client considering teaching as a career. Second, you need to remember that you could very well be wrong in your judgment and in any case have no right to try to persuade clients in one direction or another. After all, motivation and effort do indeed play a great part in reaching goals, the ''experts'' are often wrong, and the client has a perfect right to pursue any dream at all. Third, communicate only concerns that derive from objective evidence or logic, rather than from your own emotional reactions, when trying to help the client appreciate the price that will be paid for pursuing a particular course. Finally, make it clear that the decision is the client's and that you will remain supportive no matter what choice is made. Then proceed to be as helpful and as enthusiastic as you can be, assisting the client to incorporate into the plan some ways to deal with any problems that may arise.

When most of the client's options seem to be unrealistic

in some way, it is important to intervene quickly, before the client has made an emotional investment in any of the options. If you do not speak up until the client has chosen an option you believe is wrong, you are likely to come across with too much impact, rather like a judge putting the seal of disapproval on the client's choice. At best, you will run the risk of alienating the client, who will certainly wonder why you did not speak earlier, and at worst your opinion will carry too much weight and influence the client to drop the option or perhaps to pursue it in order to prove you wrong.

When only one or two options are unrealistic, there is no need to say anything, since the client might not select those for the final list. However, if most of the alternatives seem inappropriate, discuss the list with the client in terms of the contradictions or problems you observed. Doris's counselor pointed out, for example, that most of her options involved absence from the home for long periods, which did not accord with her wish to remain close to her family. Tony had no formal schooling beyond high school but chose options requiring graduate school qualifications, which were in line with his desire to "make something of myself, be somebody." When the counselor pointed out the problem she had observed, Tony explained that he had scraped through high school because he had been more interested in sports than academics and had failed to do any homework assignments. His passing grades were in fact quite an achievement since they were derived from exams for which he did not study. Tony had a lively mind, considerable academic self-confidence, and a mature understanding of what lay ahead for him. In his case, the options he selected were appropriate.

Unrealistic self-assessment often results in underrating of abilities and selection of options that will not challenge or interest the client for long. Some clients simply lack self-confidence; others allow themselves to be frightened by technological changes such as computers, believing themselves too old or stupid to cope with these devices. People who have been out of the work force for some time, especially if they are experiencing depression as a result of unemployment, tend to exaggerate the skills and efficiency of others and to downgrade themselves by comparison.

The modern preoccupation with paper qualifications can delude those without degrees and certificates into thinking that they have nothing to offer. Still other clients forget or fail to realize that the academic ability to deal with verbal and mathematical abstractions is not the only talent that exists, and in many, if not most, positions it is not the most important qualification. Interpersonal, organizational, and leadership abilities, musical or spatial talents, and hand-eye coordination are among skills that are more useful once the person gets past the initial academic entry requirements.

There are also those clients who view their current level of achievement in life as evidence of innate lack of ability, failing to realize that there are many other explanations for lack of success. Lack of interest, lack of apparent payoff to the person, adverse cultural expectations, and environmental restrictions are but a few of the reasons that clients might not have been successful in the past at either academic or other pursuits. If the client has had an unusual educational history, testing of abilities might be necessary. For example, some people have been taught at home, have no formal schooling, have lived in foreign countries, or have missed long periods of school because of illness. Essentially, these people have no academic records in this country to provide an estimate of ability.

Clearly, there is no reason why a person has to take a job that matches his or her abilities and talents if there is a good reason to do otherwise. It is, however, your responsibility to convey to the client your belief that the options selected for evaluation might not reflect what the client is capable of, together with reasons for that belief. For many people, your encouragement to try for a more difficult option will provide the needed courage. Others will need interventions at the level of their negative self-evaluations. The ultimate purpose of all interventions concerning underestimation of ability is not to persuade the client to aim higher but to ensure that the client's choices and decisions are made on a realistic basis.

For most clients who doubt their ability, experience, past and present, is the best teacher. Luke, third of five boys, had performed poorly in school, despite reasonable effort, and de-

scribed himself as "good for nothing," echoing the painful judgment of one of his teachers. The counselor had him list his activities for a week, analyzing the skills and abilities required for
each one. Luke's part-time job at the hardware store, chores
at home, and the care of his retarded youngest brother yielded
an impressive list of achievements and abilities. The counselor
was able to convince Luke that he was able to learn and could
be a valuable employee who did not need to confine his ambition to the lowest level of job he could find. This approach is
also extremely effective with older adults who, whether formally
employed or not, have a wealth of experience, knowledge, and
coping skills to draw on. If clients need some structure in assessing their abilities in this way, excellent guidance can be found
in Bolles's *What Color Is Your Parachute?* (1986).

Experience can be most persuasive. Clients who doubt
their ability to perform a task should arrange to engage in that
task, after taking any necessary instruction or refresher courses.
Those interested in teaching can, for example, volunteer their
services at a Sunday school or day-care center or can arrange
to speak on a familiar topic to high school students.

If the client finds attractive many options that contradict
his or her WRPs, the preferences need to be revised before proceeding further. It is most important, however, to discover why
the original assessment was, apparently, so inaccurate and to
avoid making the same mistakes again. It could be that the
client's situation has changed. When Clare's long custody battle
with her ex-husband ended in his favor, she was suddenly free
of constraints that had influenced her WRPs till that time. Mar-
jorie's self-confidence after taking a college course resulted in
a dramatic increase in her ambition. Nicky, on the other hand,
admitted that she had not really taken career counseling seriously
until the time came to generate options. She realized then that
she had little idea of her own desires and underwent the assessment process for a second time with more interest and effort.

Should the client be reluctant to reassess WRPs or fail
to understand your concern, it might be useful to narrow the
list to a few alternatives that you both submit to detailed evaluation. This process almost invariably results in the client's recog-

nizing that either the options are unsuitable (in which case, the client will need to return to the stage of generating alternatives, using revised criteria) or that the WRPs are inaccurate (in which case the WRP process will need to be repeated).

When clients' contact with reality results in a downward reappraisal of their abilities or the loss of a long-held self-image, confusion and depression can set in. They typically waste time on blaming others—the world for its unreasonable standards, their coach for not telling them the truth, their counselor for not being supportive. They tend to think the worst and overgeneralize, telling themselves that life is over, that there are no good options left, that they are totally without talent or worth. You will need to be alert to the possibility of this kind of distress and address it before proceeding with career counseling.

More difficult to deal with are cases where the client continues to cling to what appears to be unrealistic self-assessment or expectations and makes a choice that you have reason to believe will either be unfeasible or not produce the expected results. Diane was typical of this sort of client. She believed, on the basis of praise from a doting mother and an untalented, untrained music teacher, that she had superior musical talent. Objective information about her talent, in the form of failure to be admitted to music schools or to place in even minor competitions and the negative opinions of experts in the field, did nothing to diminish her belief in herself. She was impervious to information that in order to embark on any musical career she would have to be judged by the standards of others of her profession rather than by her own standards. When she talked to several relatively successful musicians, she was enchanted rather than put off by their struggles and declared herself willing to pay any price for the sake of her music.

The counselor realized that even the most unlikely ventures often succeed, that factors other than raw talent play a part in achievement, and that Diane's greatest asset at this point was her self-confidence, which should not be undermined. Accordingly, the counselor discussed with Diane, as tactfully and objectively as possible, the implications of the feedback she had received, the probability of success, and the obstacles she might encounter. When it was apparent that Diane still had no doubts, the counselor promised enthusiastic help in pursuing the chosen career. In similar circumstances, other counselors might have felt unable to be supportive and would have referred the client.

Client Resistance

Some clients have a low tolerance for detail work that requires careful organization and consumes a great deal of time. In effect, they become bored by the process of researching information and making lists of alternatives. Young people, especially, tend to become impatient, but your earlier encounters with the client should allow you to help him or her to anticipate problems of this nature and to take action before a crisis point is reached and the person refuses to continue. Explaining beforehand that the process can be lengthy and tedious is not likely to increase a client's enthusiasm, unless you use this explanation as a reason to work concurrently on other related issues, such as résumé writing. A tactic of this type provides the client with evidence of progress and diminishes the impact of the more tedious tasks. Your own attitude will be important in helping easily frustrated clients through the selection stages. If you continue to be enthusiastic about clients' goals and to move the focus from the present slow progress to the future when their dream might have been achieved, clients tend to make a greater investment in their present counseling activities.

When a client has great difficulty remaining on task throughout these stages, solicit his or her help in generating solutions to this problem. One effective method is to reward the completion of career counseling assignments. One client, for example, persuaded her husband to take her out to dinner at the end of any week in which she had conducted a prearranged number of interviews. Another client, more spartan, refused to allow himself to watch the ballgame at the local bar unless he had accomplished a set number of tasks.

Finally, give as much help as possible to clients having difficulty with these stages. The value the client might derive from doing all the work will be lost if boredom results in quitting.

If you can, find shortcuts, enlist the help of others, help set up interviews, provide materials for the client to read, be satisfied with less than an optimum number of alternatives—in short, do whatever is necessary to keep the client involved.

At times, clients are not so much bored as discouraged during the selection stages, when they come across information that seems to limit their dreams or when they begin to feel that their options are not as exciting as they had hoped. It can be disappointing to discover that a particular position requires an extensive apprenticeship, pays much less than was hoped, or has very few openings. With disheartened clients, first acknowledge and validate their feelings, then discourage as much as possible any negative evaluation of the options. This could be done by asking the client to look at the extent to which each alternative satisfies some of the WRPs. It is better to have the client make this judgment than to have it come from you, so that you do not appear to be persuading the client into a more positive frame of mind. You might also remind the client that a perfect outcome is unlikely but that together you should be able to arrive at a choice that satisfies many of the client's more important wishes and needs.

Difficulty Making the Choice

The most common problem that arises in the decision-making stage is failure to arrive at a choice. Salomone (1982) distinguishes between clients who are *undecided* and those who are *indecisive.* He suggests that to be undecided about one's career direction is to a large extent a developmentally appropriate state of mind for people under, say, the age of twenty-five. Gianakos and Subich (1986) report that both male and female undergraduates endorsing androgynous sex roles show high levels of career undecidedness, as might be expected because of the large number of options they perceive as available to them and because of the greater barriers and risks they would face if they were to choose a nontraditional career. For many young undecided clients, the most appropriate career counseling might well take the form of exploration, experimentation with the world of work, and pursuit of more than one option rather than a firm choice of one specific career.

Indecisive persons are those whose personal problems make not only career decisions but also many aspects of psychological functioning difficult. These are people who lack ego strength, self-esteem, and a clear sense of identity. They may also have negative attitudes toward work in general and a fear of taking the risks involved in any decision making. Chronically indecisive persons almost always experience high levels of anxiety. It is unlikely, however, that clients with such severe indecisiveness will reach the stage of making a career choice without having revealed their difficulties in this area. In all probability, these clients will already have had problems at one or more of the earlier stages, such as with goal setting or with the autonomous performance of career-related tasks. During the self-understanding stage, they might have been unable to formulate clear or realistic pictures of their interests and desires; later, they may have found it difficult to generate options, may have tended to react negatively to options, and may even have prematurely rejected all options. Because any of these responses would make it almost impossible to proceed with career counseling, we assume that counselor and client will suspend career counseling until personal problems have been resolved. The difficulties we discuss next, related to the failure to make a career choice, are therefore ones experienced by either undecided clients or by clients whose indecisiveness is relatively mild.

The reasons for indecision are many and must be understood before an effective intervention can be devised. We discuss below several common reasons for client indecisiveness.

Fear of Failure. Fear of failure is a common reason for indecisiveness (Saltoun, 1985). Some people feel that as long as they remain undecided they still have potential and that it is better to be a potentially successful person (even one who is doing nothing) than to be a person who is doing something but not doing it well enough, by whatever standards are important to that person. When their fear of failure is intense, many people will refuse to try at all rather than devote their energy to minimizing the likelihood of failure. Reality testing is an important strategy here, since the fear is often grounded in exaggerated views of the requirements for success, misinformation about the number of people who actually fail at a particular job, or a misunderstanding of the extent to which commitment and effort to a project reduce the likelihood of failure. Should it turn out that the client's fears are realistic, that might be sufficient reason to reassess the value of the particular option.

Clients with low self-esteem or an inaccurate view of their own abilities often fear failure unnecessarily. In their case, an effective antidote is success. Like many mature women who have raised families but have not been part of the paid work force, Shirley had developed the conviction that college work would be too difficult for her. The counselor suggested that it did not make sense to reject a cherished dream because of an untested assumption and persuaded Shirley to take one course, to test out her belief. Since most such women work exceptionally hard at their studies and generally do well, this was a safe suggestion and proved effective. Shirley chose a fairly easy course, and although she needed some support through the panic of the first few days and at exam time, she emerged at the end of the semester with much greater confidence and a determination to pursue her wishes.

Sam presented a different fear of failure. A brilliant honor student and star athlete, he remained undecided about a career, despite several attractive options, because he was afraid that he would not live up to his winning record. Discussion revealed that Sam's fears were ideal subjects for cognitive interventions. He believed that if he made a mistake, he would be a total failure, that the only possible alternative to failing was to be the best at everything, which he somehow defined as having the highest salary, the most prestige, the greatest number of promotions and awards, and so on. Because he doubted his ability to achieve all these from the bottom rung of a new career, it was obviously safer for him not to start at all. More probing revealed another underlying fear—that if he did not become and remain an instant success, he would not live up to the reputation of his successful older brother and would therefore lose the approval of his father.

These complex beliefs and attitudes took time to work out before Sam was able to reach a point where he was clear about such issues as how far he was willing to go to emulate his brother and please his father, what it would cost him to continue being scared to fail, and how likely his father was to love him best, regardless of how hard he tried.

Sometimes the client's fear of failure can be circumvented by anticipating areas in which mistakes can be made and working out a plan to avoid them or to handle them if they occur. Clara, for example, was unable to choose among her options because all of them involved a change from her past situation in which she had had no authority to positions in which she would be required to supervise others. She was afraid that she would alienate people by appearing too picky and demanding or that productivity would suffer because she would not be assertive enough. When the focus of fear is as specific as this, information or skill training might be all that is needed. Clara attended assertiveness training classes to increase her general skills in this area and with the counselor worked out a step-by-step plan for confronting employees, proceeding from mild to more vigorous interventions.

The Effect of Significant Others. A common reason that clients are unable to make choices lies in their relationships with other people. They might be afraid of and guilty about the adverse effects of their decision on the lives of significant others, or they might be afraid that others will disapprove of their choice and harm them in some way, perhaps by derision, perhaps by withdrawing from the relationship. The cognitive approach is perhaps the most effective in these circumstances. In effect, the client is asked for evidence that the anticipated harm will indeed occur and that it will be as harmful as expected, or evidence that others do in fact disapprove. Mabel, for example, was caught between two choices: bookkeeping, which she could do at home part-time with little disruption to her family, and nursing, where shift work would often mean leaving her children home alone and working when her husband, an interstate truck driver, was home from long drives. Mabel was far more interested in nursing as a career but could not overcome her feeling that this would be self-indulgence at the expense of others and would run counter to her beliefs about how a wife and mother should behave. The main strategy with Mabel was to persuade her to first discuss the problem with her family. A preparatory role-play focused on having Mabel explain to her family the importance of the choice to her and on teaching her how to handle possible negative reactions and how to explore with her family alternative ways to get her needs met. This discussion could also have been held as a family session in the counselor's office, but the counselor preferred to have Mabel experience the success of handling the situation herself. It turned out that her children were pleased at the prospect of some responsibility and independence, and her husband declared that he would be happy to sleep, should the end of a trip coincide with her shift.

Jenny was in a similar situation but had unfortunately trained her family to expect and demand round-the-clock service from her, so the discussion of career versus family produced feelings of anger and resentment that only increased Jenny's guilt. In her case, the counselor led Jenny to a clarification of her beliefs about what it means to be a "good" mother and wife. The counselor first acknowledged how important those roles were to Jenny so that she would not view the counselor as trying to push her toward a career at the expense of her family. Knowing that terms such as "good mother" are typically based on vague, unrealistic, and therefore unattainable criteria, the counselor asked Jenny to define her roles in practical terms, not in order to change her values but so that she would be quite clear about the basis for her decision. For example, how many hours of the day did Jenny owe to her family? When the family's interests conflicted with Jenny's, how much of the time should she give up her own wishes? If there is a limit to what a family can require from a mother, who decides that limit? If interests conflict, does it matter how important the interests are to each person? To help Jenny answer these questions for herself, the counselor asked her to identify women she admired who both worked and were mothers and to discover how much time they spent with their families, which tasks they performed and which ones they delegated, how they handled their feelings of guilt, and so on. At one point, when Jenny was still feeling that perfection was possible, she was asked to write a detailed calendar for one week, showing herself as the perfect mother she would like to be. The counselor then critiqued the calendar, pointing out where Jenny could have been more loving, more giving, more perfect. As soon as Jenny cried out, "But that's impossible, I'm human, too!" the door was open to a consideration of some realistic criteria for performing all her roles.

The issue of who should be allowed to make major decisions about a client's life often arises when younger people's ideas clash with their parents' ambitions for them; it can be handled by cognitive techniques and by traditional values clarification exercises. Sometimes neither party need "lose" if a compromise can be worked out. Jerry, for example, knew that his mother had her heart set on seeing her son become a lawyer. This was not Jerry's first career choice, but it met some of his interests, and he could see how it might be a useful first career for him, especially since law school would "only require three extra years after graduation" and his mother was willing to pay his costs. Accordingly, he decided on an unusual plan: to become a lawyer "for Mother" until he was thirty and then change careers if he still felt so inclined.

The example of Jerry introduces a caution for the counselor working with clients' values and beliefs. Jerry's counselor strongly believed that people should follow their own needs and wishes and not sacrifice them to the demands of others, whereas Jerry felt it quite reasonable to make a gift of a few years of his life to his mother. Fortunately, he was strong enough to follow his own beliefs, but many clients are vulnerable to persuasion, especially by a person they respect and feel has their best interests at heart. It is almost impossible to keep your own biases and preferences out of the picture, however much you tell clients that you are simply trying to help them explore ideas in the interest of making fully informed choices. Rather than having your attitude leak out, it is better to explain that you have a bias on a particular issue but also recognize that in a pluralistic society there is rarely if ever one ideal way to live, and you want to help clients find the way that will be most successful and feel most comfortable for them.

Desire for Perfection. Inflexibility and the desire for perfection are common reasons for indecision. Drew, age twenty-eight, felt that he was in a dead-end job with a major steel company, even though the financial rewards were satisfactory. He wanted a job with a steady salary, autonomy, and a good future and had identified three alternatives that would provide one or two but not all three of his wishes. If he accepted his father-in-law's offer of a junior executive position in a meat-packing business, he would have the salary and assured future he wanted, but little autonomy. As an independent manufacturer's representative for several steel firms, he would have autonomy and an excellent but unreliable income and almost no chance for promotion. Returning to school for an M.B.A. might get him all three of his wishes eventually, but he might also end up no better than at present. Unable to find the perfect option, Drew remained undecided.

The counselor tried several strategies to help Drew resolve his paralysis, such as reviewing the WRP list and prioritizing the various items, and suggesting that Drew set up a sequential plan of different careers, exploring each one in turn. They also looked for different options, seeking one that would provide Drew with everything he wanted. All this effort was to no avail. Drew simply could not make himself commit to a less than perfect option. Finally, the counselor suggested that in reality Drew seemed to have decided to stay in his present position, and continued to point out the obvious advantages of this choice. This comment highlighted for Drew the fact that before he chose among his three options he would need to make a preliminary choice among (1) keeping his present imperfect job, (2) moving into a different but still imperfect job, or (3) pining for a perfect job while in the meantime doing 1 or 2. Seeing the reality of the situation and realizing that remaining indecisive was also a decision, Drew was at last able to unblock himself and make a choice.

Hasty Decision Making. Another type of difficulty is encountered with the client who might be labeled "the hasty decision maker." Once the client has a list of options in hand, it can be tempting to stick a pin in the list and avoid going through the decision-making process. When the options are fairly equal, pin sticking can be as effective a way as any for making a choice, and you might not want to deter the client from this method. Usually, however, the more structured methods do help the client choose the best option, and you will want to persuade your client to slow down and use a more laborious approach, perhaps by pointing out how much the client has at stake in this decision, which should therefore be approached with more care than selecting candy at the 7–11. A discussion of the price to be paid for a bad decision can be convincing. It is also helpful to remind the client that helping people make decisions is your area of expertise and that it seems pointless to consult an expert and then ignore the recommendations. If the client is still eager for a quick decision, try to work out a compromise in which the client will complete one simplified decision-making exercise, taking no more than a single office session. Do not, however, allow the client to actually make the decision in your office. Choosing at home provides a little more time for reflection and a chance to discuss the choice with others.

Reinforcement of Indecisiveness. Occasionally, clients fail to come to a decision because their indecisiveness is being reinforced. Seventeen-year-old Peter, for example, was the first member of a large extended family to receive any form of counseling or to consider planning a career. As he hesitated in choosing among joining the army, becoming a fire fighter, and working in a local sheetmetal shop, he received more attention than ever before in his life, mostly from his female relatives, who were worried that he would be injured or taken away from the family if he selected either of his first two choices. It was not surprising that he delayed his decision in order to prolong his time in the limelight. Similarly, Jennie was unwilling to make a choice because as soon as she started to earn her own living, her parents would cease to provide her with the apartment and money for living expenses that had been hers since she had graduated from college six months before.

In dealing with the problem of indecisiveness reinforced by secondary gain, it is necessary to confront the client with what is, in effect, another decision. First acknowledge that you understand and appreciate the reasons for delaying a choice. There are many rewarding aspects to being treated with love and attention or being financially supported, and the client's behavior is, therefore, quite reasonable. The issue is, however, how long will the client let this situation go on before making a decision? Will it be the client who decides when to forgo the reinforcement, or will time, chance, or other people be in control? Convey to your client that any decision, including one to delay deciding, is acceptable, but that you, as counselor, need to know what is happening in order to plan how to proceed from this point.

Equipotentiality. There are some, usually very gifted, people who have interests and abilities in a variety of fields. Their indecisiveness arises from *equipotentiality*—that is, a situation in which no one option stands out as best and the person could take any of a number of directions and probably have a satisfying career of distinction. Although gifted people do not suffer the same negative reactions as people with few good options, they can still feel discomfort at being pulled in several directions, as well as a sense of opportunity lost if only one option can be chosen.

If interest and ability are equal, the client must use other criteria for the choice. Thus, the client might select the option with the most acceptable level of risk, the shortest path to the highest point, the greatest flexibility for moving to other options, or the greatest financial rewards, to allow for leisurely exploration of other paths. Furthermore, it is nowhere written that a person cannot go from career to career if he or she is willing to spend the time training and to lose whatever accumulated benefits might be left behind in each move. These clients might also wish to plan a first career that is in itself exploratory. For example, a stint in the armed forces can provide travel, the opportunity to practice different roles, and training in several areas. Similarly, the long summer vacations of teachers are ideal for going on archeological digs or other extended expeditions that would allow a person to explore many different interests and acquire a varied background. For some of these clients, it will be helpful to select a career that allows them free time to adopt other interests as avocations. Once clients appreciate that the paths not taken at this point can probably be taken later or in some other way, their indecisiveness disappears.

No Good Options. Perhaps the saddest reason for indecisiveness is the lack of good options. Mario was a fifty-six-year-old master watchmaker suffering from a degenerative eye disease. At his age, with no formal education and in a poor economic climate, his best options appeared to be night watchman, custodian, and jewelry clerk. Compared to the elegantly precise work of repairing watches, his choices seemed so boring that he could not bring himself to make a decision that would condemn him to a job he would dislike. Unfortunately, there are no counseling techniques to turn bad options into good ones, and it is not reassuring to mouth platitudes such as "You'll like it once you get used to it." With Mario, the counselor agreed that his options could in no way compare to the work he had loved for a lifetime. She encouraged him to develop a new attitude toward work, regarding it as a source of income rather than of satisfaction. This meant that it would make sense for Mario to choose the option that provided the greatest financial rewards or the most free time, so that he could pursue interests that gave him pleasure outside work. Alternatively, he could choose the option with the fewest negative aspects. The options remained unattractive, however, and Mario needed considerable support over the first few months of his new job in adjusting to his unwelcome fate.

A final note about the indecisive client: It is not always necessary that the client make a career choice. Sometimes the exploration of possible options is sufficient to make the existing situation seem preferable. Sometimes the client decides on a preferred option but has reasons not to implement it at this time. Sometimes the client is simply not yet ready to make a change. Whatever the case, it is important to help such clients feel as satisfied as possible with their decision, rather than feel disappointed or believe that they have somehow let someone down, such as themselves, their family, or even you. Encourage such clients to feel that they will always have options of some kind and that their current choice represents what they see as the best way to conduct their lives at present. Help them see the value of the work they have done in counseling, so that they will leave with a sense of hope and self-respect rather than with the view that their lack of decision has been another failure.

Dissatisfaction with the Choice

The most common reaction to actually making a choice is second thoughts—doubts about the wisdom of the choice or about one's ability to reach the goal. There are several helpful strategies for the counselor at this point: admit that few choices are perfect and that it is normal to have doubts; remind the client that all change involves risk, but the alternative is to stagnate; remind the client that the choice was made as rationally as possible and probably represents the best choice the client is able to make at this time; help the client look at negative aspects of the choice and determine a way to remove or diminish them; and not allow too much time to elapse before getting the client engaged in the practicality of making plans. If the doubts persist so strongly that the client is paralyzed and unable to proceed to the planning stage, it is obvious that a choice has not really been made, and you need to return to whatever previous stage seems appropriate, after discussing with the client what might be preventing decision making.

Another common reaction to having made a serious decision is fear that one is now locked into this choice for life. Usually all the help clients need with this problem is for you to point out that almost no life decisions are permanent. They still have other options on their list and should be encouraged to remain open to them should the present option not work out. For a timid client who is particularly afraid of commitment, it is wise to plan escape hatches along the route to actualizing the chosen career goal. For example, a young man who has decided to become a minister could enroll for a semester in a religious college that would allow him to do so without making a formal commitment to the religious life. Furthermore, he could take courses that would be transferable to another career option, if he should change his mind.

After all the effort involved in reaching a decision, some people have a sense of anticlimax and feel vaguely let down, even apathetic. This is especially true if the final choice is not, in fact, an exciting one but merely the best available, or if the choice involves a great deal more time and effort before it can be achieved. Although this is usually just a temporary state, the client will need energy for the next steps. Therefore, keep your client's enthusiasm high by focusing on the positive aspects of the choice, the ways in which it will improve the client's life. You can increase the client's pleasure in career counseling by eliciting an account of new skills learned, of challenges that have been met, and of any increase in self-confidence. Encourage in your client a sense of pride at having come so far in the process of taking charge of his or her life and at having accomplished so much work.

❧ 7 ❧

Making Plans

By now, the client has made a choice, but because there are different types of choices, not every client will proceed immediately to look for a job. Sometimes the choice concerns education or training rather than a particular job or career, and sometimes counseling will terminate at the end of the planning stage because the client's choice will not be acted upon until a later date. Whatever the case, clients need some form of plan—a direction, a course to follow, a series of actions and steps to be taken—either before they proceed to the next stage or before they put their choice on hold.

Many clients recognize the importance of planning and have experience making both long- and short-term plans; they will not need further assistance in this task. Others may have the necessary skills to do planning but tend to overlook the necessity of making good plans. And some clients have not yet learned either the importance or the technique of preparing a blueprint for action. Often, too, clients are so enthusiastic about their choice and so eager to go ahead at full speed to implement it that they find it hard to bring objectivity and rationality to bear on the planning process. It would be unfortunate, after all the hard work to this point, if attainment of the client's choice were made unnecessarily frustrating or even impossible because of inadequate planning. With every client, therefore, the issue of planning needs to be raised and a mutual decision made as to the extent of the counselor's involvement in this activity.

The process of making and evaluating plans is not very complicated and can generally be completed quickly, sometimes

174

in just one or two sessions, after which the client is ready to proceed. There are some factors, however, that extend the planning stage. Planning takes longer if the client has to gather more information, such as about entry requirements for a college or job or about the choice itself, if it becomes apparent that research into the alternative has been inadequate to allow detailed planning. When clients need extensive help with planning, the result can be a recurring cycle in which the client's actions lead to refinement of the overall plan, which then produces a new set of actions.

The goal of this preparation stage is for the client to leave your office with a personalized written plan of action that is feasible and that contains sufficient detail to allow goal-directed action. The plan will include sequential steps, a time line (however tentative), and some indication of the points at which the plan will be reviewed, since almost no plans are inflexible.

What to Do and Why

Three tasks must be accomplished in order to arrive at a suitable plan: selecting the appropriate type of plan, creating the plan, and evaluating the plan's feasibility.

Selecting the type of plan will be based on the client's situation, on the time frame for the choice, and on the type of choice made. To take an obvious example, it is clear that there will be considerable differences between eighteen-year-old John's plan to apprentice as a mechanic as soon as possible and twenty-eight-year-old Krista's plan to take college courses that will leave her open to several career paths—paths that will also be contingent on whether she has children in the intervening years. John's choice requires a detailed set of steps that will be acted upon at once, whereas Krista's plan must be much more open-ended and cannot be created in detail at this point.

Creating the plan is the heart of this stage of career counseling and will vary in difficulty and in need for your input according to the complexity of the client's situation and the problems that arise while the plan is being formulated. Whenever possible, the final product of planning should be written out and a copy retained by both you and the client. Without a written version, it is easy to forget details, to omit vital steps, or to get out of time sequence and thus lose some of the value of careful planning.

The feasibility of a plan includes what is possible in terms of time, the marketplace, other people's behavior, and the client's own abilities. Although clients will evaluate their own plans as much as possible, your expertise will be needed to ascertain where the client will need further help. Marvin, for example, making a mid-life career change after fifteen years in the same job, planned to use the résumé that he had used all those years ago, not realizing that it was neither current nor suitable for the type of work he planned to change to. Similarly, Alice felt that her self-confidence and eagerness were adequate preparation for interviews. When she demonstrated her skill in a simulated job interview, the counselor realized that Alice lacked the ability to present herself in the best possible light and that her bubbly enthusiasm was likely to be a handicap unless controlled and directed. In both cases, counselor input enabled clients to receive help they had not realized they needed.

Sample Procedures

Decide on the Type of Plan Needed

A plan is a map of how to reach a chosen goal by specifying a series of goal-directed activities that take place over time, from a starting point in or near the present to an end point in the future. To reduce complications, we consider only three variations of plans: straight-line, multiple, and flexible plans. The simplest type, the *straight-line plan,* is so called because it can be drawn as a straight line, with all the activities on the plan leading, without deviation, toward a single end point. Thus, a person wishing to become a physician would carry out, in sequence, the necessary steps of completing college, applying to and entering medical school, completing that schooling plus all residency requirements, and applying for a position as a fully qualified physician, until the desired end point is reached, with an M.D. after the person's name on the office door and the certificates on the wall. Should the plan be interrupted by other activities (such as two years in the Peace Corps), the steps will still be completed in the appropriate order. The person has no intention of stopping at any point to review the plan and perhaps take a different career direction with a different end point. In other words, the straight-line plan contains no decision points. Presumably, the thrust of career counseling has been to help the client reach a firm decision and proceed to implement it. As with any long-term plan, however, clients should be encouraged to recognize that, in an unknown future, anything can happen to make deviation from an original plan necessary or desirable.

Sometimes it is impossible to make a straight-line plan because of the existence of one or more impending decision points in the client's life. One option is to create a *multiple plan,* consisting of two or more straight-line plans that are independent of each other. The client is unable to make a choice between these different career options at present and must wait until a time in the future when a decision point is reached. This point is usually an outside event or a decision to be made by someone else that will determine which of the directions the client will take. For example, Jack was interested in being either a pilot or a physician and could easily have made a choice between the two and proceeded with a straight-line plan. However, he had become interested in Sue, a young woman with strong feelings against his choosing a career as a pilot; thus, Jack decided that he was willing to postpone his choice for several months to see how his relationship with Sue developed. Jack could have waited until later, made his choice, and then worked out a single straight-line plan. But because he did not want to waste the intervening time, he opted to develop a multiple plan that would start at once with any preparations he could make for jumping in either direction, such as obtaining application papers, taking physical examinations, or applying for loans. Jack developed a Y-shaped multiple plan, with the stem of the Y representing the waiting period, the two arms representing careers as a pilot and as a physician, and the place where the two arms intersect representing the choice point—that is, whether

Jack will marry Sue. The multiple plan is not, it should be noted, a way for the client to avoid making a decision, except in those circumstances where the decision is dependent on uncontrollable outside forces.

The *flexible plan* is most commonly used with younger people, who should not be encouraged to make a single career choice too early in their lives, before experience, maturity, and further education have been allowed to exert their influence (Bartsch, Yost, and Girrell, 1976). In the flexible plan, there are usually many possible end points and decision points. The client does not know yet which of the end points is most desirable, nor is it necessarily outside events that will be most influential in determining which direction the client will take at choice points. Usually, the choice points occur over an extended period of time, each one resulting in a new route and leading to a new set of choice points. Thus, the flexible plan resembles a decision tree, consisting of a series of if-then choices. It is rather like trying to plan a complex vacation that will depend on such ifs as "If George can't get away until the snow comes," "If Mother decides to come, too," "If we don't have to get a new roof for the house," "If my pregnancy is proceeding okay . . . "

The type of plan to use will depend on the client's situation. If the client has made a single choice, with a single end point and no pending events or decisions that could alter the end point, the client will be preparing a straight-line plan. Even if there is a pending event that will affect the client's career decision (you may both be aware of this from the readiness check conducted before the client made a career choice), the most appropriate plan might still be straight-line—that is, a plan in pursuit of only one new career option. Sometimes the client is attracted to only one career alternative and is prepared to remain in the present situation or even have no career at all should the pending event dictate that outcome. Elizabeth, for example, had decided to allow four more months to become pregnant. At the end of that time, she would forgo any career plans if she was pregnant and pursue her straight-line plan to become a repairer of small appliances if she was not. This did not mean that she would be inactive for several months. Most career choices and changes take time to implement, and Elizabeth's plan, contingent though it was on her pregnancy, began with steps she could carry out at once that would facilitate her career path if she took that route but that would not involve too serious a loss of resources should she not pursue her career goal. She decided, for instance, that a night school course in practical basic electricity would be valuable whatever her ultimate choice.

In another example, Dolores had taught dance at a college noted for high standards in the performing arts and would have preferred to continue doing so. However, a recent injury had presented her with the possibility that she would no longer be able to perform and would have to make a career switch to choreography. Although it would be a year before Dolores would know the extent of her recovery, she considered it important to begin the early steps of the career move just in case, since bureaucratic decisions are typically made slowly and require progress through many hoops, and Dolores could not afford to be caught unprepared. She therefore made a straight-line plan that in essence fell into two stages: the preparation stage, which would occupy the coming year while she waited for news about her health, and the implementation stage, which would occur only if she received an unfavorable checkup from her physicians.

When the client is awaiting a decisive event but has at least two attractive career choices, a multiple plan will be the most appropriate, especially if the interim can be put to good use in the service of either or both alternatives. Even if there is nothing preparatory the client can do while waiting for a choice point to arrive, it is often valuable for the client to make a plan for action, to avoid a sense of letdown. The client has been working toward a career decision for some time and is psychologically primed for movement forward. When circumstances force a delay in that movement, having a specific plan provides the promise of action and tends to forestall a loss of enthusiasm and commitment.

The client in need of a flexible plan can often be recognized by such characteristics as a general career vagueness appropriate to the person's developmental stage and the existence of pending life decisions. Flexible plans, extending over a longer period of time than straight-line or multiple ones, are generally more appropriate for younger clients. Older clients are typically in a position to set and pursue relatively clear career goals. Age itself, however, is not the decisive factor in the type of plan the client creates. For example, after fifteen years as a nun in a cloistered order, where she had had chores but no career, Gilean at age thirty-five was functionally still an adolescent as far as career development was concerned. Her departure from the convent was also an entry into a life where she must decide about marriage, children, and further education, develop self-knowledge and confidence in her skills, gain work experience, and explore her interests. Psychologically, she was not in a position to make a single career choice and pursue it, so she needed a flexible plan to accommodate exploration and development.

Develop the Plan

The purpose of a plan is to guide the client through the actions necessary to reach a certain goal in the most efficient

Exhibit 23. Steps for Developing Plans.

1. Make an overall outline plan, with beginning and end points and major intervening tasks in chronological sequence.
2. Break up major tasks, especially those to be performed first, into smaller substeps.
3. Identify choice points in the plan. Include a method for handling choice points.
4. Identify the points at which the plan will be reviewed. Decide how these review points will be handled.
5. Place the steps on a time line, with starting and ending dates, and indicate the approximate time needed for each step or substep.
6. Assess where the client might need help in carrying out the plan. Determine how this help will be obtained and from whom.
7. Troubleshoot the plan.
8. If necessary, make a detailed miniplan of the first substeps: Who will do what, when, where, how much, in what order, with whose assistance?
9. Produce written copies of the overall plan and any miniplans.

Note: At any step, further information might be needed. When this need arises, insert the gathering of specific information as a substep.

and productive way possible. To achieve this result, we offer several guidelines, which are summarized in Exhibit 23.

One way to ensure that no steps of the plan are omitted is to begin with the end point and work backward, as my (E.B.Y.) mother used to say when planning a family outing. Her process went something like this: "If we're going to spend a week at Lake Tahoe in June, there's a lot to do first." She would then list all that had to be accomplished before the date in question and sort the activities into the necessary sequence. "If we want to arrive by lunchtime on Thursday, we need to leave by six because it takes five hours. That means the car has to be packed the night before, and that means I have to do the baking on Tuesday, so I'd better shop on Monday . . ." In other words, begin with the end point the client wishes to reach and determine what step precedes that; then each preceding step should be identified until the first step is eventually reached.

A second guideline for planning is to identify substeps in detail. The further away in time the steps of a plan, the more general and vague they can be, but the steps closer to the present need to be very detailed and broken down into substeps. If this is done, there is less chance that unexpected problems will arise or that the timing of the steps will be inaccurate. Suppose, for example, that the client's plan requires saving money for further education before proceeding with the career goal. It would not be enough to write as a first step "Get money for college," because too many questions would be left unanswered. How much money will be needed? What resources will the client tap? How long will this take? What will the client do first? Is there anyone else who can help with this process? Depending on the answers to such questions, the single vague command "Get money for college" could be divided into many substeps, each taking its own amount of time. This part of the client's plan might end up containing such substeps as:

> Talk to three friends currently enrolled in three different colleges to see how much it cost them this year.
> Find out from my school counselor what loans and scholarships might be available.

Discuss with my parents the amount of money, if any, they are willing to contribute to my education.

Make a list of my most likely expenses at college.

Ask my grandparents if I can use their second car instead of buying one of my own.

The use of verbs (talk to, find out, and so on) makes the required actions clearer.

A major advantage of a detailed plan is that the client will know how to proceed and can do so one step at a time. Clients feel less overwhelmed and are less likely to procrastinate when difficult tasks are broken into smaller and therefore more feasible parts, and the sense of progress and success occurs more frequently, providing reinforcement and encouragement. When the early steps of a plan are outlined in insufficient detail, there is a danger that the client will go home, try to implement a step, fail because the tasks are not clear, and then feel inadequate or discouraged.

A final guideline concerns the flexibility of the plan. Even the simplest plan is unlikely to go without a hitch, and clients should be prepared for problems and setbacks. When the plan covers a long period of time, change is almost inevitable, both in the environment and in the client's own interests, motivation, and values. Clients may have difficulty remaining enthusiastically committed to the goal without developing such a rigidity of purpose that any change or disappointment will be treated as a major catastrophe. Clients will not necessarily continue counseling throughout the life of the plan, especially if that life is long, but there are ways to set them on the road toward a healthy balance between commitment and rigidity. One way is always to refer to the plan in flexible terms, talking, for example, about "your current plan" or "the plan that seems to be right for now." Review points inserted into the plan prepare clients for the possibility that experience and new information might produce change. When appropriate to the client, you might also make comments such as "Of course, you'll be quite a bit older then, and you may find that this path no longer interests you." Especially if you suspect that a particular career position might be difficult for the client to obtain, you will want to refer to the current choice as only one of several and remind the client that there are still other options, that there is more than one possibility to suit people, and that nowadays even the best career choice is not necessarily for life.

Creating a plan is primarily the task of the client, and your role that of consultant as needed. Often all that clients require is a review of planning guidelines, perhaps in the form of a copy of Exhibit 23, and the opportunity to discuss their plans. Following are two case examples of different types of plans.

Straight-Line Plan. We have chosen the example of Andrea because she required more of the counselor's help in making plans than is usual, thus allowing us to present the process in some detail. Andrea had decided that her goal was a career in computer programming. Her end point was a job in programming in a place with opportunities for further training and possible advancement to systems analyst. She could see no reason to make anything but a straight-line plan, as described to her by the counselor, and spent time at home making a general outline of the steps she thought she would need to take. This homework allowed the counselor to assess how much help Andrea would need with the planning process. Unfortunately, that first outline consisted of only two steps: get some training and get a job. These were indeed the steps to be taken, but the plan definitely lacked detail. Andrea was not sure how to implement her first step, nor could she estimate from her brief plan the amount of time she might need to reach her goal.

To help her prepare a more specific working plan, the counselor began with the end point of the plan and worked backward to the present, asking the following questions to elicit the important steps Andrea would need to take to reach her goal: "What has to happen before this can occur?" "What information will be needed to take this step?" "What decision or choice will you have to make at this point?"

The first tentative answers to these questions produced an expanded plan with six steps:

1. Find out about training.
2. Take training.
3. Find out about jobs.
4. Apply for jobs.
5. Interview for jobs.
6. Accept a job.

Some decisions remained, such as what type of training she wanted, which jobs to apply for, and which one to accept. These decisions needed to be inserted into the plan as separate steps, not in the interest of thoroughness but because each of these selection points might require consultation with others or a hunt for more information and thus extend the time line.

When the counselor asked what information might be needed at various steps, Andrea checked the notes she had made while gathering data on this particular career and noticed that, partly because this is a new field, there are many different types of training acceptable to employers and that programmers work in a large variety of situations. She wondered about the comparative advantages and disadvantages of various training routes and the opportunities for advancement in different places. Obviously, she needed more information and consequently added an extra step to her plan: examining the differences between various types of programmers.

When the counselor asked what had to happen before Andrea could undertake the second step, taking training, she realized that she must apply to the schools of her choice, possibly have to make a choice among them, and go through all the preparation necessary to get organized for a new kind of lifestyle as a student. Undoubtedly, this would involve her family. Andrea's next plan was more detailed and comprehensive, containing sixteen sequential steps.

At this point, Andrea realized that her debut as a computer programmer would not be quite as soon as she was hoping and would require considerable work. Since she was feeling rather overwhelmed and discouraged, her counselor suggested breaking the list into sections, with steps grouped together logically. The section closest to the present time would receive the most detailed planning attention, and more distant sections would be left to a later date. Andrea's revised list read as follows:

Immediate Steps

1. Learn about different types of computer programming and corresponding training requirements.
2. Learn about different types of training and local availability of training.
3. Decide on level and type of training needed.
4. Select desired method of training.
5. Apply for training to several places, if necessary.
6. Select training.
7. Prepare, with family, for life as a student.

Middle Steps

8. Start training.
9. Complete training.

Last Steps

10. Find out where jobs are available.
11. Get information about specific jobs that are available.
12. Select jobs to apply for.
13. Apply for jobs.
14. Interview for jobs.
15. Decide among job offers.
16. Accept job.

The next thing Andrea did was place her steps on a time line, a process that often results in the addition, deletion, or combination of steps. Starting from the present, she estimated how long each step might take. She realized that gathering information for the first two steps could probably be done at the same time. Discussion about how the information was to be acquired produced several subtasks under the now combined steps one and two: interview an instructor in computer programming at the local community college, reread material in the library on the subject, consult her uncle in New York who sold mainframes and might be informative, attend a local computer buffs' group, talk to college students currently enrolled in programming classes and ask them where they planned to work, send away for catalogs of training courses. Much of this information might have been acquired before Andrea made her career choice, but she had been impatient with the gathering of information at the earlier stage, had found it easy to make her choice, and was quite willing to do the work now that it seemed more relevant.

When the counselor had helped Andrea identify these early tasks, she was able to apply the same specificity to other steps in the first section and come up with a rough estimate that it would take her about three months to complete the immediate steps. She also estimated that it would take approximately a year to train (at this point, that is all the time she was willing to spend, but she knew that she could change her mind) and perhaps three months to complete the last section of her plan.

Next she began to look at dates. She might need more than the eighteen months her plan would seem to require, since it was then the beginning of January and new classes would not be open until summer session, at the end of May, regardless of how rapidly she completed the first steps of her plan. If she followed her plan as written, she could be employed as a computer programmer by the end of August of the following year— that is, twenty months from her starting point. She realized that she might be able to overlap some of the final steps of the plan (applying for jobs) before she graduated, but felt incapable of making accurate predictions about such a distant time, especially when she could not tell how busy she might be with finals in May, so she left her end date as August.

Generally speaking, clients should review their plans at every decision or choice point. The first of these for Andrea was at step three, where she would need to decide about training. She could go two ways at this point. She could identify the type of programming she wanted to do and then train to the extent necessary to obtain that sort of position, or she could decide how much training she was willing to take and then look for work commensurate with her training. In this field there is also the possibility of some on-the-job training, which could drastically alter her time line and might, by leading directly into a permanent job, eliminate several steps from the plan. A second review point was likely to arrive at the completion of training, assuming Andrea chose formal rather than on-the-job education. She had chosen a rapidly growing field that might change in important ways in a year's time. Her year's training might also open up hitherto unknown possibilities and interests. Thus, Andrea might need to update her information and even consider a change of direction at the end of her year.

Once the review points had been decided, Andrea and the counselor discussed how the reviews would be handled. She decided that, since she was rather apprehensive about this new venture, she would continue counseling at least through the steps prior to beginning training. Thus, the review of the plan would automatically be a part of counseling during the early steps. Andrea believed she would be able to handle the second review point alone, in consultation with her husband, since by the end of her training she expected to have both the necessary information and the decision-making skills learned in counseling.

Last, Andrea decided where she might need help in carrying out the various tasks called for by her plan. She concluded that her greatest concern was step seven, which required identifying and dealing with all the changes in her life that would be produced by her status as a student. She thought she would need help with planning her time, with teaching her children to be more helpful with chores, and with maintaining an adequate focus on her marital relationship. Suspecting, because of her inexperience, that Andrea might also need help with interview preparation, the counselor asked Andrea to role play being interviewed for entry to a specialized program in computer training. Her performance indicated that she interviewed well but was unsure just what a résumé was. She was glad to learn that if she became a student she would be able to use the services of the college placement office, since such offices often provide excellent instruction in résumé writing at no cost to the student.

Andrea's final plan, as conceived at this point, is given in Exhibit 24. Note that only the most immediate steps are completed in great detail, since to do so for later steps would make the entire plan too cumbersome. As she arrived at each step,

Andrea understood that subtasks must be identified in more detail, put into sequence, and assigned their own time line within the greater framework. These miniplans, as one might call them, resemble a "to do" list of items that can be checked off as they are completed.

Exhibit 24. Simple Plan for Career as Computer Programmer.

Part One: Outline and Time Frame

January to April of this year:

1. Get information on:
    a. types of programming.
    b. entry requirements for each type.
    c. training available.
2. Choice point: Select training.
3. Apply for training.
4. Prepare for life as a student.

May of this year to May of next year:

5. Complete necessary training.
6. Research field for types of jobs, possibilities of advancement, local opportunities, etc.
7. Prepare for job search.
8. Choice point: Decide on desired work.

Either March or May of next year:

9. Apply for and obtain employment.

Part Two: Detailed Steps for First Part of Plan

Gathering Information

Sunday	1.	Phone Uncle Louis.
This weekend	1.	Prepare list of specific questions to ask about training and different types of programming.
	2.	Draft letter to send to training institutions asking for catalogs and application forms.
Monday	1.	Make appointment with instructor at community college.
	2.	Find out when class meets and ask if okay to talk to students.
Wednesday	1.	Go to university library and read about programming in sources I glanced at before.
	2.	List training institutions. Revise my list of questions if needed.
Thursday night	1.	Go to computer group meeting, with questions.

Exhibit 24. Simple Plan for Career as Computer Programmer, cont'd.

During appointment with college instructor	1. 2.	Ask for names of places to train. Talk to at least three students.
Next weekend	1.	Mail letters to training institutions.
When information arrives	1. 2.	Discuss everything I've learned with counselor. Decide on type of training I want, and where.

Preparing for Life as a Student

For at least one week	1.	Keep a journal of how I spend my time now and how much Henry and the kids do around the house.
Weekend	1.	Talk to neighbor about how she juggles her job and running the house.
This week	1.	Call Parks and Recreation and kids' school about afterschool activities.
By end of next week	1.	Identify how much time I might need for school and what impact that will have on family (won't know for sure till I have decided what type of training I want, but can identify obvious changes).
By end of month	1. 2.	Discuss the subject with Henry and kids. Begin making small changes.

Flexible Plan. As he approached his freshman year in college, Eric felt a need for some direction in his life but did not feel willing or able to make a definitive career choice. Thorough assessment of his career priorities revealed that Eric was torn between his artistic talent and interests on the one hand and his desire to work with people on the other. However, he was not sure whether he could or would want to combine art and people and whether his interest in people was theoretical or practical. Nor was he able to say whether he was interested in extending his schooling much beyond his bachelor's degree. Decisions such as these cannot be made simply on the basis of more information. Eric, at nineteen, needed to experience various types of activities related to his interests and allow his continuing maturity throughout the college years to work its influence on his thinking about careers.

As a result of his preliminary exploration of career fields, Eric felt attracted to several options within two major career areas: art and social service. With his counselor, he designed a flexible plan that would allow him to narrow his choices over time.

Preparing a flexible plan is somewhat more complicated than preparing a straight-line plan, as it usually involves many more decision points and a greater span of time. Because Eric had only tentative end points in view and wanted to remain open to the inclusion of potential new interests, it was not possible to simply work backward from end points, as with a straight-line plan. Instead, Eric had to keep in mind the general direction he wished to pursue and work forward from the present to the next decision point in time, and from there to the next, and so on.

In arriving at a career choice centered on either art or service, Eric had acquired an adequate overview of both fields and was aware of most of the different branchings within each field. Since he preferred to live at home while completing his undergraduate work, he obtained the catalog from a nearby state college and mapped out routes to several of his career interests, noting various majors and minors, required courses and their prerequisites, electives that would fit more than one career direction, and electives that he felt might expand his horizons. From previous research notes, he compiled a list of skills and experiences that would be important in the careers that attracted him. Having assembled this information, Eric's next task was to ask himself, "Where is the first fork in the path?" and after that, "Where is the next fork?" until he reached forks that ended in a specific career. He next drew up a list of time points and review points, as with a straight-line plan. This procedure resulted in a very general flexible plan (Exhibit 25) to cover at least Eric's college years.

Eric fleshed out his overall plan with campus activities, vacation work, and volunteer experiences designed to increase his exposure to the careers that interested him and to provide him with the opportunity to develop skills and to add potentially useful entries to his résumé. However, he did not plan these activities more than a semester in advance, since he did not know how his interests might change. For the present, he learned how to make a detailed short-term plan, with substeps and a time

Exhibit 25. Sample Flexible Plan.

Choice Points	Choice to Be Made
1. By end of freshman year	General field of study: art or social service
2. By end of sophomore year	Specific major
3. By end of junior year	Whether or not to go to graduate school
4. December of senior year	Which graduate schools to apply to or which jobs to apply for

line, to carry out his first-semester goal of obtaining volunteer work in the social service area. He also developed a plan to help him prepare for his first choice point. Thus, he decided what information he would need, where he would acquire the information, what part his parents would play in the decision, and even what he would do if he did not feel ready to decide. He agreed to have his decision reviewed by someone he felt was in a position to judge the validity of his decision-making method and thought that he would probably return for at least one counseling session at the end of the year in order to revise his plan.

Eric's example illustrates both the advantages and the inevitable difficulties of a flexible plan. In his case, choice points coincided with the end of each college year, when he had to select courses for the upcoming semesters. Obviously, he was more likely to choose courses wisely when he had some idea of where he was headed and was following a plan that included in vivo experiences designed to help him with choices. There was thus less chance that he would drift aimlessly, take courses that were unrelated to his career goals (except as a planned effort to enlarge his horizons), or postpone career decisions so long that he would have to backtrack in college or settle for something of less than optimum interest. It was exciting for Eric, and provided him with a sense of confidence, to know that he had goals, however tentative. On the other hand, Eric could not be allowed to view his plan as a rigid structuring of his future. For example, his plan called for taking courses in both of his major fields of interest as a freshman and choosing between the fields at the end of that year. It was possible that Eric would be unable to make that choice after only twelve months and would need an extra semester or two. He could also be sidetracked by an entirely new interest and want time to explore that, to include it in his overall plan, or even to pursue it as a major interest.

As the years passed, other decisions, such as whether to marry, might be expected to influence Eric's career plans. In fact, he became involved in the campus newspaper, first in the art department and later, by accident, in reporting. He found in this work an ideal way to express his creative side and yet follow his interest in people, and eventually he abandoned both art and social service in favor of a career in journalism. As his interest in this field grew and crystallized during his last years at college, Eric modified his plan to incorporate the necessary education and experiences.

In essence, the flexible plan is a decision chart, and it is on the choice points of the chart that counseling will concentrate. In other words, it is not the content of the decision that counts most but rather the process of deciding. Perhaps the greatest service counselors can do for clients with long-term flexible plans is teach them a good decision-making procedure that they can use with confidence at every choice point. After the overall plan was completed, Eric's counselor taught him to prepare for upcoming decision points by asking himself what he would need in the way of information, experience, or consultation with others in order to make the best possible choice. He then learned to translate these needs into detailed plans, developed from his more general overall plan, so that he would not be caught unprepared with an important choice on his hands.

Although flexible plans are necessarily general, this fact does not obviate the need to help clients prepare specific and detailed plans for action whenever they are needed. Such detailed planning is an important skill to teach clients, since a flexible plan is likely to involve a great number of smaller plans over time, and clients should not be left feeling that they will need to consult a planning expert every time a plan is required. These detailed plans are made in the same way as flexible or straight-line plans, with their own time lines and attention to all factors in the client's life.

Evaluate the Plan

Apart from the factor of chance, which is beyond control, the execution of any plan depends on two controllable elements: the feasibility of the plan itself and the skills of the person attempting to carry out the various steps. Each of these factors needs to be evaluated before the client can feel confident that the plan has a reasonable chance of succeeding. The evaluation process is, of necessity, an ongoing part of the development of the plan, since any step that is not feasible, for whatever reason, will have to be changed and could produce alterations in the overall plan. A common result of assessing the feasibility of one part of a plan is the realization that prior steps will need to be added; thus, the act of assessment aids in the actual development of the plan.

Although the client is the person mainly responsible for formulating the plan, your input is vital to the evaluation because your experience with planning enables you to consider all the factors that could affect the plan—factors that clients often overlook or dismiss. In effect, what you will have in your mind during the planning process is a list of criteria by which each part of the plan can be measured. Suppose, for example, that a client decides on the step "Take a course in algebra at Youngly College, at night, between now and next June." The first question to ask is, can this be done? In other words, are such courses being offered, at that institution, at that time, that can be completed before that date? It is not unusual, especially among those with little experience of the world, for clients to expect that their needs will be met by educational institutions, which they view as having limitless resources and a mandate to serve individuals, rather than groups.

The second question to ask about this proposed step is, what would it take for the client to perform this step successfully? The answer requires considering the client's resources and situational constraints as they apply to the step under consideration, such as taking an algebra course at night at the local college. Obvious requirements in this case would be the educational prerequisites for the desired course, money for fees and textbooks, time to attend class and complete assignments, transportation, and energy. The resource of time is especially important in the case of returning students, who are inclined, because of their long absence from the classroom, to underestimate or overestimate the amount of time needed for studying.

The client's situation also enters into the assessment of a planned step's feasibility. Eagerness can produce tunnel vision, and the counselor's responsibility is to help the client consider all possible variables that could affect the proposed step or that could develop into trouble spots. In the case of a married woman considering night school, it would be appropriate to ask such questions as "How will your spouse's life be changed if you go to night school?" "How will he react to this change?" "If his reaction is negative, how will you handle that?" In the case of a person with a chronic illness, the counselor would naturally ask about the impact of any part of a plan on the person's health and vice versa.

When a proposed step involves skills or learning, the client's ability in this area is an important factor. Your input is valuable here because clients are not always aware of the specific skills required for particular action and might, therefore, assess themselves inaccurately. This is especially so in such career-related activities as completing applications, obtaining letters of reference, résumé writing, and interviewing. Even apparently sophisticated clients with a good deal of experience in the world of work can have misconceptions in these areas, particularly if they are moving to a different field of work. For example, an ex-actor applying for a position in an established business might well need to learn a different interviewing style. One way to check the client's ability in these areas is to ask for a sample of written materials and to conduct a diagnostic mock job interview.

In the process of assessing the client's ability to carry out plan steps, you do not want to place discouraging restraints on the client's natural desire to proceed with the career goal, nor to cause the client to doubt his or her own ability to succeed. A low-key approach with the emphasis on practicality seems to be effective. This means asking as few questions as possible, based on guesses as to possible trouble areas for the particular client. Initial assessment of coping style, for example, will have alerted you to potential difficulties in executing plans; the client's educational background will usually indicate whether a proposed training program is feasible; and your knowledge of the client's social situation will often obviate the need to assess the extent of available social support.

When the client's plan is reduced to detailed substeps that include specific names, times, dates, amounts, and so on, the feasibility of each step is often obvious, and little or no detailed evaluation is necessary. If the client needs to be asked about whether a step can be carried out, the questioning should be done in the interest of furthering success; for example: "We don't want any delays or disappointment at this stage, so let's check . . . " or "To make sure that this goes smoothly, let's not forget to look at how your children will feel about this, and then build into your plan some way to handle their concerns."

Occasionally, you will need to take a more structured or even confrontational approach to the question of whether the client can, or will, carry out the steps of a plan. Joel had a history—in relationships, in education, in recreation, and in career matters—of becoming enormously and often unrealistically enthusiastic about a plan, rushing into it without considering the feasibility, and then abandoning it at the first setback. Joel and his counselor identified this pattern in the early assessment stages of career counseling, discussed its effect on Joel's life, and worked together to use the systematic process of counseling to help him overcome his difficulty. However, the counselor was concerned lest the pattern reassert itself under the stress of carrying out the career plan and asked Joel directly how he thought he might sabotage his plans. As a result of this discussion, Joel's plan was expanded to include steps for monitoring his psychological state.

Problems and Cautions

Problems at this stage run the gamut from mild discouragement and unwillingness to embark on the plan to serious second thoughts about the chosen career goal. As with other problems, solutions depend on the causes of the difficulties.

Discouragement can occur if the client realizes that the chosen goal will take much longer to reach or will involve more effort than was anticipated. Faced with this reality, some clients tend to lose interest in their goal, make inadequate efforts to complete necessary steps, see little evidence of progress, and then become even more discouraged. Their resignation to a disappointing situation can often be eased if they can be helped to see how far they have come to this point, rather than how far is still left to go. In metaphorical terms, they have made all the preparations for their trip, and all that remains is the journey itself. You might suggest that the client break an extended plan into shorter self-contained stages, the end of each being treated as a landmark to be celebrated. Help clients create a strong fantasy about what their lives will be like when the career goal is actually reached, so that they will have a vivid dream to pull them onward.

Discouragement at the thought of the time and work ahead can also be increased by significant others. Sol's wife, Sandy, for example, was initially delighted when he planned a career change from accountancy (which she considered rather dull) to the more prestigious field of law. Somehow, she had failed to realize how long his schooling would take, and when she found out she flatly refused to be supportive of such extended training. In the face of her objections, Sol's commitment to his dream diminished, and he dragged his feet for several weeks before discussing the problem with his counselor. This case had a happy ending. After several couple counseling sessions, Sandy concluded that the advantages of Sol's career change outweighed the time they would both have to wait.

One approach to dealing with the effects of significant others is to involve them in the client's career goal, focusing on possible personal long-term gain. Clients might be able to accomplish this alone, but there can be considerable advantage to having important others attend counseling sessions to help create a sense that this is a goal of benefit to all family members, not just to the client. Such visits can also allay suspicions that the counselor and client are somehow in league to exclude the interests of the rest of the family. To be avoided is any suggestion that the significant other is being brought to counseling so that the counselor can act as a figure of authority advocating the client's point of view.

Reluctance before even starting to implement a career plan can be a mask for anticipatory anxiety. Although perhaps not aware of hidden fears, the client feels a loss of energy and interest and may express dissatisfaction or "Yes, buts" about the plan. Analysis of the client's cognitions at times when the reluctance is strongest yields anxiety and self-doubt: "I'm not good enough," "This is too ambitious," "No one will hire me," "What if I go through all that training and can't get a job?" If you know your client well you will by now be able to anticipate the concerns most likely to be upsetting and can address them before they have a chance to affect implementation of the plan. Because even the most stable and self-confident clients have doubts when facing a new venture, problems can often be forestalled by expecting these reactions and labeling them as normal. In most cases of mild cold feet, action is the best cure, and clients should be encouraged to proceed with the first steps of their plan despite mild anxieties. Severe problems with anxiety will quickly become apparent during the next stage, when clients attempt to carry out their plans, and can be dealt with at that time.

At the other end of the continuum, some clients doubt the wisdom of their career choice. Such doubts cannot be ignored, as they can sap a client's will and energy if not addressed. Naturally, you will take the client's concerns seriously, but it would be unwise to immediately assume that the client should go through the choice stage again. When the client's doubts are merely normal cold feet, there are two interventions that can resolve the doubts. First, reassure clients that such doubts are common, especially when people are considering a major change in life-style or career, and remind them that they have arrived at their current choice by a painstaking and systematic process, representing the best they can do at this time. This reassurance alone is sometimes sufficient to quell hesitation and allow clients to proceed to action. If not, it may be that client doubts are occasioned by a sense of being trapped into a career. If this is the case, remind clients that they are not locked into a single choice, that they already have a list of other feasible options, and that they need not feel guilty about changing their minds. You might even want to build into the plan a review point specifically to address the question of whether the client is still committed to the chosen path. As with so many other psychological situations, the existence of a built-in breathing space or even a possible escape route is often sufficient to remove any necessity to use it.

If these approaches fail, the client may have, in fact, made an unsuitable career choice, or new information, experiences, or circumstances may have rendered the choice inappropriate or undesirable. Clients in this situation may or may not be aware of the dilemma but will certainly find themselves reluctant to make specific plans to pursue a goal they do not want. If mild reassurances and the provision of an escape route do not help remove hesitation, and if the client continually finds fault with the planning process or openly expresses reservations about the career goal, address the possibility of finding a different career option.

8

Beginning
the Job Search

Most career counseling clients will have plans that aim at either employment or further training of some kind. Because finding work is generally more complicated than applying for training, the major focus of the next two chapters will be on how to help clients obtain a job. In this chapter we will discuss three aspects of job hunting: how to present oneself on paper (by résumé, applications, and letters of recommendation), how to search out job leads, and how to obtain desired training or education. Chapter Nine will be devoted to job interview skills and to problems and cautions relevant to the entire job search process.

Since luck, undoubtedly important in getting a job, cannot be programmed or predicted, clients need to mount a deliberate and systematic job search campaign if they wish to be successful in obtaining work. Your role is to be a behind-the-scenes director of the campaign, providing expertise in two areas: the tasks involved in an effective job search, and techniques to carry out these tasks. The role of director also requires helping clients develop attitudes conducive to success, providing psychological support during the job search, and helping clients evaluate their progress and alter strategies when necessary.

Before the job search begins, attention should be paid to the client's attitude toward the campaign. Many job hunters have the secret fantasy that someone will discover them and offer them the perfect job. They will not have to make any effort to find a job but need simply wait, quite passively, until someone

199

has the good sense to see how bright/well motivated/skilled they are and present them with the ideal offer of employment. The counselor must combat this passivity, as the most critical factor in implementing a career decision is to take action. Rational decisions and careful plans will not become a reality unless the client actively sets out to ensure their fulfillment by taking concrete steps. To get an excellent job, a person must conduct an excellent job search, which almost always entails hard work, time, and money. Time needs to be spent discussing these facts with the client, so that he or she is prepared for what can be a demanding and protracted task. If passivity lingers or recurs at any point, you may need to reiterate the necessity for action, and for patience as well.

Another attitude that can be destructive during the search for work is the client's sense of inferiority or lack of commitment resulting from such cognitions as "It is shameful to be unemployed," "A person looking for work is a second-class citizen," "Job seeking is not real work and doesn't count." Beliefs such as these undermine clients' confidence and make them embarrassed to make full use of, for example, relatives and friends who might be valuable contacts. Clients need to recognize that in actively seeking employment they are doing the best they can and that looking for work is, in itself, a laudable activity. If they approach their job campaign as if it were a full-time job, they can justifiably tell critics that they are indeed working, albeit without remuneration for now. Hal, for example, made desultory efforts to find work each day but was easily distracted by friends inviting him to go surfing or to a party. However, when he began to view his job search as a real job in its own right, he was able to resist his buddies' temptations by saying that he had to get on with his job. His self-respect increased, and naturally his campaign was more successful.

Another important aspect of preparing clients for their job search is to correct any misconceptions they may have about what counts most in being hired for a position. *Getting* a job is different from *doing* a good job, which in turn is different from *keeping* a job. These are three distinct situations that require three distinct sets of skills. Doing a good job involves competence and industry—that is, working hard and well. Except in cases of gross incompetency, keeping a job primarily involves getting along with the boss and with co-workers. There are many incompetent people who, year after year, hang onto their jobs because they get along with everyone and never cause trouble. Getting a job, on the other hand, often depends less on people's competence to do the work than on other factors, such as who they know, how they present themselves, and how persistent they are in looking for employment. Clients need to understand this distinction so that they will not misdirect their energies or become unduly discouraged when their qualifications alone are not sufficient to attract the attention of employers.

There are several tasks to complete in a job search campaign. Job seekers must first know very specifically what they want in a position and must be able to talk intelligently about the work involved. They must then find out where actual and potential jobs exist and make necessary contacts. The third task is to present themselves effectively to people who are in a position to do hiring. Each of these tasks can be approached in a variety of ways.

Matters of primary importance in the job search are strategies for finding out about available jobs, for creating new jobs, and for making contacts. Efforts are directed at two different sources of jobs: the traditional job market and the hidden job market.

The traditional market is reached through familiar job search methods, including looking through newspaper and trade-paper want ads, using employment agencies or university placement offices, placing "work wanted" advertisements, sending out cover letters and résumés to organizations of interest, going to company personnel offices, and filling out applications. For a variety of reasons, these traditional procedures are not highly regarded by most experts (Bolles, 1986; Djeddah, 1978; Irish, 1973). For example, because the main task of personnel offices is not to hire people but to screen them out, most experts advise that the serious job hunter avoid them. Another of the problems encountered by job seekers who use traditional methods is the fact that many advertised jobs are not as available as they appear. An employer may, in fact, have already decided on the person to fill the opening, and the job is being advertised only to comply with Equal Employment Opportunity regulations. Recognizing that the job interview is the primary source of job offers, Bostwick (1985) asked 300 major U.S. companies about their methods of initiating job interviews. He learned that 12 percent of interviews resulted from employment agency contacts, 21 percent from advertising, and a whopping 67 percent from either direct negotiation between employer and candidate or other initiatives of the candidate. A final reservation about using traditional methods of job hunting is that only about 20 percent of jobs are publicized through advertisements and other traditional avenues.

This last fact means that about 80 percent of all jobs are obtained through what is known as the *hidden job market,* which is reached through friends, relatives, work associates, and direct contact with employers (Djeddah, 1978). There are two major advantages to using the hidden job market. First, the person who makes contact with a potential employer before a job is advertised arrives ahead of the crowd, does not have to compete with other applicants, and might be offered a job before anyone else has had an opportunity to apply for it. Second, half of all potential jobs cannot be advertised because they do not yet exist (Djeddah, 1978). Such positions are created when a person available to work sits face to face with a potential employer and convinces that employer that he or she is too good to lose. An effective job search must therefore focus primarily on making contacts with prospective employers via the insider or hidden job market and only secondarily on more traditional methods.

Once a contact is made, an interview is arranged and clients must embark on the third important task of the job search campaign, selling themselves to the prospective employer. Selling oneself occurs not only in interviews but also on paper by means of an application or a résumé, a cover letter, and letters of recommendation. How appropriate each of these will be depends on the type of position being sought. A person applying for a job as a short-order cook will likely need to fill out an application but may not need a résumé, whereas a person applying for a position as an accountant would probably need a résumé. Some positions will require three or four letters of recommendation, while others will need none or perhaps only a telephone call to a person listed as a reference on the application form. Because the manner of presentation can be more important in obtaining a job than the client's actual qualifications, one of the most important tasks of the career counselor at the job search stage is to help clients present themselves to prospective employers in the best possible light, both in person and on paper.

There are several excellent books available that deal solely with the subject of job search: (Bolles, 1986; Djeddah, 1978; Figler, 1979b; Irish, 1973; Jackson, 1978; Marcon and Worthington, 1984; Schuman and Lewis, 1986; Yate, 1985); they can be used, whole or in part, to good advantage by both client and counselor. Clients might follow one of the manuals on their own, using the counselor as consultant, or the counselor might use one or more of the manuals as a resource.

Accurate records are a vital part of an effective job-hunting campaign. They are required so that the client will know his or her progress and status at any given time, will avoid duplicating efforts, and will not forget to follow up a situation that might result in a job offer. At first it may seem to the client that it would be impossible to forget a name, a location, or the fact that a résumé was sent. But as time goes on and the client makes many contacts, it becomes easy to forget such information. Clients should keep all letters received as well as copies of all letters sent, and if they have more than one résumé, they should keep records of which version was sent to which prospective employer. They should also keep notes on any telephone conversations. Some people find it an excellent learning device to keep a special record of job interviews, including the interviewer's name, other people they met, what they were asked, how they responded, what they said that went well, and what they said that was less than effective. The time to start keeping records is at the beginning of the job search, and the time to set up the record-keeping system is before the job search begins. We suggest that you discuss with your client the sort of records he or she would like to keep and then work out a record-keeping system. A very simple system is presented in Exhibit 26.

Exhibit 26. Sample Record-Keeping Form.

Date	Company Name	Person Contacted and Title	Action Taken
5/17	Jamison Enterprises	Virginia Crocker Secretary to R. Hanson	Attending all-day meeting. Call tomorrow.
5/17	Knudsen Data Service	Arthur Knudsen, C.E.O.	Interviewed for info. Left résumé.
5/18	Pitney, Haskins & Polk	George Cox Manager, Tax Division	Interviewed for junior tax accountant position.
5/18	Knudsen Data Service	Arthur Knudsen, C.E.O.	Wrote thank you letter for 5/17 interview.
5/18	Jamison Enterprises	Virginia Crocker Secretary to R. Hanson	Asked about status of my application.

Presenting Oneself on Paper

Résumé. A résumé is a written summary of personal, educational, and experience qualifications intended to demonstrate an applicant's fitness for a particular position. A résumé is almost always expected for the applicant seeking a professional, technical, administrative, or managerial job and has recently been recommended for people seeking nonprofessional positions as well (Azrin, Flores, and Kaplan, 1975; Flannagan, 1977). In the last two years, for example, the owner/manager of hardware stores in a Southwestern city has adopted the policy of ignoring applications, even for jobs as clerk and stocker, that are not accompanied by a résumé, simply because the high rate of unemployment has produced more applicants than he has time to process. He considers that whatever a person's experience or education, a résumé provides evidence of serious intent to seek work and a willingness to do a little bit extra, both of which are desirable characteristics in an employee (Dalton, personal communication, 1986).

Although a résumé can serve as a calling card, an agenda for an interview, and a means of jogging a prospective employer's mind after an interview (Bolles, 1986), its major purpose is to obtain the job interview in the first place. A carefully executed résumé can be the key to getting an important job interview; a bad résumé can eliminate a person from the running. Because the résumé is a personal advertisement that creates a first impression for the client, it is important enough to spend time creating. Clients should be led to expect that its preparation will require several drafts.

When writing a résumé, it is important to attend not only to the content—that is, the client's qualifications and experience—but also to design and format. A résumé that is not pleasant to look at and easy to read is likely to receive scant attention from employers and therefore fail in its purpose. However, there is no one right method or format for writing a résumé. Different fields of employment vary in their requirements regarding résumé type, format, and length. Advice about résumés appropriate to specific positions or occupations can best be obtained by consulting people responsible for hiring, personnel offices, or professional organizations.

There is no rule saying that a person can have only one résumé. The client who is applying for a number of different types of positions might consider fashioning a generic résumé and then tailoring it to fit each job possibility, highlighting those items likely to have the greatest impact. Maxine, for example, at age fifty had had a variety of work experiences. She created one rather long résumé detailing all of them, as well as her educational achievements, extracurricular training, and volunteer activities. From this basis she derived a second somewhat shorter résumé that emphasized her service and teaching activities and credentials and merely summarized other experiences. A third résumé focused on administrative and business experience while still including her other work.

The specifics of résumé format and design are beyond the scope of this volume. In addition to the job search manuals referred to previously, there are many good books devoted to the subject of résumé writing. Both you and the client would do well to familiarize yourselves with one or more of these references before proceeding to design a résumé. Because fashions change, it is wise to choose guidebooks that are no more than a few years old.

It is a major task of the counselor to help the client with content, rather than with format. Whatever format the client chooses, the résumé should be individually designed to highlight the client's accomplishments while minimizing limitations, and it should be tailored to meet the needs and qualifications required by the job the client is seeking. Many people tend to downplay what they have done and underrate their accomplishments. In particular, people who have had little or no work experience tend to overlook the skills they have developed in nonwork settings. As a result, clients often produce material for the résumé that is flat and uninteresting, that does not represent them well, and that does not sell. You can help the client identify all work experience, whether paid, volunteer, or educationally related, and translate this experience into action-packed descriptions designed to make the most of the client's experience and to adequately market the client. Exhibit 27 presents examples of clients' work experience statements and the translations made by the counselor.

Cover Letter. When responding to a job advertisement or when conducting a direct-mail campaign, the client needs to send a cover letter with the résumé. The purpose of the cover letter is to entice the prospective employer into reading the résumé. Each cover letter should be individually tailored to the particular situation and should be addressed, by name, to a particular person. If the letter is in response to an advertisement, it should be addressed to the person whose name appears in the ad; if the letter is part of a direct-mail campaign, it should be addressed to someone with the power to hire. The letter describes the type of position for which the person is applying, briefly states how the person's background and experience qualify him or her for the position, and closes by requesting a personal interview. Most guidebooks that teach résumé writing also discuss cover letters. The specifics of writing these letters, along with examples, can be found there.

Exhibit 27. Translating Work Experiences.

Client's Experience	Résumé Description
Volunteer for Red Cross	Public Relations Director, American Red Cross, Suva Chapter. Developed P.R. program that increased contributions by 20 percent in one year.
Waitress/kitchen aide	Supervised crew of four in food preparation for 200-seat café.
Production manager	Initiated new inventory control system; responsible for purchasing, production schedule.
Temporary clerk	Demonstrated flexibility in adapting to different styles of management; developed integrated office record-keeping system.
Housewife	Promoted and organized seven-block garage sale that grossed $3,600. Managed finances for extended family of fifteen, including budgeting and loan repayment.
Bank teller	Promoted to head teller in one year. Trained and supervised eight new tellers.
Sales promotion	Monitored $1.5 million budget. Developed international sales program servicing nineteen countries in Europe and the Far East. Sales increased fifteen percent in three years.

Application Form. In many cases an application form is required in lieu of or in addition to a résumé. Although the questions on the form may appear to be straightforward, not requiring the assistance of a counselor, some people need to be taught exactly what to put in each blank (Srebaluᵉ, Marinelli, and Messing, 1982). In addition, some employers have applicants fill out the form on the spot, rather than taking it home, which means that the person must be able to recall all the relevant information.

The counselor can help by providing the client with a list of typical information items required on application forms: names and dates of previous employment; addresses and telephone numbers of former employers; dates of military service; names, addresses, and telephone numbers of personal references, and so on. The client should take the list home and gather all the necessary information. The client's responses to the list items can then be used as a reference for filling out either take-home or on-site applications.

You should also have mock application forms available for the client to fill out. Because it is unlikely that any single application form will contain all the questions that a client is likely to encounter, you might consider developing a composite form that contains questions from a number of forms. Have the client practice filling out the form using the information list, and then check the form for accuracy, legibility, spelling and grammatical errors, acceptable reasons given for leaving previous employment, and so on, and provide the client with feedback. Also check to make sure that the client has obtained permission from each listed reference to use his or her name.

Whenever an application form is required, advise the client to make a copy of the form to use for practice. The client can then show the copy to you or to friends and get feedback before filling out the original.

Letters of Recommendation. When employers request letters of reference, applicants are at the mercy of the referee. They do not know whether the referee will remember enough about them for the letter to be relevant, whether the letter will be favorable, or whether the referee will get the letter in the mail on time. Although the applicant cannot guarantee the referee's cooperation, there are some actions the applicant can take to increase the probability of obtaining effective letters.

Clients should choose as referees people who hold a title of importance and who also have firsthand knowledge of their work. A more difficult task is to choose people who will view them favorably and not provide negative information. Ideally, the applicant would approach a potential referee, simply state that he or she is applying for a particular position, and ask whether the person is willing to provide a favorable recommendation. Unfortunately, such a straightforward approach is not likely to be successful. Few applicants would agree to ask the question, and few potential referees would be willing to look an applicant in the eye and say, "No, I won't write you a favorable recommendation." The best the client can do is to carefully consider a number of possible referees and choose those who are most likely to view the client favorably and least likely to make unfavorable comments. It is better to receive a positive recommendation from a person of lesser status than an unfavorable one from someone of high status. However, there is little value in a fistful of letters from personal friends, however glowing, when the employer is interested in the client's technical skills and experiences rather than ability to relate to others.

Having identified suitable referees, the client's next task is to arrange matters so that the letters include the most important material. One method is to provide the referee with an outline of this material—that is, performance highlights, a reminder of under what circumstances and for how long the person has known the client, and a list of any favorable comments or judgments the person may have made about the client's performance. Most referees are delighted to receive such an outline, as it makes the task of writing the letter much easier. A sample outline is presented in Exhibit 28.

Exhibit 28. Outline for Request for Letter of Reference.

1. Position for which letter of reference is needed:
   Branch manager of Consolidated Credit Union, Tucson, Arizona.
2. Addressee of letter of reference:
   Charles Houghton, Regional Director
   Consolidated Credit Unions
   6565 Tempe Boulevard, Phoenix, Arizona 88843
3. Circumstances under which referee knew applicant:
   I took Accounting 401 and Business Administration 522 from you and obtained A's in both classes. On my paper on modern economics you wrote: "This is an imaginative, original approach. You have clearly expended extra effort in researching and thinking about this topic." From August 1982 to May 1983 you supervised my independent study. During that year, I designed a new system to manage accounts receivable at the YMCA and later helped you incorporate this system into Chapter 10 of your book *Modern Accounting*. I enclose a copy of the report you made on me at the end of the internship.
4. Focus of letter of reference:
   Please focus as much as you can on my ability to work autonomously and to take responsibility, and on any experience and skills you believe I have that would make me suitable for a managerial position.
5. Time frame:
   Please mail the letter directly to Phoenix by June 30.

To ensure that the letter is mailed promptly, the client might simply ask the person, at the time the letter is requested, "May I telephone your secretary in a few days to see if you've had time to write the letter?"

Obtaining Job Leads

Exploring Traditional Methods. Even though 80 percent of job leads are gained via the hidden job market, that still leaves 20 percent that are identified in traditional ways—ways that should not be overlooked. Perhaps the most obvious method of locating job leads is through advertisements in periodicals such as trade journals and trade newspapers, the Sunday *New York Times,* the *Wall Street Journal,* newspapers from cities in which the client would like to work, and local newspapers. The procedure is for the client to respond to the advertisement with a brief letter, being careful to comply with any requests made in the ad, and hope for an interview, although waiting could certainly be coupled with making a call inquiring as to the status of the application. Advice from one expert indicates that since 80 percent of all advertised positions are filled by people who did not have the specified qualifications, people should apply for any job that they think they can do, whether or not they have the formal qualifications (Djeddah, 1978).

Another source of job leads might be the client's college or university alumni placement office or technical/professional society placement service. Some professional organizations sponsor a placement service at their major meetings, where interested candidates can be interviewed by prospective employers. For university students, being interviewed on campus by recruiters for major companies is a job search method that is often effective, especially for those who have been wise enough to major in a field for which there is a demand and who stack up well against their peers.

Placing a "position wanted" ad in a newspaper announcing one's availability to work is a time-honored method of locating job leads, although it is also well known to be virtually useless. If your client is a specialist in a particular area, it might, however, be worth advertising in a professional trade journal read by people in the field. Thus, with little expense of time or money the client will have covered one more base.

Although high-level positions are rarely handled by employment agencies, clients seeking lower- or mid-level positions might consider using an agency to set up interviews. The agency selected should be one known to produce results, willing to contract to collect a reasonable fee only if the client is placed, and careful about confidentiality, in the sense of protecting the present position of clients who are still employed.

Sending out blind letters to companies the client might like to work for, in hopes that there will be an opening, is occasionally productive, although this tactic should be used only if the client lives so far from the targeted company that she or he is unable to make a personal call.

The client should be encouraged to make a list of the possible sources of leads for the type of position she or he will be looking for. Once the list is made, work with the client to identify additional sources and to eliminate sources that do not look like good bets, and then discuss with the client methods of utilizing each of the sources on the list. The client should be prompted to rapidly and systematically set about using each of the listed sources. For example, the client could subscribe to the local newspaper and routinely respond to the advertisements that look interesting. The client should respond quickly and efficiently so as not to take away time from the task of exploring the hidden job market, an endeavor that is more likely to be fruitful.

Exploring the Hidden Market. Because the majority of jobs are reputed to be obtained through the hidden job market, the client should spend most of his or her time exploring this market. To discover leads, the client must talk with a great many people, some of whom the client already knows and some the client has yet to meet. A job campaign plan must be developed that employs a great variety of people.

The first step in generating such a plan is to build a contact list. This list ultimately is to include the names of influential people at or close to the top in the client's target area—that is, those people who have the power to hire. Client and counselor begin by making a list of all the people who might be of help to the client, including friends, acquaintances, relatives, business associates, former teachers and professors, neighbors, former employers, the client's minister or rabbi, and so on. Many people are reluctant to "use" people in this manner, and the counselor may need to do some creative marketing, convincing clients that (1) this is the most productive and efficient method of locating a job, (2) the practice is not unusual, occurring in 80 percent of cases where people obtain jobs, although perhaps not as systematically as in career counseling, (3) they will not be "using" people as long as they are honest about their purposes and give the other person a choice of whether to cooperate, and (4) most people enjoy being in a position to be helpful.

The next step is for the client to systematically approach everyone on the list with a number of requests. The client should tell contact people the kind of job that he or she wants and ask whether they know of present openings or will let the client know if they hear of a future opening. In some cases clients might want to ask permission to use the contact person as a reference on application forms or for an open letter of recommendation. The client should always ask the contact person to suggest names of executives to interview who work in their field of interest and request permission to call back at a later time. These new names are then added to the list. Most persons approached will not be aware of open positions and are contacted only as sources of job leads, but if the person does know of a job and is able to make an introduction, it serves as an endorsement and gives the client an advantage over other candidates.

If the contact list has been exhausted and has not generated sufficient job interviews with authorities in the client's field of interest, the client will need to dig deeper into his or her arsenal of acquaintances or take steps to meet people whom she or he does not know. The counselor can help clients identify people with whom they have something in common. For example, they might obtain a listing of members of their college or university alumni association, or they could use the register of any organization (professional, fraternal, social) to which they belong. Some clients might have to join such organizations in order to make sufficient contacts. The client should then follow the same procedure of communicating with each contact, arranging a personal interview, and asking for assistance in finding job leads.

If the list is still insufficient, clients must utilize people whom they do not know personally (Mencke and Hummel, 1984). Through library or other research, the client can identify influential men and women in the target field, then make an appointment with each person, asking for a brief interview (ten minutes or so) in order to discuss what he or she is doing in the particular area of concern.

During the interview, the client asks two or three specific questions, prepared in advance, about the organization and shows interest in the answers, demonstrating an enthusiasm for what the organization is doing. Next, the client asks the person's advice on where to look for jobs in the field. When applicable, the client might also ask who in the organization is responsible for the kind of work he or she is most interested in and then get in touch with that person. It is important that the client not come right out and ask for a job, as doing so will change the tone of the interview and put the executive off. Before leaving, the client should ask for the names of several other people to interview.

All interviews should be followed up with a thank you note. The client should make notes after each interview in order to remember specifics that the executive said and refer to these specifics in the note. Thus, a note might read "Thank you for your time yesterday. I found your comments on————particularly interesting and will follow up on your suggestion to contact Dr. Smith for further information." The note will bring the client to the person's mind again, acting as a second encounter (Djeddah, 1978).

The Long-Distance Job Search

It is not uncommon for a person living in one town to want to work in another and consequently to be in the unfortunate position of conducting a long-distance job search. The major difficulty with such a search is that the client must conduct interviews over the telephone or by mail—far less satisfactory than in person because it is not possible for the interviewer to size up the client, because it is more difficult to get information, especially valuable covert job information, and because the client is less likely to be remembered.

Assuming that the person cannot move to the desired location, one approach to the long-distance job search is to do as much at home as possible and then visit the place where employment is desired. Thus, while still at home the client would use the mails and the telephone to develop contacts and set up interviews and then travel to the desired location, staying at least long enough to complete the scheduled interviews.

Another approach would be to take a substantial period of time off work to go to the preferred locale and conduct a complete job search, making contacts, scheduling interviews, and taking advantage of face-to-face encounters with prospective employers. The client might need to be advised that this is not the time to niggle about money—to fuss about pay lost, the cost of a trip or an extended visit, or the price of long-distance telephone calls. A job search is often expensive, and its cost should be considered an investment in one's future.

Executing Plans to Obtain Training and Education

Should the client's plan either include or consist entirely of obtaining further training or education, there are several factors to consider. Typically, clients have limited information about what is available, tending to be knowledgeable about the more obvious and conventional ways to prepare formally for a career or job but ignorant of alternatives that can be just as effective and that might in fact be more appropriate for them. They may also have unreasonable prejudices about a certain method of education—believing, for example, that the absolute best way to prepare for any career in business is by obtaining an M.B.A. A third aspect to consider is the currency and completeness of information and access to sources for the most up-to-date material. It is not always necessary to guide clients through every detail of preparing for and obtaining further training, but it is important to spend some time checking out whether the client has the knowledge and skills to proceed alone and, if not, what your part will be in helping. This is a good time to encourage the client to use outside counseling sources, at schools and colleges, for example. Because some of the information the client needs can be quite specialized, it is valuable to consult those whose daily job it is to keep current with information and who are in a position to evaluate training opportunities.

Often, your most important task is performed before clients investigate educational opportunities: helping them clarify their purpose in seeking training, their personal limitations, what sort of information they need, and where they intend to look for it. With this clarification, many clients can proceed alone. Individual needs will determine the extent to which you will either monitor progress or actively assist clients from this point on.

When evaluating training situations, clients need to be clear about what they expect the training to accomplish for them, since purpose often determines what training will be most suitable. Does the client want to learn as much as possible? In that case, a thorough and intense type of program should be selected. Does the client simply want to obtain any sort of paper qualifications at a certain level? Then there might be little reason to seek anything but the easiest, fastest, and cheapest program available. Is the training intended to lead to further training at a later date (such as an M.S. now, a Ph.D. later)? Then it is important to look at a chosen program from the point of view of its credentialing and potential to lead to other levels or types of training. In a highly competitive field, training might be needed to enable the client to stand out as either above or different from other applicants for jobs, in which case the name and reputation of the training institution or its teachers can be of the greatest importance. If the purpose of training is to obtain a job, it is entirely possible that the client might be better advised to look not so much at academic types of education as at more practical training, such as an apprenticeship or on-the-job training. In looking at the purpose of training, clients should also consider how much they would like to keep their options open in case of future changes in direction or interest.

If a client is not clear about what purpose training will serve, clarification should be obtained by gathering further information. Probably the best source is people already in the chosen field, both workers and those responsible for hiring. They can be asked such things as "What training do you like to see on a résumé?" "What training makes you select one person over another?" "How far can a person go and how fast with different types of training?" "Is there any other route to work in this field?" "What doors are opened or closed by various types of training?" "How much of what I need to know to do a good job will I learn from academic training and how much on the job?"

Once the purpose of training is clear, clients should consider their personal limitations vis-à-vis training. In other words, is the client limited by such factors as time, money, geography, or entry qualifications? As counselor, you need to ascertain that the client's limitations are real. Many barriers thought to be insurmountable can in fact be overcome, especially the barrier that causes perhaps the most hesitation—money. Many kinds of scholarships, loans, and financial aid are available, and large sums of money set aside for education and training go unused each year. This is partly because many people decide, on the basis of poor information, that they would be ineligible, and partly because they do not know how to identify sources of these funds. It would be unreasonable to expect a counselor whose field is not career counseling to have detailed knowledge of these sources, but the least you can do is tell clients that they cannot assume their ineligibility and point them toward people who can help them identify where financial aid can be obtained. Before accepting limitations, therefore, discuss some possible ways to overcome them, especially if they severely reduce the training opportunities open to the client.

Sources of information about training institutions are varied. State departments of education can provide details about approved institutions at all levels within the state. A good general starting place is national organizations associated with various jobs. The *Occupational Outlook Handbook* lists some of these at the end of each job description as sources for information about training and career opportunities. Trade journals also advertise training institutions, and clients can ask personnel managers and employment officers within their chosen field for recommendations and information. Careful thought should enable the client to inquire of and apply to only the most suitable programs and to obtain the most complete personalized information.

Clients also need to decide what sort of information they need. When an institution puts out a catalog, most of the relevant information is supplied, but sometimes it is necessary to request missing details. With less formal types of training, almost all information must be acquired through personal contact. Clients generally need to discover how long the program lasts, what fees are charged (for application, training, and examinations), what degree or certificate the institution confers, its affiliation with official certifying organizations, and the application and admissions process (Is there an intake interview? When are applications accepted? How long does it take for a decision to be made? What are the entry requirements?). Some clients need specialized information and should obtain it as soon as possible. A person who must work during the day and can attend only night classes, for example, needs to know where this is possible.

There are two major cautions regarding training programs. First, persuade your clients to obtain the most recent information. A pamphlet, catalog, or brochure that has been sitting in a file cabinet for a couple of years is likely to be out of date, and clients will need to obtain more recent material. The second caution concerns time. The whole process of researching and applying for training can take months and be both tedious and frustrating. Clients should be prepared for this expenditure of time and energy and should build it into their plan.

You will need to ensure that the client can satisfactorily complete the application process itself. If an interview is part of the application, prepare the client by discussing the probable content of the interview and by practicing mock interviews, if necessary. Obviously, the application forms must be filled out legibly and completely. Many applications include sections that call for either judgment or "free" writing—for example, a brief essay on a subject of interest in the chosen field, an explanation of why this program was chosen, or a discussion of the person's career goals. Two considerations are important here: the applicant should select essay material that is appropriate to the program and institution, and all responses involving selectivity or opinion should be reviewed by an objective and knowledgeable outsider before the application is sent. The reviewer should focus on how appropriate the material is for the particular program or place, on clarity of style, and on tone, keeping in mind that decisions about applicants are often made by busy people who devote no more than a few minutes to each form and are unlikely to hunt for a prospective candidate's good qualities through writing that is unclear, unfocused, or irrelevant. Again, however, there is no necessity that you be the reviewer. Your role is merely to check that the client recognizes the need to take this step and has a reviewer available.

❧ 9 ❧

Preparing
for Job Interviews

The point at which the client gets a job interview is the culmination of the career counseling process, since the interview is the predominant means by which employers make hiring decisions. In his research into a large number of American companies, Bostwick (1985) discovered that one person was hired for every five to six interviews granted. In fact, the job interview is the single most important factor in landing a job. In the course of a typical twenty- to thirty-minute preliminary interview, the client hopes to make a favorable impression on the interviewer, resulting in further, more specific interviews (with department managers, for example) or an actual job offer. Most applicants who do not achieve their purpose in interviews do so because they do not promote themselves satisfactorily, failing either to present a self-assured and positive image or to convince the interviewer that they possess the necessary skills and characteristics for the position.

In this chapter, we address some methods of teaching clients how to prepare for, survive (even enjoy), and evaluate their job interviews. We also discuss difficulties that can arise during the stage of searching for a job.

The importance of the interview is attested to by the extensive advice that has been printed on the subject. Certainly, more has been written than can be discussed here. Although we present basic information that will allow you to do a reasonable job of preparing clients for interviews, you are encouraged to consult other sources for more detailed coverage of the topic.

Preparing for the Job Interview

Although it is obvious that clients vary in the help they will need with interviewing, it is difficult to know in advance what sort of help each client will need. Furthermore, some clients believe they have more skill in this area than actually exists, have forgotten minor details, or need help with organizing themselves for interviews. You certainly do not want to risk insulting the client by discussing small points that should, indeed, be obvious. We suggest, therefore, that you fashion a handout, similar to the one presented in Exhibit 29, containing organizational and procedural items that need no discussion. This handout can be given to the client as homework to read, with the preface that it serves only as a reminder, since the client is likely to know most of the material. However, the client should be invited to mark any points that need discussion.

Exhibit 29. Job Interview Information.

Preparation for the Interview

1. Make note of the following information, being certain that it is accurate, and keep the notation with you:
   a. Interviewer's name and title and how to pronounce the interviewer's name (if in doubt, ask the secretary).
   b. The full name of the organization.
   c. The exact place and time of the interview.
   d. The route you will take to get to the interview, or the bus schedule if traveling by bus.
   e. A generous estimation of the maximum time it will take to get there.
2. Plan what you will wear to the interview by finding out what clothes are appropriate for the setting in which you will be interviewing, and make sure that your clothing is ready (clean, pressed) so that you will not need to think about it during the interview.
3. Do whatever else is necessary to look your best—for example, get a haircut, get enough sleep the night before—and then dismiss the issue from your mind and concentrate on the interview itself.
4. It is wise to take the following items to the interview:
   a. A pen and note paper, kept out of sight, in case you want to jot down something the interviewer tells you—the name of someone you are scheduled to meet later, for example.

Exhibit 29. Job Interview Information, Cont'd.

---

   b. Two or more copies of your résumé. Although you have probably already sent your résumé to the prospective employer, it might have been mislaid, or you might be interviewed by more than one person. Moreover, if the interviewer starts going over your résumé item by item, you can follow along with your own copy.

   c. A list of relevant information (names and addresses of references, dates of former employment, addresses of former employers, Social Security number) in case you need to fill out employment applications.

5. Plan to arrive at least fifteen minutes early. Your interviewer could be ahead of schedule; if not, you can use the extra time to compose yourself and mentally review the reasons why you want this job and would be good at it and the questions you will ask about the position.

The Interview

1. Walk into the office briskly and greet the interviewer by name.
2. Take your cue from the interviewer: If the interviewer moves to shake hands, do so, but not unless he or she makes the first gesture. Wait until the interviewer offers you a chair before you sit down.
3. Your handshake should be firm and dry. Make sure your right hand is free.
4. From time to time look the interviewer in the eye rather than stare at the floor, at the ceiling, or into the middle distance.
5. Smile at appropriate times. It makes you look friendly and confident.

Ending the Interview

1. Be alert to signals that the interview is almost at an end; sum up your interest briefly, and stop.
2. Ask when the decision will be made regarding the position and whether you might telephone on a particular date at a certain time to inquire about the decision.
3. Smile, express appreciation for the interviewer's time, and leave promptly.
4. Be sure to thank the employer's secretary or receptionist on the way out.

Don'ts

1. Never take anyone with you to the job interview.
2. Don't try to be funny, and don't chew gum or smoke, even if the interviewer invites you to.
3. Don't pile your belongings on the interviewer's desk or move the chair around when you sit down.
4. Don't say "I'll do anything" or ask someone to employ you because you need a job.
5. Never make a slighting reference about a former employer, professor, acquaintance, or anyone else.
6. Don't volunteer negative information about yourself.
7. Avoid discussing topics unrelated to the job. The interviewer who says, "Tell me about yourself" is not asking about your hobbies or your children but about your ability to do the job in question.
8. Avoid showing strong feelings. An interview is not the place to become emotional.

Exhibit 29. Job Interview Information, Cont'd.

---

9.   Don't argue with the interviewer. You are not in a position to win. Don't discuss inflammatory subjects unless you are asked directly, and then briefly state your views without emotion.

After the Interview

1.   As soon as possible after finishing an interview, analyze what happened. Identify what went well and what seemed to turn off the interviewer, and try to figure out why. Consistently analyzing your interviews will help you handle subsequent interviews better.
2.   Write a brief note to the interviewer expressing appreciation for the time he or she gave you and explaining in as few words as possible your continuing interest in the position. If possible, include some updated data.
3.   Certainly if you arranged to do so, and even if you did not, telephone the interviewer a few days later and inquire about the status of your application.

In helping clients make the best of their interviews, teach them to look at the interview as a three-stage process, comprising preparation for the interview, the interview itself, and post-interview activities. Because the actual interview is usually stressful and requires, in effect, a dramatic performance, many clients see the interview itself as all important, not realizing that the best interpersonal skills and most appropriate training and experience can be undermined by failure to spend time and effort both preparing for the interview and following up afterward.

There are two types of preparation for interviews, general and specific. In general, clients need to know before their first interview exactly what they want out of a job, why they want these things, and what skills and experience they have to offer that make them a potentially valuable employee. They should be able to communicate all this information clearly and confidently. More specific preparation relates to each particular job interview, before which clients need to have researched the organization, decided on questions to ask of the interviewer, and planned how to express their wishes and qualifications in order to fit the specific situation.

As a preliminary exercise to help clients with the general preparation they need, we recommend the job advertisement

Exhibit 30. Job Advertisement Exercise.

Part One

Compose a twenty-five- to forty-word advertisement for a position that you would like and that, with your qualifications, you could reasonably expect to obtain. Be specific, concrete, and realistic. You must include the duties and responsibilities and the type of organization. You may include, if you like, a description of colleagues or supervisors, working conditions, location, and salary. Do not include information on fringe benefits and promotions. Try to squeeze everything you want in a job into this advertisement.

Example:

> WANTED: Counselor to join close-knit team of ten psychologists, counselors, and social workers in rural mental health center. Duties include family and group counseling and consultation with local schools. Excellent outdoor recreational area adjacent to Yellowstone National Park.

Part Two

Phrase by phrase, or word by word, pull apart your job advertisement. In the left-hand column write each word or phrase on a separate line. In the middle column indicate what interests you about that particular aspect of the position. In the right-hand column (when applicable) show how you qualify for the position.

Word or Phrase	Interest	Experience or Demonstrated Ability

Part Three

This is an example of how the form in Part Two might be filled out for the sample advertisement in Part One.

Word or Phrase	Interest	Experience or Demonstrated Ability
Close-knit team	Can consult and give better client service.	Have practiced many team roles and done well in all.
Psychologists, social workers, and counselors	Like working with people of varied backgrounds and orientations.	Worked in several countries and had to adjust to different cultures.

Exhibit 30. Job Advertisement Exercise, Cont'd.

Rural	Like rural people and the things that interest them.	Taught for ten years in country schools.
Family counseling	Variety of problems. Can have impact on many lives.	Experienced in church, MHC, and agency settings. Started HS family agency.
Group counseling	Variety, quicker progress. Lots of fun.	Have conducted groups with university women, the elderly, parents, and high school students.
Consultation with schools	Enjoy my own expertise. Enjoy offering practical help.	Lots of experience. Can emphathize with both students and teachers.
Outdoor recreation	Like to hike, canoe, snowshoe, ski, and be in unpolluted and quiet atmosphere.	

exercise presented in Exhibit 30. In the first part of the exercise, clients are asked to invent a short job advertisement for a position they would like. In the second part, they isolate the separate elements of the advertisement and then, with the help of the counselor, identify what interests them about each element and how they think they qualify for each. (Part Three provides some sample answers for Part Two.) Although this exercise can be used as a homework assignment, it is important that the counselor review it with clients by conducting an in-depth interview to analyze each part of the advertisement. An interview such as this, audiotaped or videotaped to facilitate feedback, can also be used to provide clients with practice in discussing their qualifications and interests related to a job. The ability to do so effectively will form the backbone of later job interviews. Exhibit 31 presents an example of a counselor interviewing a client about the sample job advertisement from Exhibit 30.

Clients who have specific job interviews scheduled often find it helpful to complete Part Two of job advertisement exercise

Exhibit 31. Job Advertisement Exercise Interview.

Counselor:	You've done a good job pulling apart your job advertisement and listing the key concepts or aspects of the position. The next step will be to take each concept separately and identify what it is about that aspect of the job that interests you and then to identify what it is that qualifies you for that aspect of the job. Let's begin with the first concept that you mention, which is "close-knit team." What is it about a close-knit team that interests you?
Client:	I like to work with a team because you get the opportunity to consult with other people. You don't feel so alone, and there's a chance of producing much better service for your clients because you've got a lot of brains working on something.
Counselor:	I can understand that you want to be part of a team, but what in your experience indicates that you could be a contributing member of this team?
Client:	My very different experiences with different types of teams indicates to me that I'd be a reasonably good team member.
Counselor:	Would you be more specific about just what is it about you that makes you a good team member?
Client:	If I'm in charge of the team, I'm able to motivate people to work, I can get people enthusiastic about a project, I can keep them going through the rough times, and I'm reasonably good at picking out the people who can do different types of tasks best.
Counselor:	You identified leadership abilities; what about being a member of a team?
Client:	I've known the various roles of a team and I've practiced them all. Feedback from others has been good. I'm reliable and conscientious, and pleasant to work with. I'm not bossy when I'm the leader and I don't shirk responsibility when I'm a follower.
Counselor:	Much better answer. You have down here as one phrase that is important "psychologists, counselors, and social workers." What is it that interests you in working with them?
Client:	I like the idea of having people with different backgrounds and orientations because I think you can provide a better service.
Counselor:	Anything else?
Client:	Well, yes. I'd like to be supervised by psychologists, but I'm not sure that's okay to say, because I'm leaving out social workers.
Counselor:	What do you like about social workers?
Client:	I like their medical perspective. It's one that I haven't been trained in much and I'd like to be able to think the way they do.
Counselor:	Good. Now, put it all together and you'll have a good answer to why

Exhibit 31. Job Advertisement Exercise Interview, Cont'd.

	you'd like to work with people of varied backgrounds and orientations. From your experience, how do you think you would be able to work with people as varied as this?
Client:	I've worked in four different countries, which has required flexibility in adjusting to different cultures. I think that experience would translate well to a team situation such as I describe in my ad.
Counselor:	Excellent. Now, let's move on to the word "rural." What is your interest in a rural setting?
Client:	Oh, I hate cities. They're noisy, they're dirty, they're too big, it takes too long to get anywhere.
Counselor:	You're telling me what you don't like about cities, not what you do like about a rural setting.
Client:	It's just the opposite of what I said. In the country you get fresh air, you're closer to outdoor recreation.
Counselor:	Anything else you especially like about a rural atmosphere?
Client:	On the whole, I like rural people; I like them and the things that interest them, like crafts and gardening and the outdoors.
Counselor:	Next time, put all your reasons together and stay with the positive. What about your experience working with rural people?
Client:	My experience comes from teaching for over ten years in country schools. I had a lot of contact with the community because I was frequently involved in community affairs. So I'm well aware of the sort of problems they have.
Counselor:	Moving down the list, why is doing family counseling of particular interest to you?
Client:	I think it's a bit boring to work with individuals all the time. You get more going with a family.
Counselor:	Again, you put your answer in the negative. Try it again using a positive approach.
Client:	I like to work with families because I think there's a lot going on in a family. And it's possible to make interventions that really make a difference in a lot of people's lives. You get a great variety of problems in a family: school problems, bed-wetting problems. It's very interesting and stimulating.
Counselor:	Good. Now, what makes you think you would be able to do family counseling?
Client:	I've had a certain amount of experience with family counseling, and I came from a really large family, so there was a lot of close interaction, and people were always solving problems within the family.

Exhibit 31. Job Advertisement Exercise Interview, Cont'd.

Counselor: Most people come from families; it doesn't sound as if your experience was unique. Better stick to your experience with family counseling.

Client: I've done family counseling. The problems got solved.

Counselor: Could you elaborate? Tell me about what you've done.

Client: I've dealt with a variety of families, from really quite high functioning families who just wanted things to be a little better, who just wanted some communication skills, to families suffering from severe abuse and poverty. And I seem to have been able to establish rapport with all members of the families. I seem to have had success in helping them solve problems, even those that were quite difficult and of long standing. For example, an eight-year-old child who was encopretic had suffered multiple sexual abuse at the hands of her older brothers and came from an extremely narrow-minded and religious family who thought that she was a sinner because of the sex, and we managed to get to the point where the child was succeeding in school, the family was more close knit, there was much better communication between all members of the family.

Counselor: The first part of your answer was excellent, but I think it's best not to describe a particular case unless you're asked to do so. Maybe you could identify the number of different locations in which you did family counseling in making a general answer, and then if the interviewer wants to ask you specifically about any particular setting, you could bring up one of the cases. It tends to sound as if that's the only case you've had, unless you make a general statement first.

Client: So what you mean is something more like, I've done family counseling out of a church setting, out of a mental health center, out of a private counseling agency, and I started and administered a family counseling center operating out of a high school.

Counselor: Exactly. That sounds much more as if you'd be able to do family counseling than your explaining in detail how you handled just one case. Let's move on to group counseling. What is your interest in group counseling?

Client: My interest is probably for the same reasons that I like family counseling. You get a lot of variety and I think it's stimulating and you see much quicker progress. Besides, I like to relate to a larger group of people. Groups are fun.

Counselor: What is your experience or demonstrated ability in doing group work?

Client: Actually, I've had very little group experience at all when it comes right down to it. I've run many parent study groups, teaching parents how to manage their children's behavior, and a lot of career counseling groups with students from twelve to eighteen, and a support group of university women, and groups with the elderly depressed. These

Exhibit 31. Job Advertisement Exercise Interview, Cont'd.

---

were different kinds of groups. Some were support groups, some were specifically educational, some were career, some interactional, some were using cognitive therapy.

Counselor: Now, let's analyze what you just said. In the first part you said, ''Oh I haven't had much group experience at all,'' and then you named five different groups that you have led. You could just as easily have started off by saying, ''I've conducted several different types of groups'' and then gone on to list some of the groups you have conducted. It sounds much more positive, and all you've changed is the first sentence. Always start with a positive, never a negative.

Client: And I've also indicated that there's lots more if the person wants to ask.

Counselor: Right. Lets move on to consultation with schools. What is your interest in this activity?

Client: I'm interested in consulting in the schools partly because I've been both a teacher and a school counselor; I know what goes on in schools. I've seen both sides of the fence and am able to empathize with both teachers and students. My experience gives me considerable expertise, and I enjoy being in a position of being able to offer very practical help.

Counselor: Well, that answers both your interest in and your ability to provide consultation to the schools. The last item on your list is ''outdoor recreation.'' I don't think that your ability to engage in outdoor recreation is of concern, but what about your interest?

Client: My interest is very strong. I like to hike, I like to canoe, I like to snowshoe, I like to cross-country ski, I like to have a garden, and I like to live in a place that's open and relatively unpolluted and quiet, where I can see animal tracks and follow animal tracks. And it would be very nice to live in a place where I could have chickens.

Counselor: Well, there's no question that you're enthusiastic about outdoor recreation. Let's take it, again, from the top, changing the parts that we discussed; this time try to be as enthusiastic about various aspects of the job description as you are about outdoor recreation.

---

for each position in question, first listing each function involved in the job and then identifying what interests them about each function and how they qualify for each function.

A critical preparation that clients can make for each interview is to research the organization, keeping in mind that they are looking for the type of job they want, rather than for an organization willing to hire them. Specifically, clients should try to discover what problems the organization has that they, with their unique set of skills, might be able to solve. To do this, clients will need to find out as much as possible about the company's products, management philosophy, plans, current problems, and triumphs. What has been happening in the department for which the client is applying? Who is in charge of that department, what problems is it trying to solve, in what direction is it heading? Backed by this kind of research, clients are in a position to speak the company's language, framing their responses to indicate how their skills match the company's needs.

Information about a company can best be gleaned by talking to people who work for the company. Clients should use friends and acquaintances to locate someone who works for the company and then arrange a meeting with that person for the purpose of finding out inside information about the company. Information can also be acquired from written sources, such as the company's annual report or publications whose sole purpose is to provide information about corporations and industries. These sources can be consulted in public libraries, using the expertise of the reference librarian. Clients need not overburden themselves with information about every aspect of a company but rather should concentrate on the section, department, or office that is their job target.

When research on a company is complete, the client needs to prepare specific, well-thought-out questions to ask during the interview. Appropriate questions might center on opportunities for and routes to advancement, new directions the company is taking, and the people with whom the client would be working. You should review the client's list of questions, mainly to monitor the attitude the client is likely to convey by asking them. Employers are not interested, for example, in interviewees who present themselves as expert diagnosticians of company problems or critics of organizational policy. The questions should simply show the client's intelligent and informed interest in relevant areas.

The final step in preparing for interviews is to consider the sorts of questions that might be asked in an interview and plan tentative answers. Clients should be discouraged from memorizing answers to questions, as these responses usually sound stilted and insincere; rather, clients should be able to adapt basic material to answer questions framed in several ways. This process is analogous to preparing for an examination requiring essay rather than multiple-choice answers. Exhibit 32 contains nineteen commonly asked interview questions. You and your clients may also wish to consult books and chapters devoted to the subject of interview questions. Particularly helpful in both format and content is Yate (1985).

Exhibit 32. Job Interview Questions.

1. What are your major strengths?
2. What is your major weakness?
3. What can you do for us?
4. Tell me about yourself.
5. What starting salary do you expect?
6. What do you see yourself working at three to five years from now?
7. Why do you want to work for us?
8. What job in our company would you like eventually?
9. What future vocational plans do you have?
10. What are the personal characteristics necessary for success in your field?
11. What do you know about our company?
12. What would you like to know about our company? About our competitors?
13. What are you looking for in a job?
14. What is the minimum salary you would accept?
15. How much money do you expect to be earning in five years? Ten years?
16. What have you learned from previous jobs you have held?
17. Why did you leave your last job?
18. In what areas do you think you need additional experience?
19. Which particular aspect of this job appeals to you most?

After preparation comes the interview itself. During this encounter, both content and demeanor are important. Essentially, clients have to sell themselves to prospective employers by making sure they communicate their good points as clearly as possible. Clients should not assume that the interviewer can learn this information from the résumé or from the client's nonverbal behavior. In fact, if the interviewer hasn't asked "Why should we hire you?" within the first five minutes of the interview, it is up to the client to supply this information, stressing assets but without blustering or bragging.

At the first opportunity, clients should tell the interviewer specifically and briefly why they are interested in the position and what they can offer, using material from their preparatory job advertisement exercise as a guide. It is best to mention good qualities in relation to something concrete. Rather than saying, "I'm always eager to learn," it would be more informative to tell the interviewer about all the extra workshops and seminars the client has taken. Work skills should also be described, using the appropriate terminology for the particular job for which the person is applying.

Clients should be given some general guidelines to follow when answering questions posed by the interviewer. First, they must take care to listen to each question carefully and to answer, or at least appear to answer, the question. If necessary, they can ask for clarification; for example: "As I understand it, you are interested in my growth on the job rather than in the tasks I performed. Is that right?" This technique also gives clients a moment's breather during which to frame an answer. A second guideline is to answer questions fully but without rambling detail and without diverging from the question. Interviewers do not want to feel as if they have to pull information out of applicants, nor do they want to hear irrelevant information. Third, clients should take time in answering questions. It is not necessarily impressive to have a quick response ready for every question, and interviewers appreciate the self-confidence and thoughtfulness of an interviewee whose first response, at least occasionally, is along the lines of "That's an important question, and I don't have a quick answer for it. However, I've given it some thought and one of my ideas is . . ."

Often, toward the end of the interview, the interviewer will ask whether the applicant has any questions. Even if not given this opportunity, the client should find a way to ask one or two of the questions prepared from research into the company. There are, of course, some questions that should not be asked. It is unwise to ask about salary, vacations, pension plans, and other employee benefits during the first interview, since employers expect applicants to be more interested in the work they will be doing than in salary and the other benefits they will receive. These questions should be raised only after a firm job offer has been made.

During the interview, clients are most likely to make a good impression if they remain alert, pleasant, and businesslike and convey the attitude that, although they have other irons in the fire, this particular job is the one they find especially interesting. It is essential for clients to both feel and communicate enthusiasm, which is not always easy when a person is anxious about the interview, lacking in self-confidence, discouraged after many rejections, or even finding the interviewer aversive. However, few employers want to hire someone who is indifferent to the company or just shopping around, so it is worthwhile to teach clients how to manufacture and convey enthusiasm. Before the start of the interview, the client should review all the reasons for wanting the job and during the interview should communicate these reasons. Other ways to demonstrate enthusiasm include asking relevant questions about the job; continuing to make remarks indicative of interest even if the interviewer digresses into the history of the company or other topics not especially relevant to the client; showing knowledge of the company; calling back after the interview to inquire about the position; and writing a thank you note to the interviewer.

Some problems can arise during the interview, and clients need to be prepared for at least the most likely ones. One problem is interviewer incompetence. Not all people who do job interviewing are skilled. Sometimes they do all the talking, never asking a question that would allow applicants to sell themselves. There are several techniques that can be used in this type of situation: (1) If there is a break in the conversation, the applicant can say, "I'd like to share with you some of the things that I've been doing most recently." (2) In response to something the interviewer says, the applicant could comment, "I was interested in your description of . . . because I have done . . . I can really identify with your interest in . . . because . . . " (3) At the end of the interview, the applicant might say, "Before I go, perhaps you would be interested in knowing [fill in one or two assets]."

A second difficulty that can arise during an interview is dealing with a job offer, although such offers are rarely made in the first interview. If an offer is made, the client should ask for time to consider the decision; overnight is long enough if the decision is an easy one. In any case, the interviewer should be given a firm date by which the decision will be communicated. The employer will almost certainly understand the need for time to think over such an important decision. If the client is exploring several possibilities, this should be mentioned: "I am extremely interested in your offer and in the company, but I am waiting for the outcome of other interviews." Sometimes a person becomes more attractive to the employer as a result of others being interested.

Job Interview Techniques for Clients with Special Problems

Clients who have had little experience or little education, or who are very old, who have had a contagious disease but are now recovered, who have been fired from a previous job or otherwise have a poor history, who have been patients in psychiatric hospitals, who have physical handicaps, or who have prison records fall into the category of people with special problems. The employment interviewing guidelines we have already discussed apply to clients with unusual problems; however, they will also need to learn how to handle questions about their problems on application forms and how to explain their problems to prospective employers in such a way that they are not turned down for the position before they are even considered.

For some of these clients, extra practice in job interviewing will be required. For example, prisoners and mental patients, especially those whose confinement has been prolonged, have had little opportunity to practice their social skills and have often lost the self-monitoring behaviors normal to most people not confined to institutional settings. Under these circumstances, it is not uncommon for people to develop nervous or asocial mannerisms, such as scratching, sniffing, an extremely loud tone of voice, and so on. It would be wise to try to help these people recognize the inappropriateness of their habits and learn how to control them when they are applying for work.

Another problem common to clients who have spent time in mental hospitals or prisons is that they have often become accustomed to talking at length about their problems to psychologists, social workers, parole officers, and others. In the course of these discussions, they have learned to use psychological or sociological jargon and to focus almost exclusively on their own past and current difficulties. You will need to help these clients practice using a more everyday type of language and a more objective focus. In particular, clients should not take up interview time in extensive descriptions of and explanations for personal problems. It might be necessary to explain that an employer's first concern is whether an individual has the skills to do a particular job and will be a good employee. Problems the client had in the past, or even current difficulties, are important to the employer only as they might affect that person's ability to perform on the job for which he or she is now applying. Clients should be cautioned that this attitude is reasonable, given the employer's role, and that they should not be overly sensitive to whether or not the employer cares about them on a personal level. Interviewing practice should be directed at having these clients discuss assets rather than liabilities, the future rather than the past, and the desired job rather than personal concerns.

The first step in helping a client with a special problem is to identify with the client those aspects of his or her record that might cause difficulties in the job search process. The next step is to discuss with the client how these aspects will be handled on the application or the résumé. Questions about problem areas on an application form ("Have you ever been in prison?") are made even more difficult because there is never enough space to explain that the client has recovered or changed since the problem occurred. Such questions can be handled by admitting the problem, denying the problem, leaving the question blank on the application and explaining it in the interview, or denying the problem on the application and then, after obtaining the job and establishing a good work record, attempting to straighten out the record.

The clear advantage to admitting the problem is that the client would be being honest and have nothing to hide should he or she get the job; the disadvantage is that the client might very well never get to the interview stage.

A decision to deny the problem might be based on an evaluation of whether the problem is characteristic of the client and could offer the interviewer valid information. For example, it probably would not make much sense for a person who spent a brief period of time in a mental hospital many years before and has not needed psychological or psychiatric help since to write "yes" to mental illness on an application. One disadvantage to lying on the application blank is that the employer might find out and fire the person; thus, the decision to use the denial method should take into consideration how thoroughly the employer is likely to check details of the applicant's background. Denying the problem at first and admitting it after a period of employment implies that the employer will not do a thorough check before hiring. Obviously there is no way to tell whether, at the time of a later disclosure, the client's work record will outweigh the employer's reaction to being deceived.

Although it is possible that leaving the question blank might eliminate the applicant from the running simply because the form is not complete, it is more likely that admitting the problem on the form would result in elimination. If the client does obtain an interview, he or she can then explain simply and directly why the question was left blank—for example, "I left that question blank because I thought I could explain the answer better in person." Discuss the advantages and disadvantages of each approach with your client, but leave the final choice up to the client. Your task is to help the client evaluate the methods as carefully as possible.

The next step is to work with the client to list as many questions as possible that the client would have trouble answering and then identify acceptable answers to each question. Answers should avoid medical or psychological jargon, should be short, and should end with a positive statement about the client's ability to do the work despite the problem, in order to leave the employer with a sense of what the client *can* do rather than what the client *cannot* do. Thus, the client needs to identify something to be said about the problem that is not negative (such as that the problem once existed but no longer does) and to state that he or she has the ability to do this particular job without difficulty.

If a problem is visible to the interviewer (such as age or a physical handicap), the client should bring up the subject within the first few minutes of the interview, before the interviewer (who may be reluctant to ask) makes a negative judgment on the basis of the problem without hearing how the client can do the job despite limitations. Finally, the client should rehearse the answers to the questions until he or she can answer them in a quietly confident manner.

Practicing Job Interviews

Job candidates who are relaxed, skilled, and confident in the employment interview are more competitive than those who are not, but these skills have to be learned. Simply knowing what to do is rarely enough, and most clients will need assistance in practicing how best to market themselves in the interview situation.

The major tool used to teach the necessary skills is mock interviews in the counseling session. These practice interviews have two major purposes: to lower the client's anxiety, and to teach interview behavior. Some clients already know how to interview but need practice to eliminate nervous mannerisms and to polish their presentations. For these people the opportunity to rehearse, together with focused feedback on their own performance, may be all that is required. Other clients, usually those with little interview experience, need to be taught the basic process of interviewing. They need a model before beginning to practice, for without modeling they will make too many mistakes and the process will be unnecessarily tedious. You can model the interiew yourself in the session, or, if you have access to the equipment, you could make a videotape to be used with career counseling clients. The tape could be of an exemplary interview or could perhaps present an inept interview and then an ideal one. Many career development centers in universities and colleges have such tapes, and it might be possible for you to arrange for clients to view model interview tapes.

Whether or not you make a prototype job interview videotape, you might consider purchasing video equipment for job
interview practice. Although your feedback can be extremely
helpful to clients, it is not the same as seeing oneself on videotape.

The procedure for practicing interviews consists of three
steps. Since it is much more effective to conduct this practice
in groups, the following procedure is designed for at least five
people, including the counselor, who acts as director of the role-
play. The procedure can be modified to be conducted with just
one client.

1. Either show a tape of a model interview or model a desirable
    interview yourself, asking one of the group to play the part
    of interviewer, using a list of prepared questions such as those
    presented in Exhibit 32. Allow time following the modeling
    for discussion and clarification before proceeding to the
    actual practice.
2. To prepare for the actual practice, make up a list of possi-
    ble interview questions, tailored to the clients' particular
    situations. Then assign four roles to the members of the
    group: interviewer, applicant, receptionist, and one or more
    observers. Explain the tasks required of each role: (a) The
    receptionist is to greet the applicant and usher him or her
    in to see the interviewer. (b) Using both the applicant's
    résumé and the list of interview questions as guides, the inter-
    viewer is to conduct the interview, asking the applicant ques-
    tions. (c) It is the applicant's task to do the best job possible
    of presenting himself or herself. (d) It is the observers' job
    to watch the interview and take notes on good and bad points
    of the applicant's behavior. (If not specifically instructed
    otherwise, observers are apt to focus on both applicant and
    interviewer behavior. Therefore, it may be necessary to ex-
    plain that in this exercise the interviewer can do no wrong;
    since in real life there are good and bad interviewers, in prac-
    tice there should also be good and bad interviewers. So it
    does not matter what the interviewer does, only what the
    applicant does.) Next, tell participants to assume that the
    applicant has sent his or her résumé to the interviewer in

advance of the interview; then establish the job for which
the applicant is applying, the company the interviewer
represents, and the position the interviewer holds. Arrange
the physical setting. For example, have the interviewer
seated at a table with an empty chair for the applicant, create
an outer area where the receptionist sits, and identify the
location of doors. Instruct the applicant to review his or
her résumé and job advertisement exercise and to identify
what questions he or she will ask the interviewer about the
company. Direct the interviewer to look over the list of interview questions (Exhibit 32) and decide how to conduct the
interview, and to stop the interview after about ten minutes.
Tell the observers to situate themselves so that they can see
both the applicant and the interviewer and to take very
specific notes on what the applicant said. Instruct the receptionist to decide how to treat the applicant (require that the
applicant wait, escort the applicant right in, or whatever).
Begin the rehearsal by having the applicant approach the
receptionist and request to see the interviewer. If the rehearsal is not going well, stop it, make suggestions for
improvement (or elicit them from the observers and interviewer), then start it again.

3.   After the mock interview, elicit feedback first from the
observers, second from the interviewer, and last from yourself. Make certain that the feedback from observers and
interviewer is specific enough to be useful; clarify it if
necessary. Negative feedback should be accompanied by
suggestions for other ways of handling the situation. For
example, the comment ''You looked too nervous'' should
be followed by specific advice, such as ''Don't twist your
pen around in your hands; keep them together, below the
level of the desk top.'' To assist the observers in giving
specific feedback, you might provide a list of behaviors to
watch for, such as body posture, nervous mannerisms, tone
and volume of voice, and facial expression. To ensure that
applicants really listen to the feedback, tell them that they
will be asked to summarize the feedback they receive. It
is best not to ask for feedback from applicants, as they are

apt to justify their behavior rather than listen to the feedback of others. If videotape is used, feedback can occur in a variety of formats. For example, at the end of the interview, you could play the tape and stop it from time to time to interject comments. The tape could also be played without your comments, or it could be used in addition to feedback from the observers.

After one client has had the opportunity to practice, you can go on to the next person who needs practice, as long as the experience went fairly well. You might also decide to repeat the interview so that the applicant can practice the new behaviors suggested by the feedback. Or it might be decided to have the same applicant practice with another interviewer in order to broaden his or her experience. In any case, make certain that the applicant ends with a relatively successful interview. Roles should be rotated and the process repeated until each person has had an opportunity to rehearse.

Problems and Cautions

The job-hunting process almost always has built-in difficulties: the client's natural sense of urgency is usually frustrated by the amount of time it takes to set up and attend interviews, and, except in rare cases, the client will be rejected for jobs several times and tend after a while to feel that the job situation is hopeless or that he or she is unemployable. Initial enthusiasm, realistic expectations, and a certain amount of good luck will carry most clients over their moments of doubt and depression, but this is not always so, and it is important to recognize when the situation has reached the stage of a problem requiring intervention.

The most obvious signal that there is a problem is failure of the client to carry out any of the steps of the plan. Or the client will follow the outlined steps but in a reluctant, downhearted, or negative manner that seriously affects performance. For example, Nate reported that his interview with an influential employer had gone badly. Upon analysis, the counselor discovered that Nate had arrived barely on time, had been unprepared for the interview, and had forgotten to ask key questions and to volunteer information about himself. A reenactment of part of the interview demonstrated that Nate had probably appeared somewhat sullen and indifferent—not at all like the rather personable self he had presented during interview practice. As proof that the interview had indeed been a failure and that his account was not simply a matter of poor self-confidence, Nate reported that the interview, planned for thirty minutes, was over in ten and that the employer had acknowledged that Nate had the right qualifications but even so had held out little hope of a job.

Although any interview can go badly, you should suspect problems if the client seems to be making a minimum effort to succeed or if poor interviews seem to be the norm for this client, despite adequate rehearsal. There are also grounds to investigate if the client's body language expresses increasing discouragement, if you hear a great deal of complaining and hopelessness, and if you find yourself needing to supply ever-increasing amounts of psychological support. In other words, when your enthusiasm and interest, rather than the client's, become the prime motivators for the client's continued job hunt, there is something wrong.

It is to be hoped that you will not wait until the client has almost given up before intervening. We suggest that at the first sign of failure to follow the plan with eagerness and efficiency you take time out to troubleshoot. Attacked early enough, some problems can be solved quickly and have no chance to develop into major difficulties. Clients will also learn for themselves how to troubleshoot situations and can thus rely increasingly on themselves rather than on you.

Perhaps the easiest source of trouble to correct is the plan itself. Ascertain whether the client actually followed the steps of the plan, in the assigned order and manner. If not, find out why the plan was not followed exactly as specified. One possible reason lies with the client, who may not have had the necessary skills or attitude to perform a step in the plan. If this is so, you will need to help the client acquire the skills and find some way of dealing with negative reactions, such as acute procrastination, the tendency to feel overwhelmed at the least setback, or crippling anxiety at interviews. Other common reasons that people do not follow plans are: (1) they do not really understand exactly what has to be done or how; (2) the necessary resources are not available; and (3) the plan itself is at fault—a step is missing, the time required or how much others will help has been misjudged, or the requirements of a particular move have been misunderstood. Usually, an investigation into these factors is sufficient to pinpoint weaknesses in the plan that can then be remedied by increased specificity concerning precisely what will be done, where, when, by whom, and for how long.

If clients' problems do not originate with the plan itself or with their own ability to do what is necessary to carry out the plan, the cause may lie with unexpected roadblocks, such as sickness in the family, the unavailability of contacts, slow mail · delivery, or a sudden change in the economy. In 1986 a rapid drastic drop in oil prices, for example, resulted in dramatic changes in the oil industry itself and in related industries and businesses. A client looking for a position in this area would have found that what had seemed a promising and relatively stable work field was suddenly in confusion. Job hunting would have been more difficult because of increased layoffs and reorganization, but there was no way to have reliably predicted these changes in the industry.

In helping clients deal with the unexpected, you need to address both practical and psychological issues. When a client reports an unexpected block, assess where help will be needed most by asking how the client feels about the problem and proposes to handle it. According to need, work with the client to make necessary alterations in the plan, such as changing the order of substeps, adjusting time lines, or developing alternative methods to achieve the desired results. Whenever possible, the client's ideas should be the ones adopted, especially if these ideas are drawn from successful past experience. In the process of dealing with the practical side of the problem, you are also teaching the client problem-solving skills to increase independence in the future.

If clients' emotional reactions to setbacks are sufficiently negative to affect performance, you will need to help them develop an attitude that promotes persistence and problem solving rather than helplessness and giving up when they encounter unforeseen difficulties. Analyze clients' cognitions, emotional and physical reactions, and overt behavior when faced with unexpected problems in order to discover where intervention is needed. Also ask clients what they have done in similar past situations, to discover what has worked or not worked. You will then be in a position to help the client develop effective coping strategies, which will, of course, be highly individualized. Some people, for example, are helped most when they view a plan not in its entirety but in very small portions, each complete in itself. If something goes wrong with one portion, there is no sense that the overall plan or the final goal is in jeopardy, and the client feels able to make necessary adjustments in order to handle problems within the limited segment of the plan. Other people prefer to view each step of the plan as a personal challenge, gaining reinforcement from the very process of overcoming difficulties. Yet other clients find it more useful to focus on their own record of successful problem solving and to draw confidence from the use of methods that have worked before. Sometimes clients feel more confident about dealing with setbacks if they have assembled a list of resources that they can turn to for help in a crisis. Finally, for some clients the most helpful approach to a setback is to vent negative emotions as completely as possible, even to the point of giving themselves permission to give up. Once the storm has died down, they can return to the problem ready to take a new approach.

It is important to wean clients off reactions to difficulties that make the situation worse. Doris's most reliable reaction to any crisis was to overindulge in sugar products. Although she did not have an eating disorder requiring intervention for its own sake, her emergency sugar fixes always resulted in unpleasant physical side effects, such as lassitude, irritability, constipation, and facial acne. Thus, at times when she needed to function well, she guaranteed that she would feel below par and unattractive. Doris was unwilling to give up the solace of eating in a crisis but found that dinner at a good restaurant with a congenial friend made an acceptable substitute for sugar binges, without any of the unpleasant side effects.

Similarly, Carl's typical pattern of responding to difficulties made it harder for him to begin problem solving. First, he exaggerated the magnitude of the problem, then he predicted disaster far into the future and far beyond the scope of the current trouble. These are not unusual cognitive reactions to a problem, but Carl ensured their longevity by telling all his friends that he had abandoned his original goal or plan and was, definitely, headed in a different direction. After this dramatic announcement, he found it difficult to continue with his original idea without looking foolish in front of his friends. An obvious intervention to try with Carl, and one that proved effective, was to have him record his dire predictions and change of plans on a tape recorder instead of talking to friends. The taped monologue also, incidentally, provided excellent material to use in helping Carl deal with his negative cognitions in therapy.

One of the most serious problems that arises when clients are looking for a position is discouragement in response to the reality of the marketplace. It can be long months and many rejections before a client finds a job, and the longer it takes, the more of a failure the client can feel—unproductive, unwanted, valueless. Clients can begin to doubt their skills and ability, devalue their experience, and present themselves with less and less enthusiasm and confidence. When the failure to find a job is accompanied by economic hardship or withdrawal of support from significant others, anxiety and depression are difficult to avoid.

It is not hard to see when this sort of discouragement is setting in. Just the passage of time is sufficient to make you ask clients whether they are becoming upset with their lack of progress, but usually they are all too clear in expressing their frustrations and worries. There are several strategies, discussed below,

to help clients with their sense of discouragement over not getting a job. Although you will presumably have tried to prepare
clients for the negative responses and the expenditure of time
and energy that can be part of job hunting, the message will
probably have to be repeated that "no" is to be expected, that
getting a job is a full-time job in itself, that many people find
job searching unpalatable, and that most people who keep looking do eventually find work. This last is the most vital point
to make. If the client discontinues the hunt, failure is guaranteed,
but persistence usually pays off in the end. In a program designed
to provide support, practical assistance, and tips on finding work,
Azrin and his associates (1975) required clients to be occupied
full time in activities related to obtaining employment. Within
two months, 90 percent of the counseled job hunters, compared
with 55 percent of noncounseled job seekers, had found work,
and of those in the counseling group the only ones who did not
find work were those who did not regularly attend sessions or
perform the job-hunting activities regularly.

An important contribution to the success of the program
developed by Azrin and colleagues (1975) was the support of
other group members. Clients met daily to practice skills, share
job leads, review résumés, assist each other with transportation,
and help in any other way related to the search for work. Buddies gave each other individual attention and support, and the
group experience provided a sense of commonality and psychological support not available to those who look for work in isolation. If it is at all possible, therefore, clients should be put in
touch with others who are also seeking work. Ideally, you would
want a supervised group in which the focus is, quite simply,
on obtaining work, but even one other person who is in the same
situation as the client could be of value in warding off discouragement.

Rather than continuing what looks to be an extended and
hopeless full-time search for desirable work, it might be wise
for some clients to take the first job they can obtain and plan
to spend time, while employed, on the search for a better position. Consider this option if clients are in severe economic need,

if they have been unemployed for a long time, or if it seems that their self-confidence will be increased by the evidence that they can at least obtain work of some kind. There is an additional advantage to job searching from a current position in that prospective employers tend to view the employed person as someone whose skills are in demand and who is therefore more attractive than someone who is unemployed. Furthermore, a temporary position that bears some relation to the job the client really wants will most probably provide an opportunity to gain experience and even develop an area of expertise that can increase the client's attractiveness to employers in the desired field.

Sometimes clients view the prospect of an interim job as a deviation from the true career goal, and their discouragement increases. In this case, help clients decide about an interim job by assessing the comparative pros and cons of remaining unemployed versus taking less-than-perfect work. An important point that should be taken into consideration here is the fact that conducting a successful job search is probably not compatible with working a forty-hour week. Clients might therefore prefer to choose part-time employment while they are conducting a job search.

Final Note

Counseling for career choice carries its own special difficulties. The sheer amount of information processed, the limitations imposed by economic realities, and the need for a progressive and structured approach can sometimes cause client and even counselor to feel lost in a mass of detail or discouraged by tedium and slow progress. When this occurs, it is easy to forget that the essence of career counseling is making dreams happen. To preserve a client's dreams as a central focus in counseling, we have found it valuable to give prominence to the Work-Related Preferences (WRPs). By summarizing all that a client wants and can reasonably expect to obtain in a job or career, the WRPs provide a kind of blueprint for the dream and should guide each step of the process. Thus, the major purpose of assessment is to help clients discover, articulate, and refine their career aspirations; the reason for interventions must be to help clients realize their hopes and ambitions.

It is important, too, to maintain a humanistic attitude while moving through the steps of the process. We hope that we have conveyed in this book our belief in the necessity of adapting techniques to individual needs and in the value and significance of all kinds of work.

Finally, we hope that you will discover, as we have, the rewards of helping clients toward choices that will have a major impact on their lives.

❧ Resource A ❧

Test Information and Addresses for Tests

Jackson Vocational Interest Survey
Research Psychology Press, Inc.
P.O. Box 984
Port Huron, Michigan 48060

Kuder Occupational Interest Survey
Science Research Associates, Inc.
155 N. Wacker Drive
Chicago, Illinois 60606

Occupational Card Sorts
Career Research and Testing
2005 Hamilton Avenue #250
San Jose, California 95125

Self Directed Search
Consulting Psychology Press, Inc.
577 College Avenue
Palo Alto, California 94306

Strong-Campbell Interest Inventory
Stanford University Press
Stanford, California 94305

Ninth Mental Measurements Yearbook
J. V. Mitchell, Editor
Buros Institute of Mental Measurement
University of Nebraska-Lincoln
Lincoln, Nebraska 68508

Tests in Print III
J. V. Mitchell, Editor
Buros Institute of Mental Measurement
University of Nebraska-Lincoln
Lincoln, Nebraska 68508

❧ Resource B ❧

Sample Directories

At regular intervals, often annually, hundreds of directories are published that contain information on virtually every industry, trade, profession, institution, organization, and association, both abroad and in the United States. These resources may list the names of executives or contact personnel, provide details about job openings and training requirements, or discuss trends and business potential. Because directories vary greatly in both price and usefulness, we suggest that readers consult public or university libraries to see which directories are available. The large number of publications makes it impractical to adequately represent the field here, but we list fifteen selected directories as examples of the wealth of information that is available.

American Hospital Association Guide to the Health Care Field
Chicago, Ill.: American Hospital Association.
Provides an extensive guide to the health care field.

Community Resources Directory
Detroit, Mich.: Gale Research.
Covers all aspects of volunteerism in America: funding, management, training, publications, and programs.

Directory of American Firms Operating in Foreign Countries
New York: World Trade Academy Press.
Lists approximately 3,200 American corporations and factories that conduct business outside the United States.

Directory of Directories
Detroit, Mich.: Gale Research.
Serves as an annual guide to directories in all fields.

Directory of Internships, Work Experience Programs and On-the-Job Training Opportunities
Thousand Oaks, Calif.: Specialized Index.
Lists internship opportunities for high school and college students, alphabetically, geographically, and by subject.

Directory of Museums and Living Displays
New York: Stockton Press.
Provides names, locations, and exhibit details for museums, zoos, and aquaria throughout the world.

Encyclopedia of Business Information Sources
Detroit, Mich.: Gale Research.
Provides detailed lists of major sources of information related to business, including books, directories, bibliographies, and organizations.

Guide to International Venture Capital
New York: Simon & Schuster.
Lists firms actively involved in providing capital for new businesses in the United States, Canada, the United Kingdom, Europe, Asia, and Israel. Information includes project preferences for each firm in terms of location, industry, and stage of financing.

Industrial Outlook: Prospects from 350 Manufacturing and Service Industries.
Washington, D.C.: International Trade Administration, U.S. Department of Commerce.
Provides economic, import-export, and product data as well as projections for 350 specific manufacturing and service industries.

Magazine Publishing Career Directory
New York: Career Publishing Corporation.

Describes all aspects of work in magazine publishing, including expected job openings for the coming year with 100 major publishers.

Peterson's Annual Guides to Graduate Study: Graduate and Professional Programs
Princeton, N.J.: Peterson's Guides.
Covers U.S. and Canadian graduate programs in the humanities and social sciences; biological, agricultural, and health sciences; the physical sciences; and engineering and applied sciences. Organized by field of study. Includes a description of each program, degree requirements, and faculty qualifications.

Scientific and Technical Organizations and Agencies Directory
Detroit, Mich.: Gale Research.
Guide to approximately 12,000 organizations and agencies concerned with physical sciences, engineering, and technology.

Standard & Poor's Register of Corporations, Directors and Executives
New York: Standard & Poors.
Covers more than 45,000 U.S. corporations. Includes number of employees, names of accountants, primary banks, primary law firms, outside directors, and biographies of directors and executives.

Thomas Register of American Manufacturers
New York: Thomas Publishing.
Profiles over 120,000 manufacturing firms in the United States. Describes companies, lists products, and includes bound catalogs of manufacturers. Entries provide toll-free telephone numbers.

Yearbook of International Organizations
Brussels, Belgium: Union of International Associations.
Describes nearly 20,000 organizations that are active in at least three countries. Entries include name of director, history, goals, structure, number of members, publications, and place and dates of meetings.

References

American Personnel and Guidance Association. *Ethical Standards.* (Rev. ed.) Falls Church, Va.: American Personnel and Guidance Association, 1981.

American Psychological Association. *Standards for Educational and Psychological Tests.* Prepared by a joint committee of the American Psychological Association, the American Educational Research Association, and the National Council on Measurement in Education, 1974.

American Psychological Association. *Ethical Principles of Psychologists.* (Rev. ed.) Washington, D.C.: American Psychological Association, 1981.

Azrin, N. H., Flores, T., and Kaplan, S. J. "Job-Finding Club: A Group-Assisted Program for Obtaining Employment." *Behavior Research and Therapy,* 1975, *13,* 17–27.

Bartsch, K., Yost, E. B., and Girrell, K. *Effective Personal and Career Decision Making.* New York: Westinghouse Learning Corporation, 1976.

Beck, A. T., Rush, A. J., Shaw, B. F., and Emery, G. *Cognitive Therapy of Depression.* New York: Guilford, 1979.

Bolles, R. N. *What Color Is Your Parachute? A Practical Manual for Job-Hunters and Career-Changers.* (Rev. ed.) Berkeley, Calif.: Ten Speed Press, 1986.

253

Bostwick, B. E. *Résumé Writing.* New York: Wiley, 1985.

Brooks, L. "Career Counseling Methods and Practice." In D. Brown and L. Brooks (eds.), *Career Choice and Development: Applying Contemporary Theories to Practice.* San Francisco: Jossey-Bass, 1984.

Brown, D. "Summary, Comparison, and Critique of Major Theories." In D. Brown and L. Brooks (eds.), *Career Choice and Development: Applying Contemporary Theories to Practice.* San Francisco: Jossey-Bass, 1984.

Brown, D. "Career Counseling: Before, After or Instead of Personal Counseling?" *Vocational Guidance Quarterly,* Mar. 1985, pp. 197–201.

Buehler, C. *Der menschliche Lebenslauf als psychologisches Problem* [The human life span as a psychological problem]. Leipzig: Hirzel, 1933.

Burck, H. D. "Facilitating Career Development: Past Events, Current Scenes, and the Future." In H. D. Burck and R. C. Reardon (eds.), *Career Development Interventions.* Springfield, Ill.: Thomas, 1984.

Campbell, D. P. *Manual for the Strong-Campbell Interest Inventory.* (Rev. ed.) Stanford, Calif.: Stanford University Press, 1977.

Cornell University Career Center. *Where to Start: An Annotated Career Planning Bibliography.* (4th ed.) Ithaca, N.Y.: Cornell University Career Center, 1983.

Crites, J. O. *Career Maturity Inventory.* Monterey, Calif.: CTB/McGraw-Hill, 1978.

Crites, J. O. *Career Counseling: Models, Methods and Materials.* New York: McGraw-Hill, 1981.

Djeddah, E. *Moving Up: How to Get High-Salaried Jobs.* (Rev. ed.) Berkeley, Calif.: Ten Speed Press, 1978.

Dolliver, R. H. "An Adaptation of the Tyler Vocational Card Sort." *Personnel and Guidance Journal,* 1967, *45* (9), 916–920.

Ellis, A. *Reason and Emotion in Psychotherapy.* New York: Stuart, 1962.

Emery, G., Hollon, S. D., and Bedrosian, R. C. *New Directions in Cognitive Therapy.* New York: Guilford, 1981.

Figler, H. E. *Path: A Career Workbook for Liberal Arts Students.* (2nd ed.) Cranston, R.I.: Carroll Press, 1979a.

Figler, H. E. *The Complete Job-Search Handbook*. New York: Holt, Rinehart & Winston, 1979b.

Fitzgerald, L. F., and Crites, J. O. "Toward a Career Psychology of Women: What Do We Know? What Do We Need to Know?" *Journal of Counseling Psychology*, 1980, *27*, 44–62.

Flannagan, T. W. "Placement Beyond the Obvious." *Rehabilitation Counseling Bulletin*, 1977, *21*, 116–120.

Foreyt, J. P., and Rathjen, D. P. *Cognitive Behavior Therapy: Research and Application*. New York: Plenum, 1978.

Freeman, A. (ed.). *Cognitive Therapy with Couples and Groups*. New York: Plenum, 1983.

Gainer, H. N., and Stark, S. L. *Choice or Change: A Guide to Career Planning*. New York: McGraw-Hill, 1979.

Gianakos, I., and Subich, L. M. "The Relationship of Gender and Sex-Role Orientation to Vocational Undecidedness." *Journal of Vocational Behavior*, 1986, *29* (1), 42–50.

Ginzberg, E. "Toward a Theory of Occupational Choice: A Restatement." *Vocational Guidance Quarterly*, 1972, *20* (3), 169–176.

Ginzberg, E. "Career Development." In D. Brown and L. Brooks (eds.), *Career Choice and Development: Applying Contemporary Theories to Practice*. San Francisco: Jossey-Bass, 1984.

Ginzberg, E., Ginsburg, S. W., Axelrad, S., and Herma, J. L. *Occupational Choice: An Approach to a General Theory*. New York: Columbia University Press, 1951.

Goldman, L. *Using Tests in Counseling*. (2nd ed.) Englewood Cliffs, N.J.: Prentice-Hall, 1971.

Gross, S. "Professional Disclosure: An Alternative to Licensure." *Personnel and Guidance Journal*, 1977, *55*, 586–588.

Gysbers, N. C., and Moore, E. J. *Career Counseling: Skills and Techniques for Practitioners*. Englewood Cliffs, N.J.: Prentice-Hall, 1987.

Harren, V. A. "A Model of Career Decision Making for College Students." *Journal of Vocational Behavior*, 1979, *14*, 119–135.

Hazler, R. J., and Roberts, G. "Decision Making in Vocational Theory: Evolution and Implications." *Personnel and Guidance Journal*, 1984, *62* (7), 408–410.

Hennig, M., and Jardim, A. *The Managerial Woman.* New York: Pocket Books, 1976.

Hogan, D. B. *The Regulation of Psychotherapists: A Handbook of State Licensure Laws.* 4 vols. Cambridge, Mass.: Ballinger, 1979.

Holland, J. L. "A Theory of Vocational Choice." *Journal of Counseling Psychology,* 1959, *6,* 35–45.

Holland, J. L. *Making Vocational Choices: A Theory of Careers.* Englewood Cliffs, N.J.: Prentice-Hall, 1973.

Holland, J. L. *The Occupations Finder.* Palo Alto, Calif.: Consulting Psychologists Press, 1977a.

Holland, J. L. *Self Directed Search: A Guide to Educational and Vocational Planning.* Palo Alto, Calif.: Consulting Psychologists Press, 1977b.

Holland, J. L. *Making Vocational Choices: A Theory of Vocational Personalities and Work Environments.* Englewood Cliffs, N.J.: Prentice-Hall, 1985.

Hoppock, R. *Occupational Information.* (4th ed.) New York: McGraw-Hill, 1976.

Irish, R. K. *Go Hire Yourself an Employer.* Garden City, N.Y.: Anchor, 1973.

Isaacson, L. E. *Career Information in Counseling and Teaching.* (3rd ed.) Newton, Mass.: Allyn & Bacon, 1977.

Isaacson, L. E. *Basics of Career Counseling.* Newton, Mass.: Allyn & Bacon, 1985.

Jackson, D. N. *Jackson Vocational Interest Survey Manual.* Port Huron, Mich.: Research Psychologists Press, 1977.

Jackson, T. *Guerrilla Tactics in the Job Market.* New York: Bantam, 1978.

Kendall, P. C., and Hollon, S. D. *Cognitive-Behavioral Interventions: Theory, Research, and Procedures.* Orlando, Fla.: Academic Press, 1979.

Krumboltz, J. D. "A Social Learning Theory of Career Selection." *The Counseling Psychologist,* 1976, *6* (1), 71–81.

Krumboltz, J. D., and Thoresen, C. E. *Behavioral Counseling: Cases and Techniques.* New York: Holt, Rinehart & Winston, 1969.

Kuder, G. F. "A Rationale for Evaluating Interests." *Educational and Psychological Measurement,* 1963, *23,* 3–10.

Kuder, G. F. "The Occupational Interest Survey." *Personnel and Guidance Journal,* 1966, *45,* 72–77.

Kuder, G. F. *Kuder Occupational Interest Survey, Revised: General Manual.* Chicago: Science Research Associates, 1979.

LeGendre, S. L. "A Comparison of Methods for Presenting Consumer Information to Clients in Counseling." Unpublished master's thesis, Department of Counseling and Guidance, University of Arizona, 1978.

Loniello, M., Sugimoto, L., and Jackson, G. *The Job Game: A Career Handbook.* Dubuque, Iowa: Gorsuch, 1984.

Mahoney, M. J. *Cognition and Behavior Modification.* Cambridge, Mass.: Ballinger, 1974.

Marcon, M., and Worthington, M. *Twelve Steps to Finding a Job Under $30,000 in Four Weeks.* Englewood Cliffs, N.J.: Prentice-Hall, 1984.

Maslow, A. H. *Motivation and Personality.* New York: Harper & Row, 1954.

Mayerson, N. H. "Preparing Clients for Group Therapy: A Critical Review and Theoretical Formulation." *Clinical Psychology Review,* 1984, *4,* 191–213.

Meichenbaum, D. *Cognitive-Behavior Modification: An Integrative Approach.* New York: Plenum, 1977.

Mencke, R., and Hummel, R. L. *Career Planning for the 80s.* Monterey, Calif.: Brooks/Cole, 1984.

Mendonca, J. D., and Siess, T. F. "Counseling for Indecisiveness: Problem Solving and Anxiety Management Training." *Journal of Counseling Psychology,* 1976, *23,* 339–347.

National Vocational Guidance Association. "Guidelines for the Preparation and Evaluation of Career Information Media." *Vocational Guidance Quarterly,* 1980, *28* (4), 291–296.

Norris, W., Hatch, R. N., Engeles, J. R., and Winborn, B. B. *The Career Information Service.* (4th ed.) Chicago: Rand McNally, 1979.

Osipow, S. H. *Theories of Career Development.* (2nd ed.) East Norwalk, Conn.: Appleton-Century-Crofts, 1973.

Overs, R. P. "Covert Occupational Information." *Vocational Guidance Quarterly,* 1967, *16* (1), 7–12.

Parsons, F. *Choosing a Vocation.* Boston: Houghton Mifflin, 1909.

Paterson, D. G., and others. *Minnesota Occupational Rating Scales and Counseling Profile.* Chicago: Science Research Associates, 1941.

Phillips, S. D., Friedlander, M. L., Pazienza, N. J., and Kost, P. P. "A Factor Analytic Investigation of Career Decision-Making Styles." *Journal of Vocational Behavior,* 1985, *26* (1), 106–115.

Prediger, D. J. "Getting 'Ideas' out of the DOT and into Vocational Guidance." *Vocational Guidance Quarterly,* 1981, *20,* 293–306.

Radin, R. J. *Full Potential: Your Career and Life Planning Workbook.* New York: McGraw-Hill, 1983.

Reardon, R. C. "Use of Information in Career Counseling." In H. D. Burck and R. C. Reardon (eds.), *Career Development Interventions.* Springfield, Ill.: Thomas, 1984.

Rockcastle, J. *Where to Start: An Annotated Career Planning Bibliography.* (5th ed.) Ithaca, N.Y.: Cornell University Career Center, 1985.

Roe, A. *The Psychology of Occupations.* New York: Wiley, 1956.

Roe, A. "Perspectives on Vocational Development." In J. M. Whiteley and A. Resnikoff (eds.), *Perspectives on Vocational Development.* Washington, D.C.: American Personnel and Guidance Association, 1972.

Salomone, P. R. "Difficult Cases in Career Counseling: II: The Indecisive Client." *Personnel and Guidance Journal,* Apr. 1982, pp. 496–499.

Saltoun, J. "Fear of Failure in Career Development." *Vocational Guidance Quarterly,* Sept. 1985, pp. 35–41.

Sank, L. I., and Shaffer, C. S. *A Therapist's Manual for Cognitive Behavior Therapy in Groups.* New York: Plenum, 1984.

Schuman, N., and Lewis, W. *Revising Your Résumé.* New York: Wiley, 1986.

Srebalus, D. J., Marinelli, R. P., and Messing, J. K. *Career Development: Concepts and Procedures.* Monterey, Calif.: Brooks/Cole, 1982.

Suinn, R, M. *Anxiety Management Training Manual.* Fort Collins, Colo.: Rocky Mountain Behavioral Science Institute, 1972.

Super, D. E. *The Psychology of Careers.* New York: Harper & Row, 1957.

Super, D. E. "Vocational Development Theory: Persons, Positions and Processes." *Counseling Psychologist,* 1969, *1,* 2–9.

Super, D. E., and others. *Career Development Inventory.* New York: Columbia University Press, 1979.

Terkel, S. *Working.* New York: Pantheon, 1972.

Tiedeman, D. V. "Decision and Vocational Development: A Paradigm and Its Implications." *Personnel and Guidance Journal,* 1961, *40,* 15–20.

Tiedeman, D. V., and O'Hara, R. P. *Career Development: Choice and Adjustment.* New York: College Entrance Examination Board, 1963.

Tyler, L. E. "Research Explorations in the Realm of Choice." *Journal of Counseling Psychology,* 1961, *8,* 195–201.

Tyler, L. E. *The Work of the Counselor.* (3rd ed.) East Norwalk, Conn.: Appleton-Century-Crofts, 1969.

U.S. Department of Labor. *Dictionary of Occupational Titles.* (4th ed.) Washington, D.C.: U.S. Government Printing Office, 1977.

U.S. Department of Labor. *Occupational Outlook Handbook, 1984–85.* Washington, D.C.: U.S. Government Printing Office, 1984.

Williamson, E. G. *How to Counsel Students.* New York: McGraw-Hill, 1939.

Williamson, E. G. *Vocational Counseling.* New York: McGraw-Hill, 1965.

Winborn, B. B. "Honest Labeling and Other Procedures for the Protection of Consumers of Counseling." *Personnel and Guidance Journal,* 1977, *56* (4), 206–209.

Yate, M. J. *Knock 'Em Dead with Great Answers to Tough Interview Questions.* Boston: Bob Adams, 1985.

Yost, E. B. (ed.). "Field Tested Vocational Decision Making Programs: A Guidebook for Counselors and Vocational Education Teachers." Unpublished manuscript, University of Arizona, 1976.

Yost, E. B., Beutler, L. E., Corbishley, M. A., and Allender, J. R. *Group Cognitive Therapy: A Treatment Approach for Depressed Older Adults.* New York: Pergamon, 1986.

Zunker, V. G. *Career Counseling: Applied Concepts of Life Planning.* (2nd ed.) Monterey, Calif.: Brooks/Cole, 1985.

Index